ULTIMATE X4

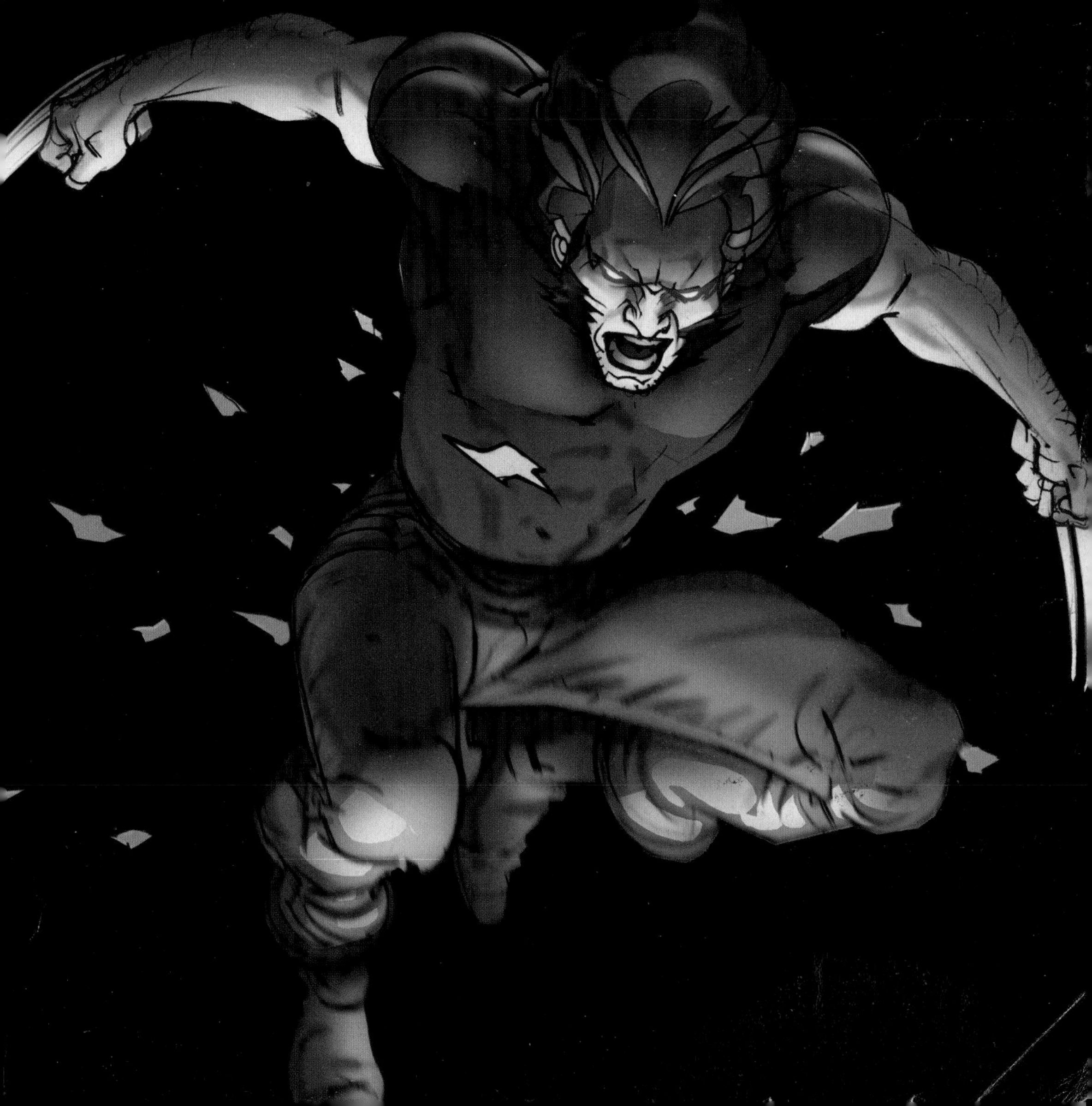

ULTIMATE X4

writer: **MIKE CAREY**
artist: **PASQUAL FERRY**
additional art: **LEINIL FRANCIS YU**
colorists: **DAVE MCCAIG WITH PAUL MOUNTS,**
ROB SCHWAGER, GURU EFX & JUNE CHUNG
letters: **CHRIS ELIOPOULOS**
covers: **PASQUAL FERRY**
assistant editor: **NICOLE BOOSE**
associate editor: **JOHN BARBER**
editor: **RALPH MACCHIO**

the offical handbook to the ultimate marvel universe:
SPIDER-MAN & FANTASTIC FOUR
head writers/coordinators: **STUART VANDAL
& SEAN MCQUAID**
writers: **RONALD BYRD, BILL LENTZ,
MARK O'ENGLISH & BARRY REESE**
cover artists: **MARK BAGLEY
& MORRY HOLLOWELL**
art reconstruction: **POND SCUM**
select coloring: **CHRIS SOTOMAYOR**
special thanks to Jeff Christiansen, Wale Ekunsumi,
John Barber, Tom Brevoort & Adam Rottenberg

the official handbook to the ultimate marvel universe:
X-MEN & THE ULTIMATES
head writer/coodinator: **STUART VANDAL**
writers: **SEAN MCQUAID,
RONALD BYRD & CHRIS BIGGS**
cover artists: **MARK BAGLEY &
MORRY HOLLOWELL**
special thanks to the guys at the Appendix
(www.marvunapp.com) and the gang at
Comix-Fan (www.comixfan.com),
Wale Ekunsumi, Tom Brevoort,
John Barber & Nathan Doyle

collection editor: **JENNIFER GRÜNWALD**
assistant editor: **MICHAEL SHORT**
senior editor, special projects:
JEFF YOUNGQUIST
vice president of sales: **DAVID GABRIEL**
book designer: **DAYLE CHESLER**
special thanks: **JENNIE HAN**
vice president of creative: **TOM MARVELLI**

editor in chief: **JOE QUESADA**
publisher: **DAN BUCKLEY**

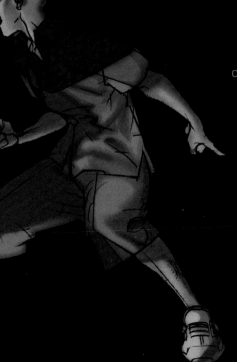

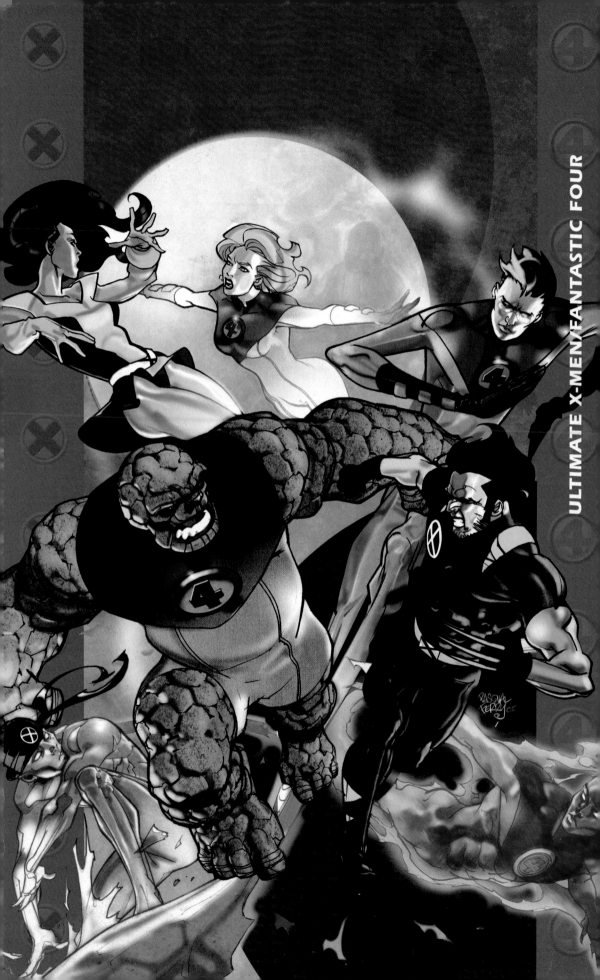

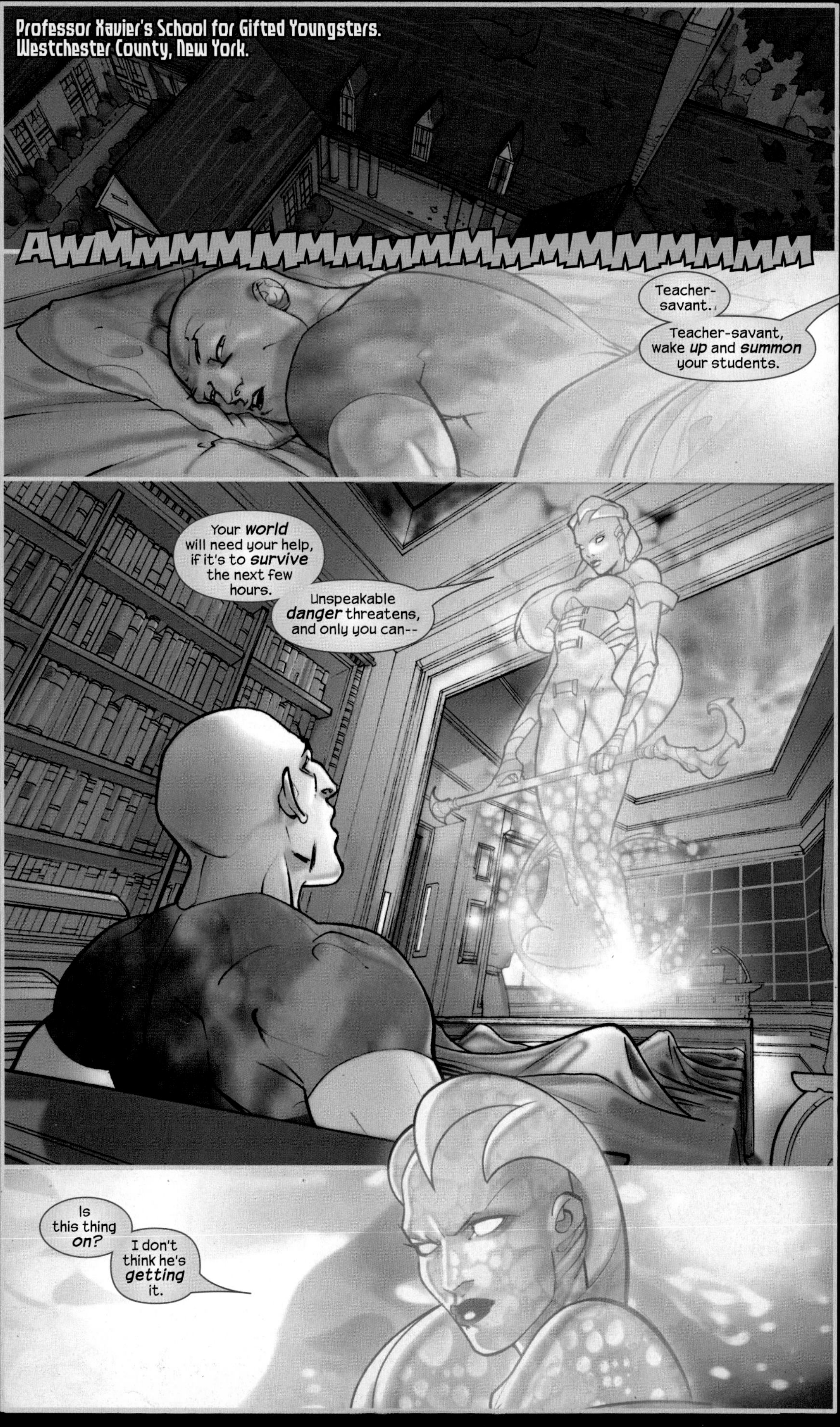
Professor Xavier's School for Gifted Youngsters.
Westchester County, New York.
AWMMMMMMMMMMMMMMMMMMMM
Teacher-savant.
Teacher-savant, wake up and summon your students.
Your world will need your help, if it's to survive the next few hours.
Unspeakable danger threatens, and only you can--
Is this thing on?
I don't think he's getting it.

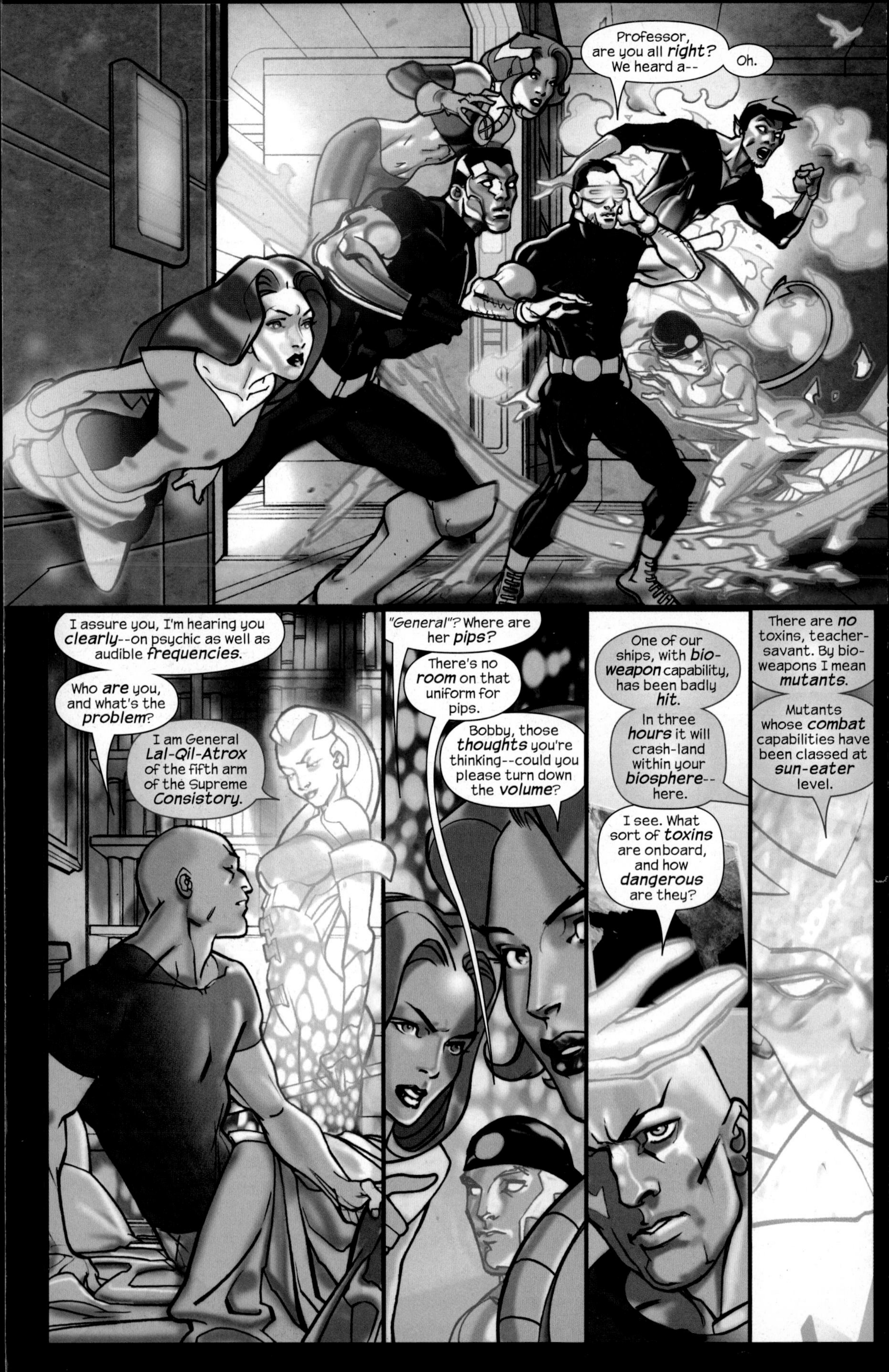
Professor, are you all right? We heard a--
Oh.
I assure you, I'm hearing you clearly--on psychic as well as audible frequencies.
Who are you, and what's the problem?
I am General Lal-Qil-Atrox of the fifth arm of the Supreme Consistory.
"General"? Where are her pips?
There's no room on that uniform for pips.
Bobby, those thoughts you're thinking--could you please turn down the volume?
One of our ships, with bio-weapon capability, has been badly hit.
In three hours it will crash-land within your biosphere--here.
I see. What sort of toxins are onboard, and how dangerous are they?
There are no toxins, teacher-savant. By bio-weapons I mean mutants.
Mutants whose combat capabilities have been classed at sun-eater level.

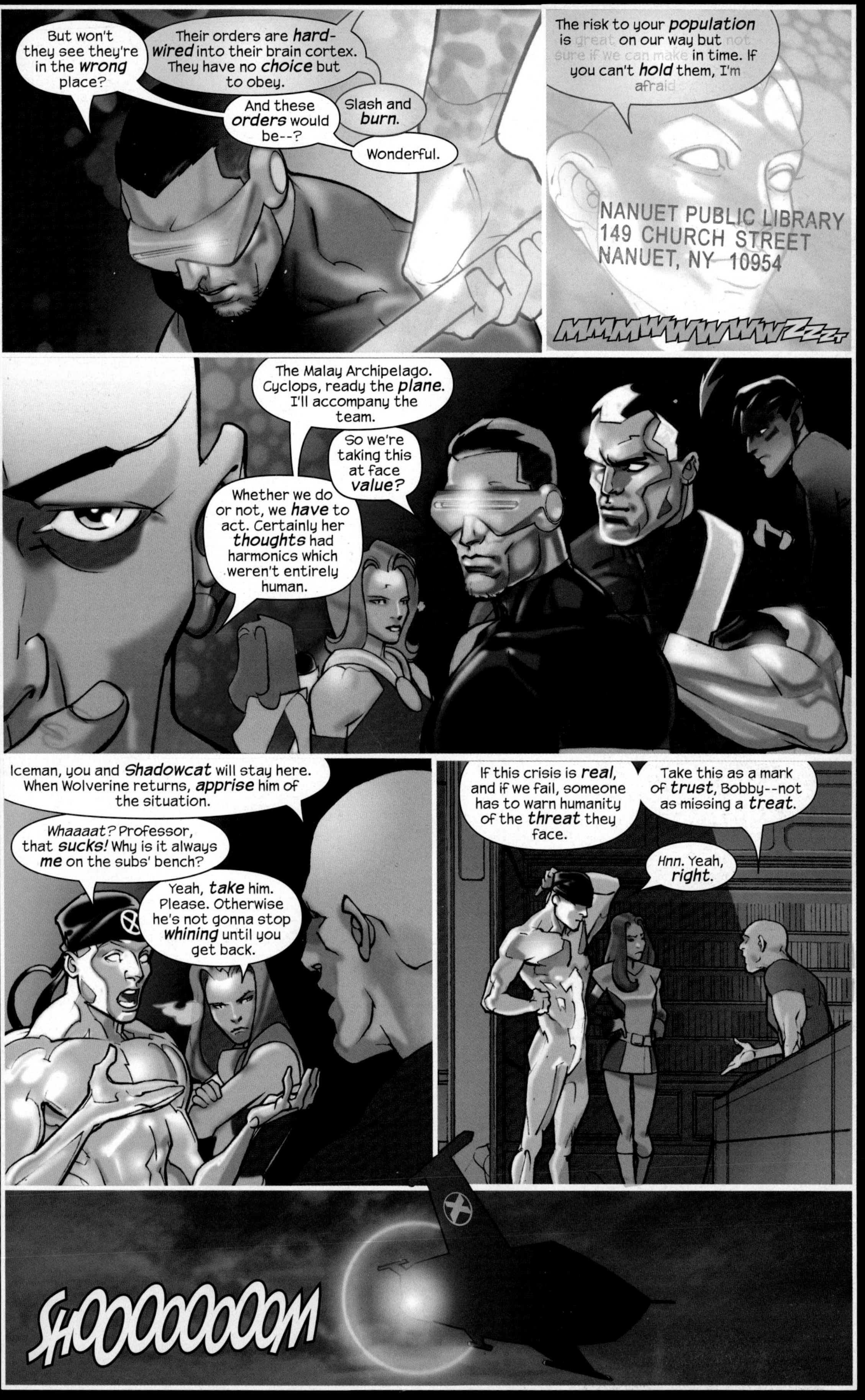
But won't they see they're in the *wrong* place?
Their orders are *hard-wired* into their brain cortex. They have no *choice* but to obey.
And these *orders* would be--?
Slash and *burn*.
Wonderful.
The risk to your *population* is great on our way but not sure if we can make in time. If you can't *hold* them, I'm afraid
MMMWWWWWWZZZT
The Malay Archipelago. Cyclops, ready the *plane*. I'll accompany the team.
So we're taking this at face *value?*
Whether we do or not, we *have* to act. Certainly her *thoughts* had harmonics which weren't entirely human.
Iceman, you and *Shadowcat* will stay here. When Wolverine returns, *apprise* him of the situation.
Whaaaat? Professor, that *sucks!* Why is it always *me* on the subs' bench?
Yeah, *take* him. Please. Otherwise he's not gonna stop *whining* until you get back.
If this crisis is *real*, and if we fail, someone has to warn humanity of the *threat* they face.
Take this as a mark of *trust*, Bobby--not as missing a *treat*.
Hnn. Yeah, *right*.
SHOOOOOOOOM

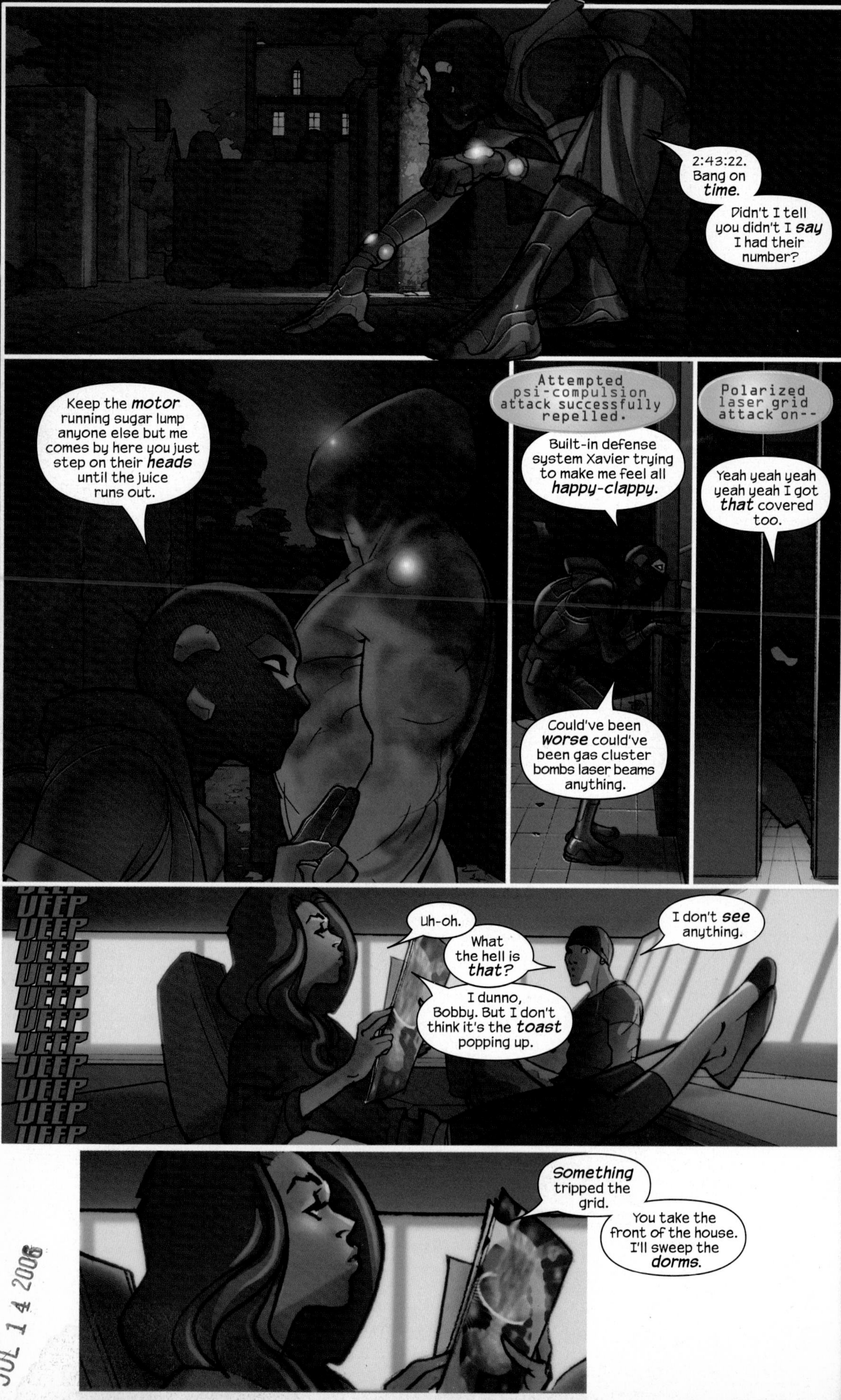

2:43:22. Bang on time.
Didn't I tell you didn't I say I had their number?
Keep the motor running sugar lump anyone else but me comes by here you just step on their heads until the juice runs out.
Attempted psi-compulsion attack successfully repelled.
Built-in defense system Xavier trying to make me feel all happy-clappy.
Could've been worse could've been gas cluster bombs laser beams anything.
Polarized laser grid attack on--
Yeah yeah yeah yeah yeah I got that covered too.
VEEP VEEP VEEP VEEP VEEP VEEP VEEP VEEP VEEP VEEP VEEP
Uh-oh.
What the hell is that?
I don't see anything.
I dunno, Bobby. But I don't think it's the toast popping up.
Something tripped the grid.
You take the front of the house. I'll sweep the dorms.

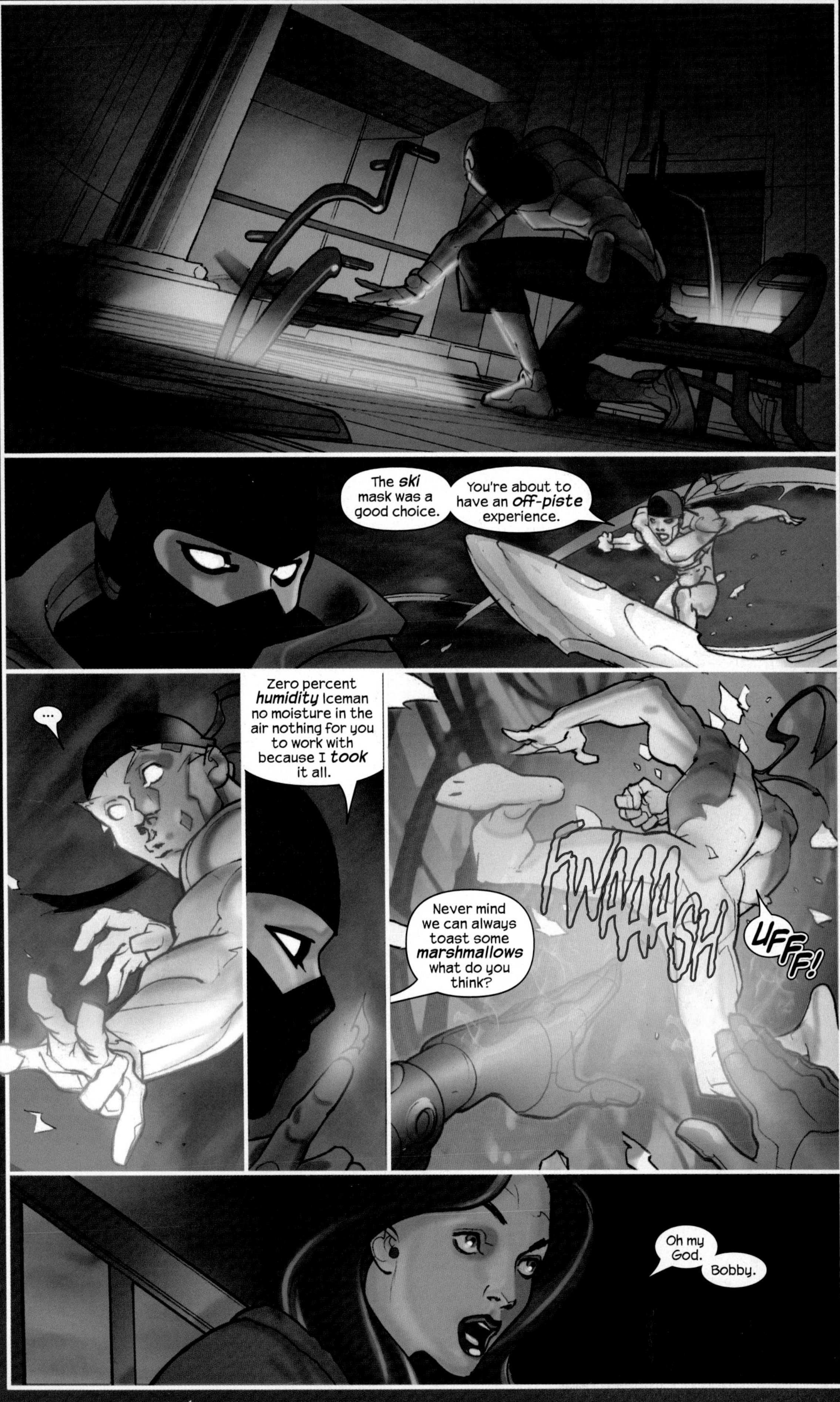

The ski mask was a good choice.
You're about to have an off-piste experience.
...
Zero percent humidity Iceman no moisture in the air nothing for you to work with because I took it all.
Never mind we can always toast some marshmallows what do you think?
FWAAASH
UFFFF!
Oh my God.
Bobby.

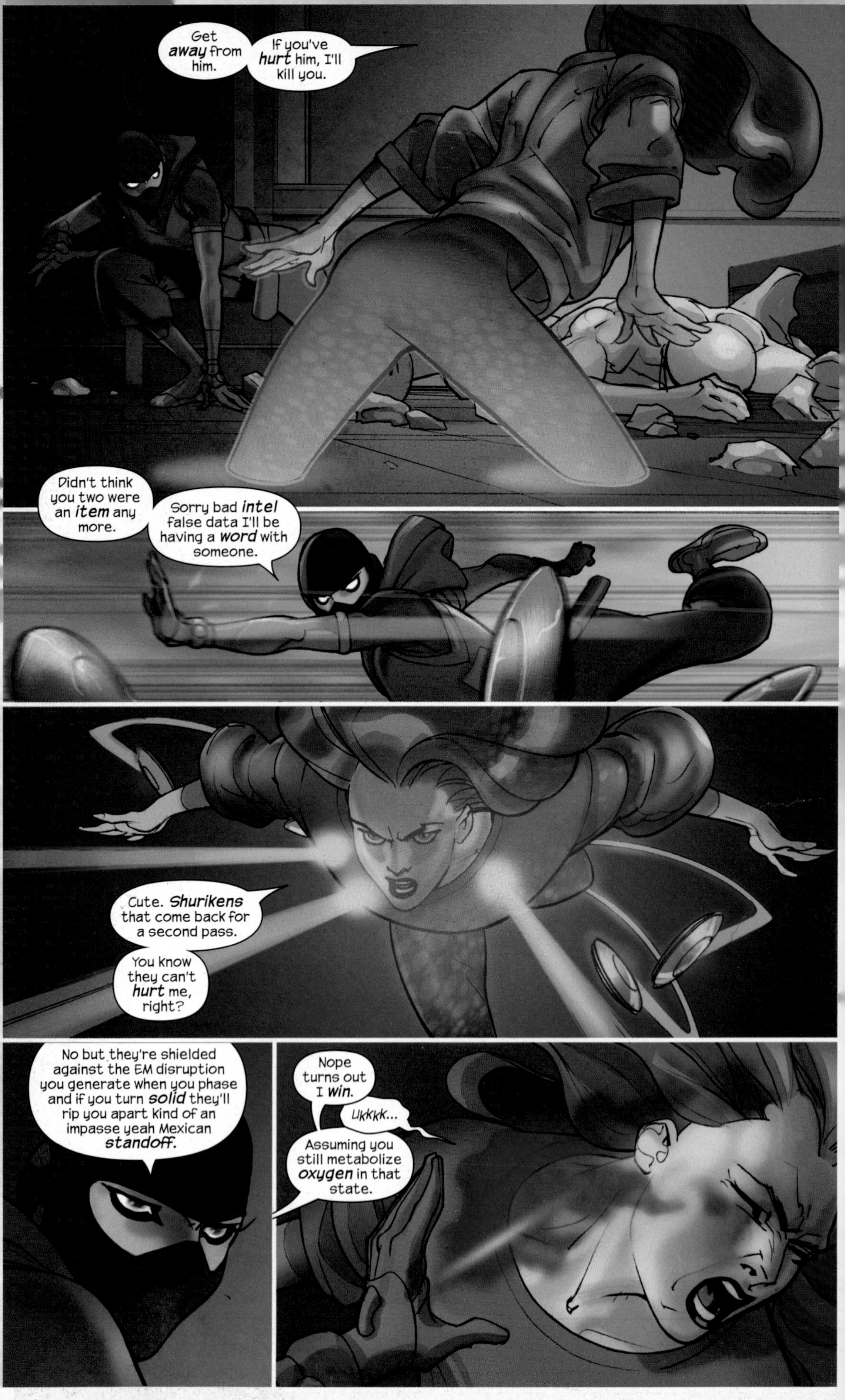
Get away from him.
If you've hurt him, I'll kill you.
Didn't think you two were an item any more.
Sorry bad intel false data I'll be having a word with someone.
Cute. Shurikens that come back for a second pass.
You know they can't hurt me, right?
No but they're shielded against the EM disruption you generate when you phase and if you turn solid they'll rip you apart kind of an impasse yeah Mexican standoff.
Nope turns out I win.
UKKKK...
Assuming you still metabolize oxygen in that state.

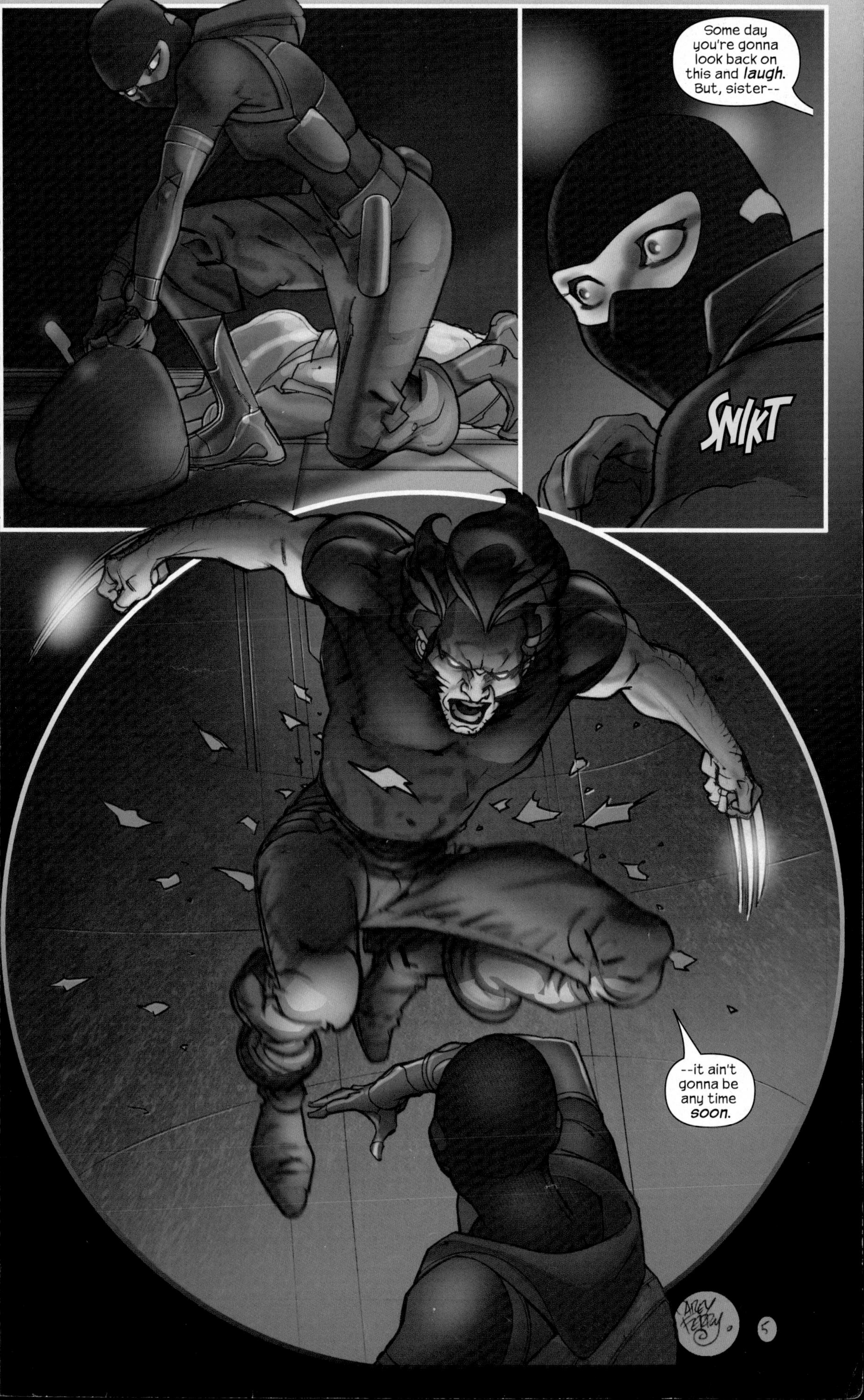
Some day you're gonna look back on this and *laugh*. But, sister--
SNIKT
--it ain't gonna be any time *soon*.

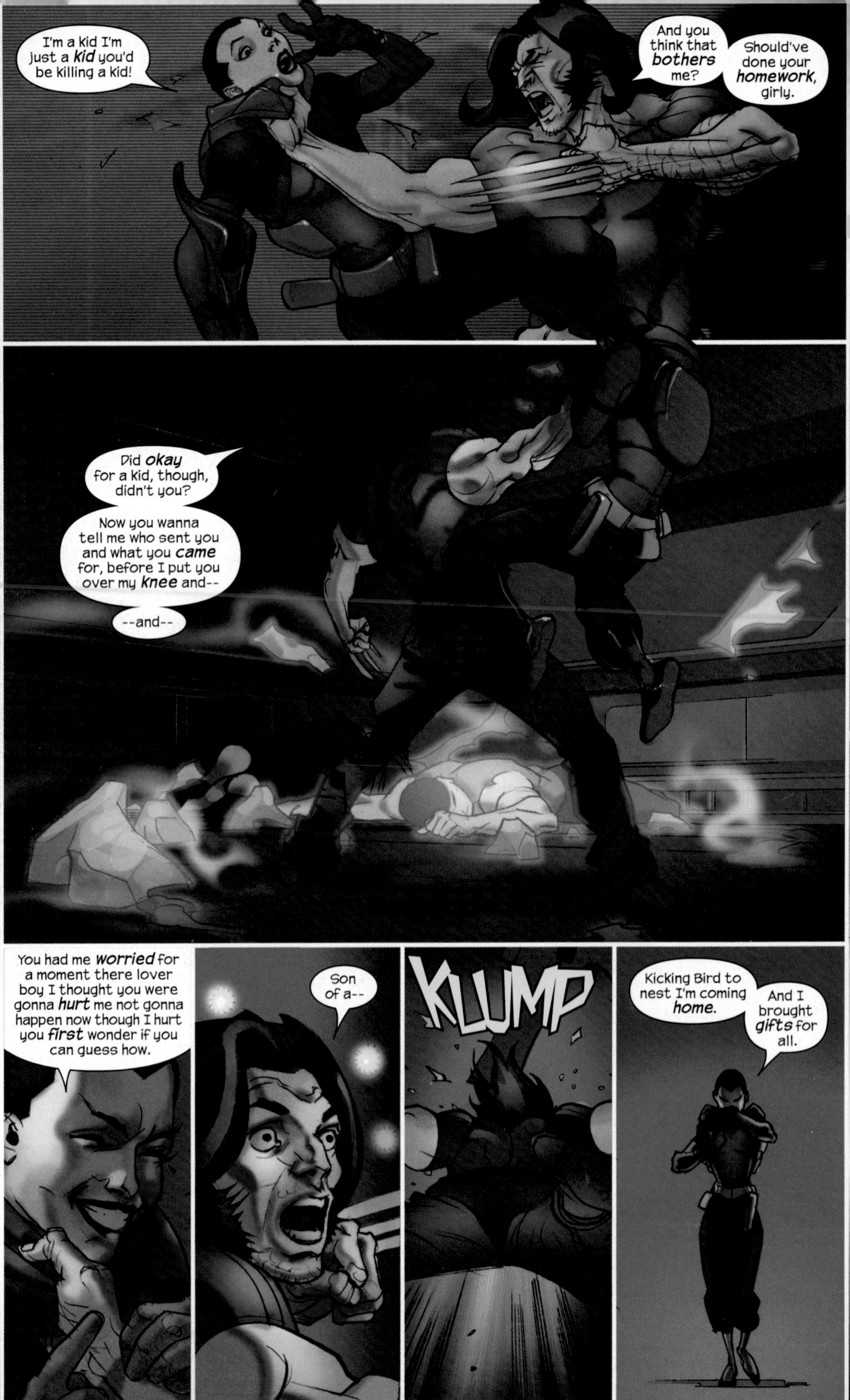
I'm a kid I'm just a *kid* you'd be killing a kid!
And you think that *bothers* me?
Should've done your *homework,* girly.
Did *okay* for a kid, though, didn't you?
Now you wanna tell me who sent you and what you *came* for, before I put you over my *knee* and--
--and--
You had me *worried* for a moment there lover boy I thought you were gonna *hurt* me not gonna happen now though I hurt you *first* wonder if you can guess how.
Son of a--
KLUMP
Kicking Bird to nest I'm coming *home.*
And I brought *gifts* for all.

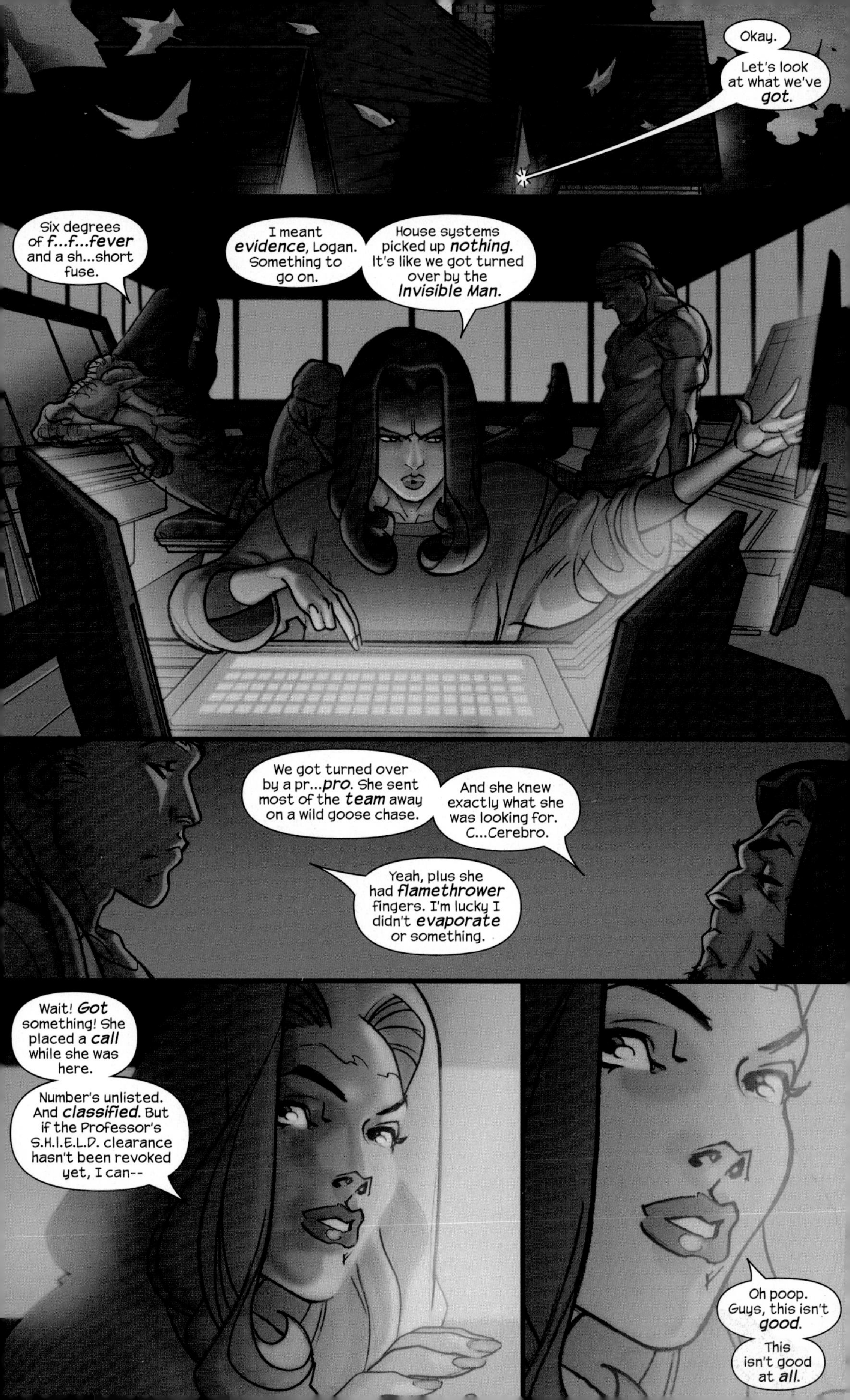

Okay.
Let's look at what we've got.
Six degrees of f...f...fever and a sh...short fuse.
I meant evidence, Logan. Something to go on.
House systems picked up nothing. It's like we got turned over by the Invisible Man.
We got turned over by a pr...pro. She sent most of the team away on a wild goose chase.
And she knew exactly what she was looking for. C...Cerebro.
Yeah, plus she had flamethrower fingers. I'm lucky I didn't evaporate or something.
Wait! Got something! She placed a call while she was here.
Number's unlisted. And classified. But if the Professor's S.H.I.E.L.D. clearance hasn't been revoked yet, I can--
Oh poop. Guys, this isn't good.
This isn't good at all.

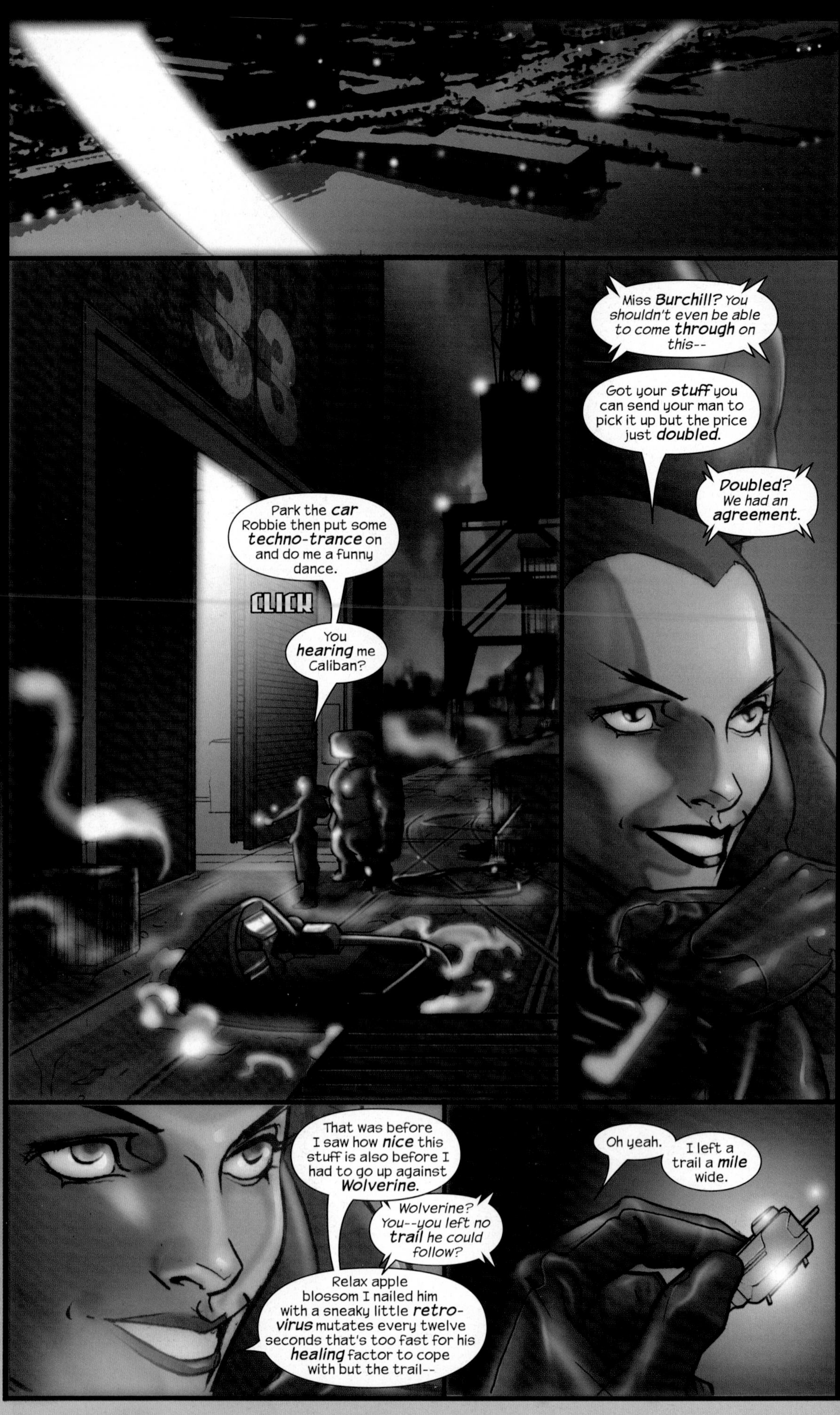
Park the car Robbie then put some techno-trance on and do me a funny dance.
CLICK
You hearing me Caliban?
Miss Burchill? You shouldn't even be able to come through on this--
Got your stuff you can send your man to pick it up but the price just doubled.
Doubled? We had an agreement.
That was before I saw how nice this stuff is also before I had to go up against Wolverine.
Wolverine? You--you left no trail he could follow?
Relax apple blossom I nailed him with a sneaky little retro-virus mutates every twelve seconds that's too fast for his healing factor to cope with but the trail--
Oh yeah.
I left a trail a mile wide.

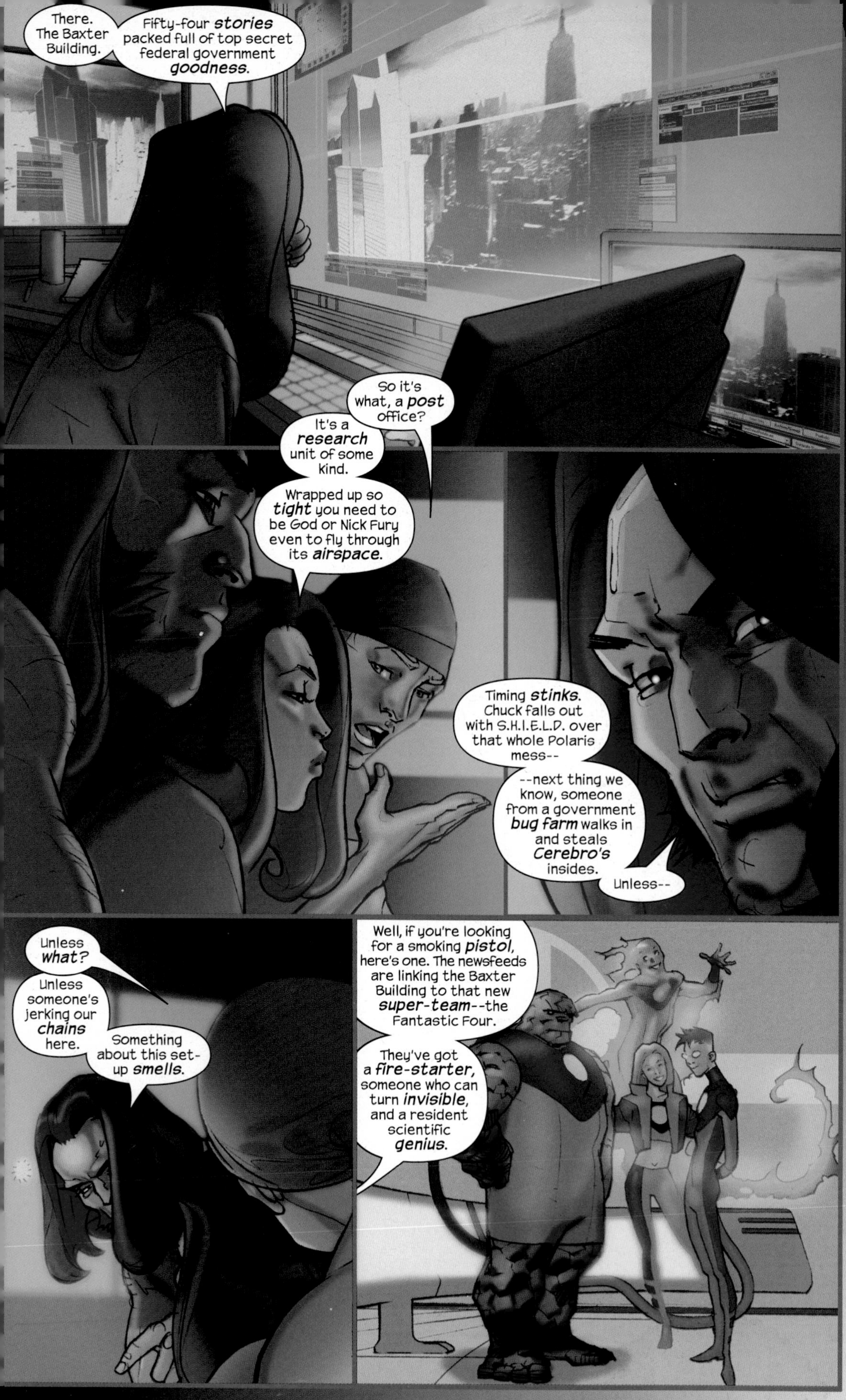
There. The Baxter Building.
Fifty-four stories packed full of top secret federal government goodness.
So it's what, a post office?
It's a research unit of some kind.
Wrapped up so tight you need to be God or Nick Fury even to fly through its airspace.
Timing stinks. Chuck falls out with S.H.I.E.L.D. over that whole Polaris mess--
--next thing we know, someone from a government bug farm walks in and steals Cerebro's insides.
Unless--
Unless what?
Unless someone's jerking our chains here.
Something about this set-up smells.
Well, if you're looking for a smoking pistol, here's one. The newsfeeds are linking the Baxter Building to that new super-team--the Fantastic Four.
They've got a fire-starter, someone who can turn invisible, and a resident scientific genius.

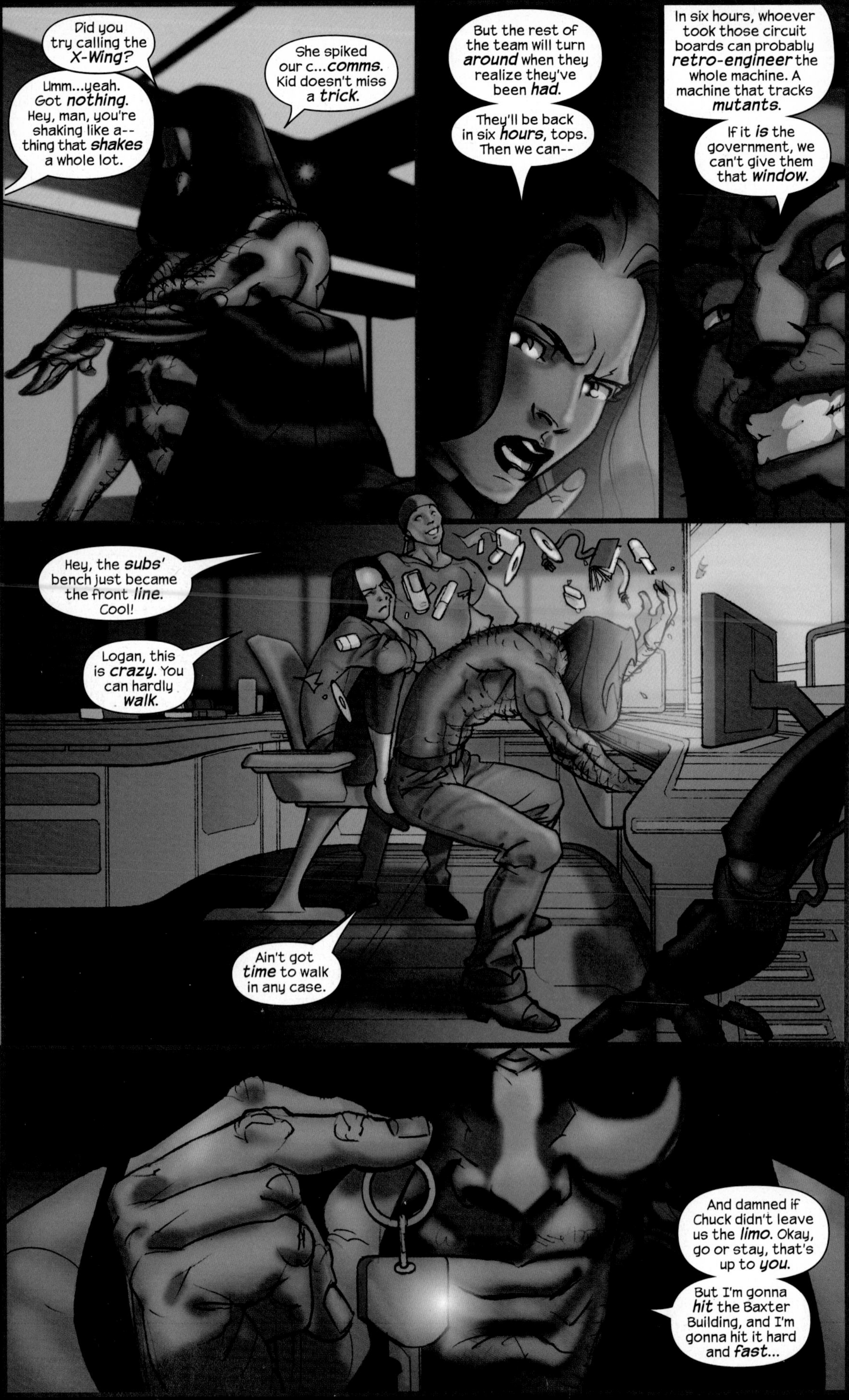
Did you try calling the *X-Wing?*
Umm...yeah. Got *nothing*. Hey, man, you're shaking like a--thing that *shakes* a whole lot.
She spiked our c...*comms*. Kid doesn't miss a *trick*.
But the rest of the team will turn *around* when they realize they've been *had*.
They'll be back in six *hours*, tops. Then we can--
In six hours, whoever took those circuit boards can probably *retro-engineer* the whole machine. A machine that tracks *mutants*.
If it *is* the government, we can't give them that *window*.
Hey, the *subs'* bench just became the front *line*. Cool!
Logan, this is *crazy*. You can hardly *walk*.
Ain't got *time* to walk in any case.
And damned if Chuck didn't leave us the *limo*. Okay, go or stay, that's up to *you*.
But I'm gonna *hit* the Baxter Building, and I'm gonna hit it hard and *fast*...

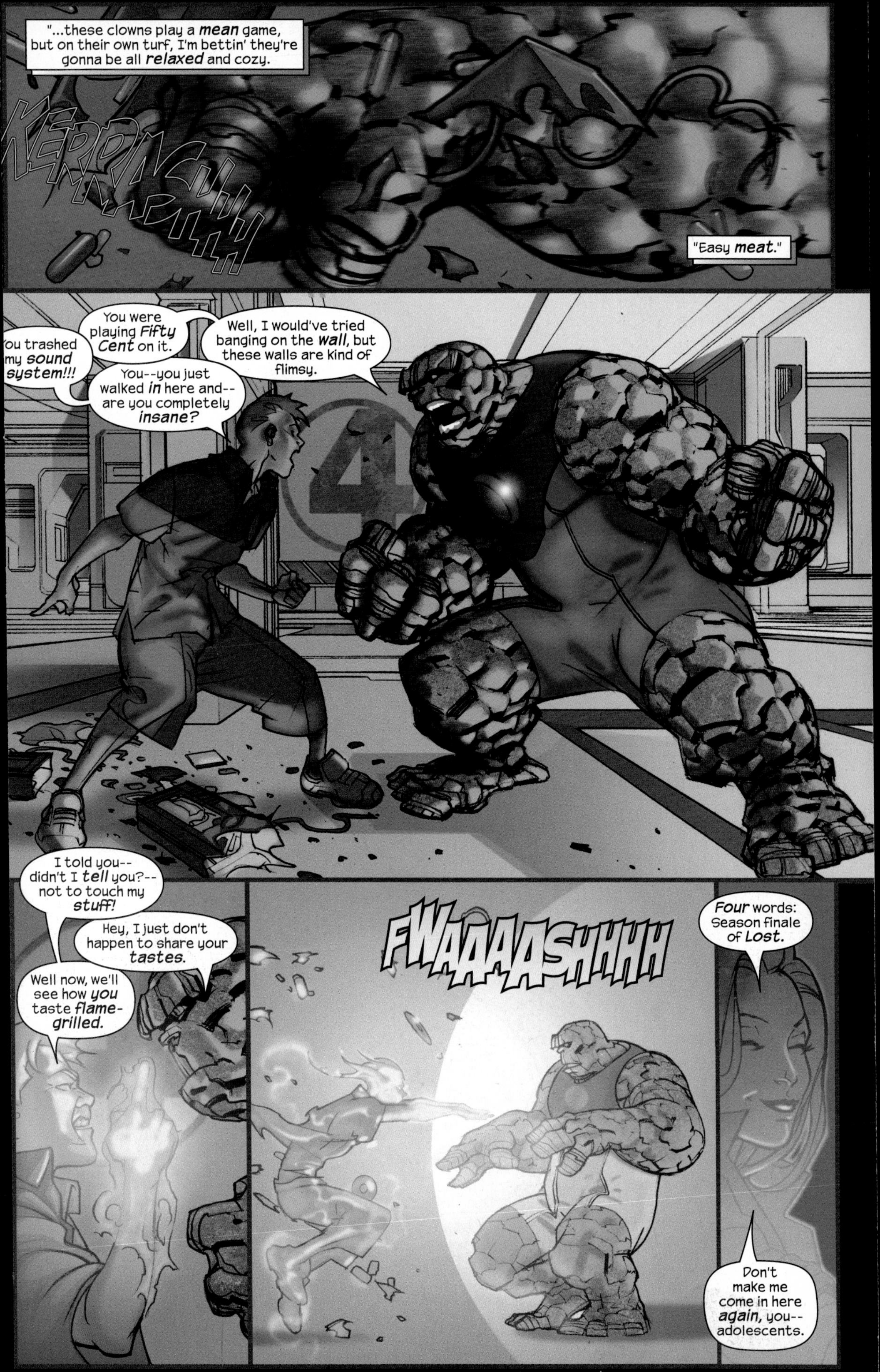

"...these clowns play a mean game, but on their own turf, I'm bettin' they're gonna be all relaxed and cozy.
KERRUNCHH
"Easy meat."
You trashed my sound system!!!
You were playing Fifty Cent on it.
Well, I would've tried banging on the wall, but these walls are kind of flimsy.
You--you just walked in here and--are you completely insane?
I told you--didn't I tell you?--not to touch my stuff!
Hey, I just don't happen to share your tastes.
Well now, we'll see how you taste flame-grilled.
FWAAAASHHHH
Four words: Season finale of Lost.
Don't make me come in here again, you--adolescents.

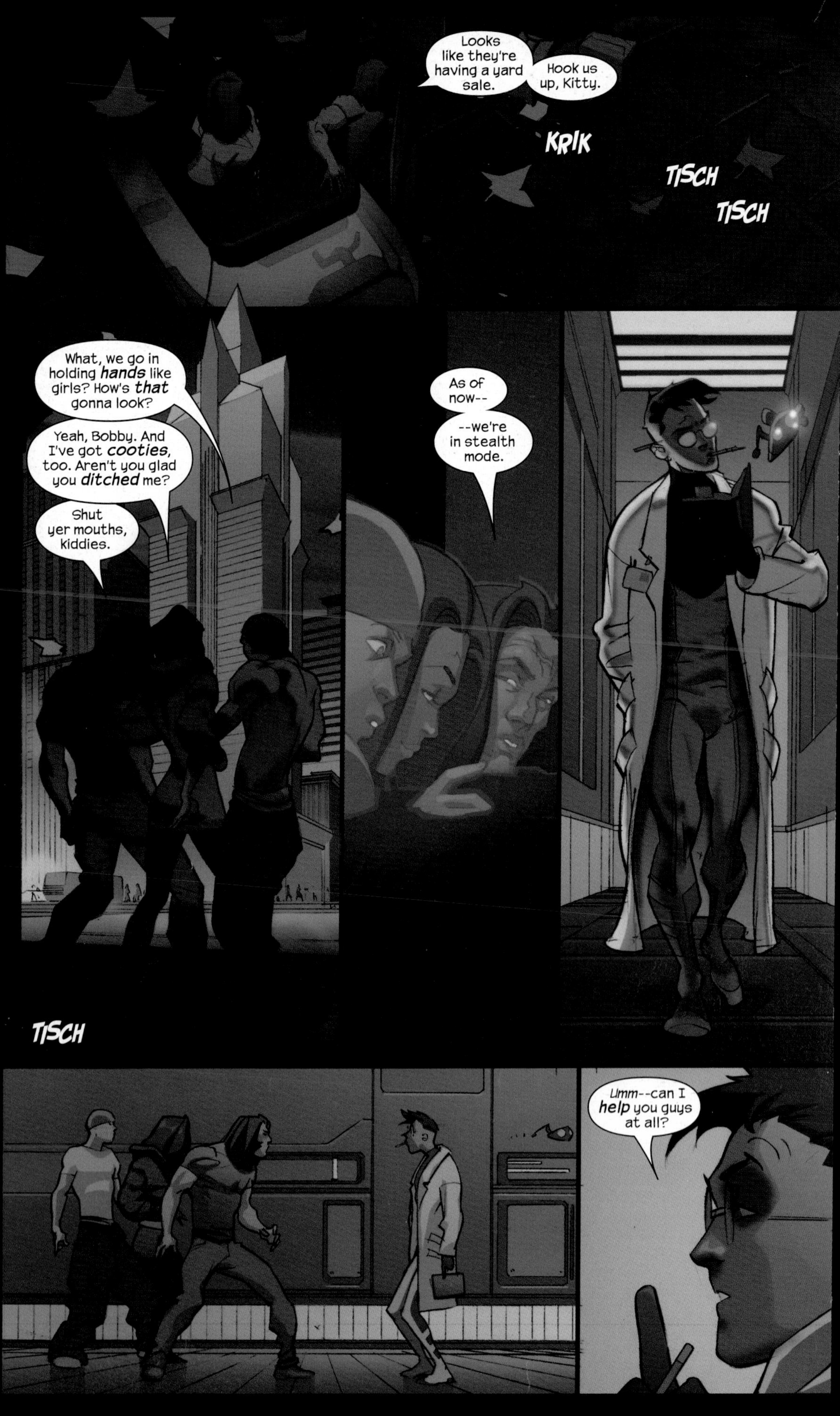

Looks like they're having a yard sale.
Hook us up, Kitty.
KRIK
TISCH
TISCH
What, we go in holding hands like girls? How's that gonna look?
Yeah, Bobby. And I've got cooties, too. Aren't you glad you ditched me?
Shut yer mouths, kiddies.
As of now--
--we're in stealth mode.
TISCH
Umm--can I help you guys at all?

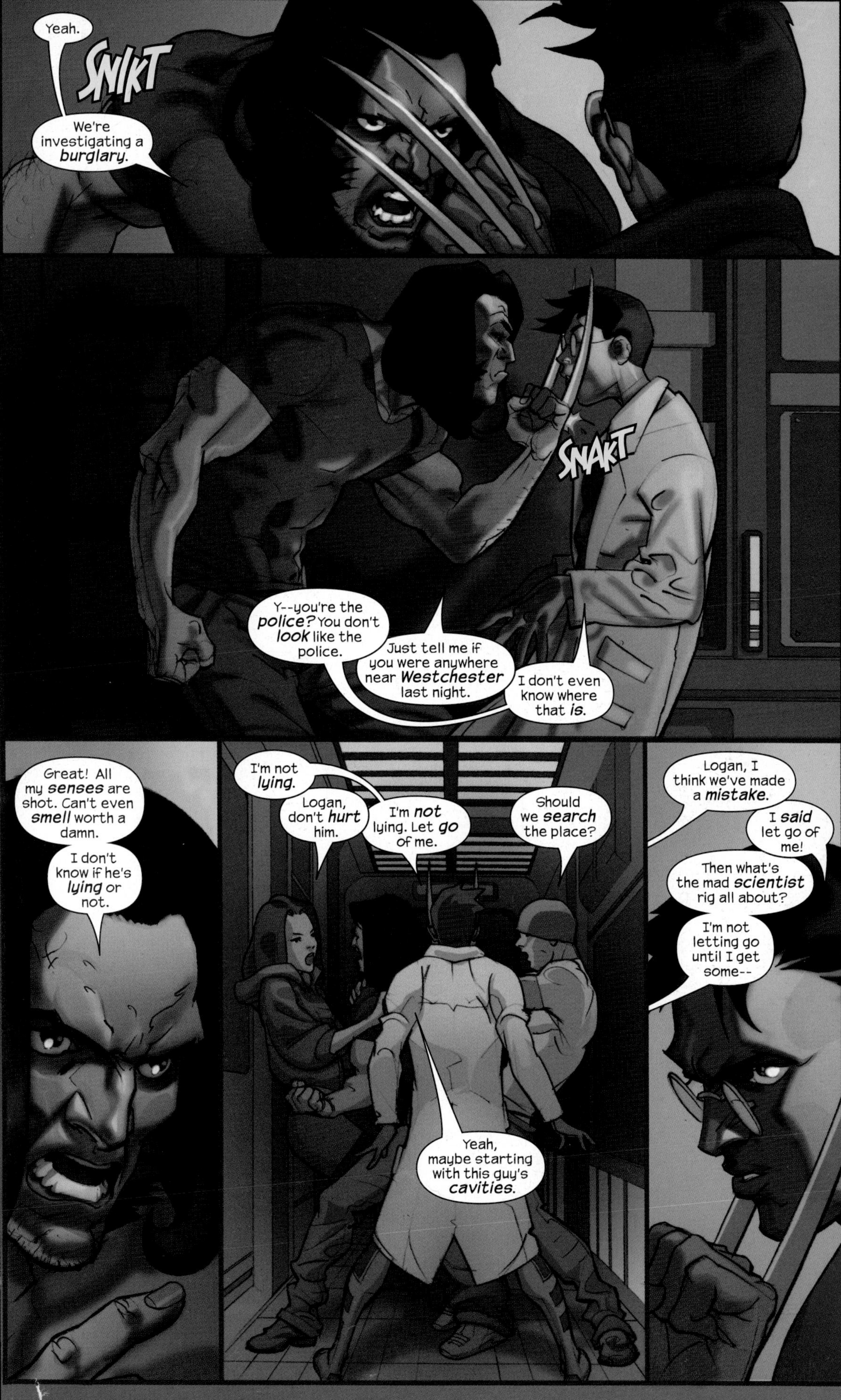
Yeah.
SNIKT
We're investigating a burglary.
SNAKT
Y--you're the police? You don't look like the police.
Just tell me if you were anywhere near Westchester last night.
I don't even know where that is.
Great! All my senses are shot. Can't even smell worth a damn.
I don't know if he's lying or not.
I'm not lying.
Logan, don't hurt him.
I'm not lying. Let go of me.
Should we search the place?
Yeah, maybe starting with this guy's cavities.
Logan, I think we've made a mistake.
I said let go of me!
Then what's the mad scientist rig all about?
I'm not letting go until I get some--

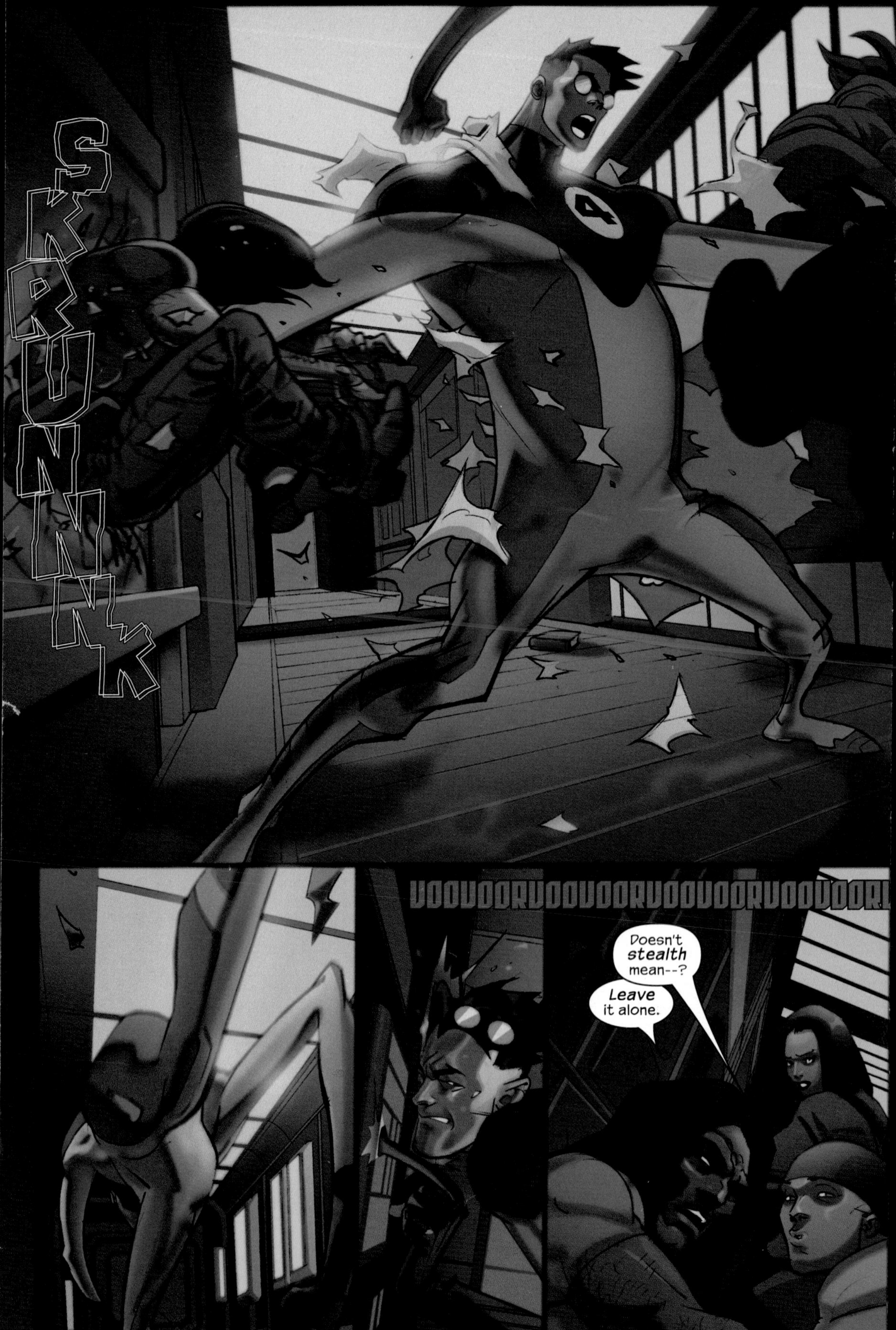
SKRUNNK
VOOVOORVOOVOORVOOVOORVOODOOR
Doesn't stealth mean--?
Leave it alone.

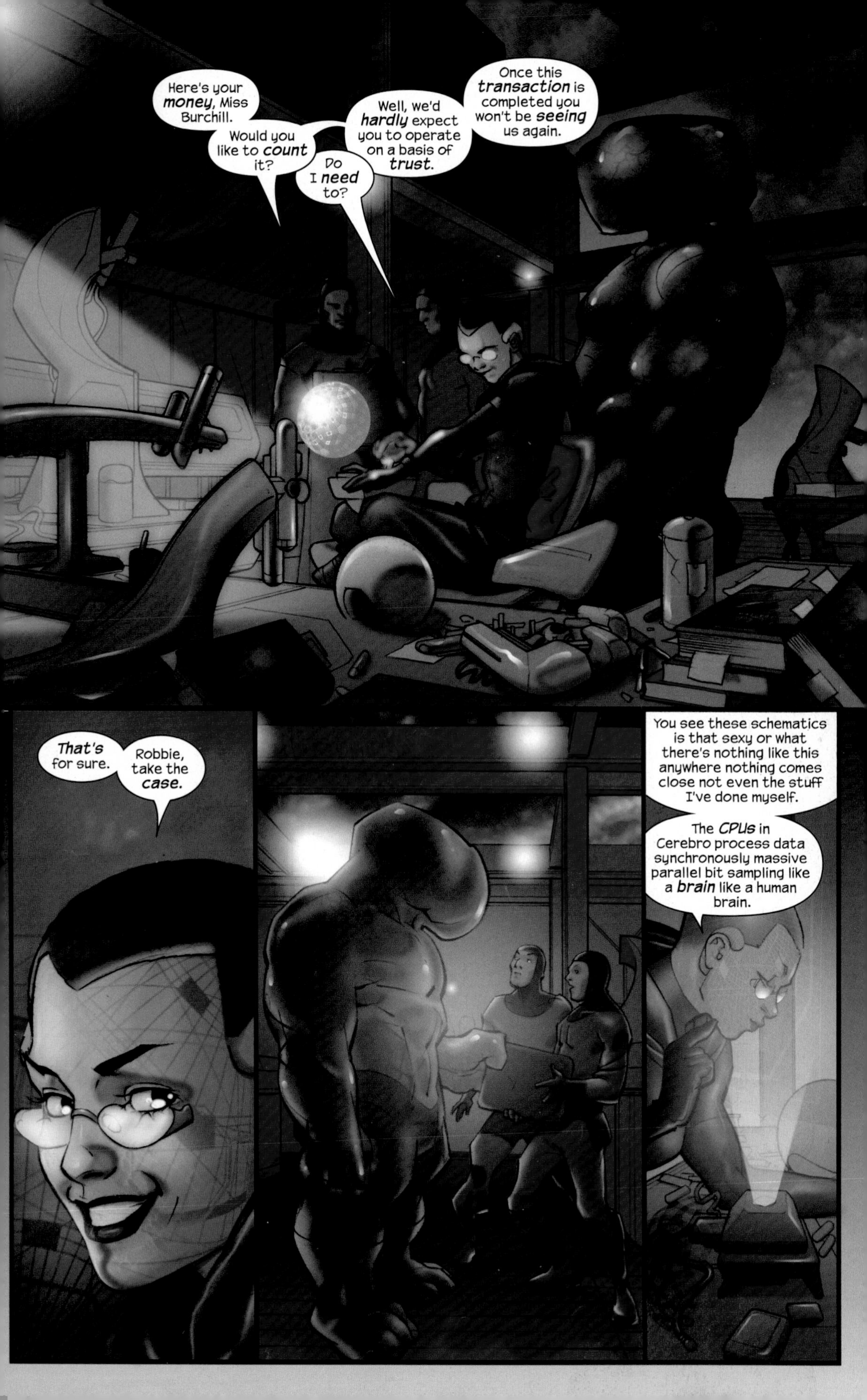
Here's your money, Miss Burchill.
Would you like to count it?
Do I need to?
Well, we'd hardly expect you to operate on a basis of trust.
Once this transaction is completed you won't be seeing us again.
That's for sure.
Robbie, take the case.
You see these schematics is that sexy or what there's nothing like this anywhere nothing comes close not even the stuff I've done myself.
The CPUs in Cerebro process data synchronously massive parallel bit sampling like a brain like a human brain.

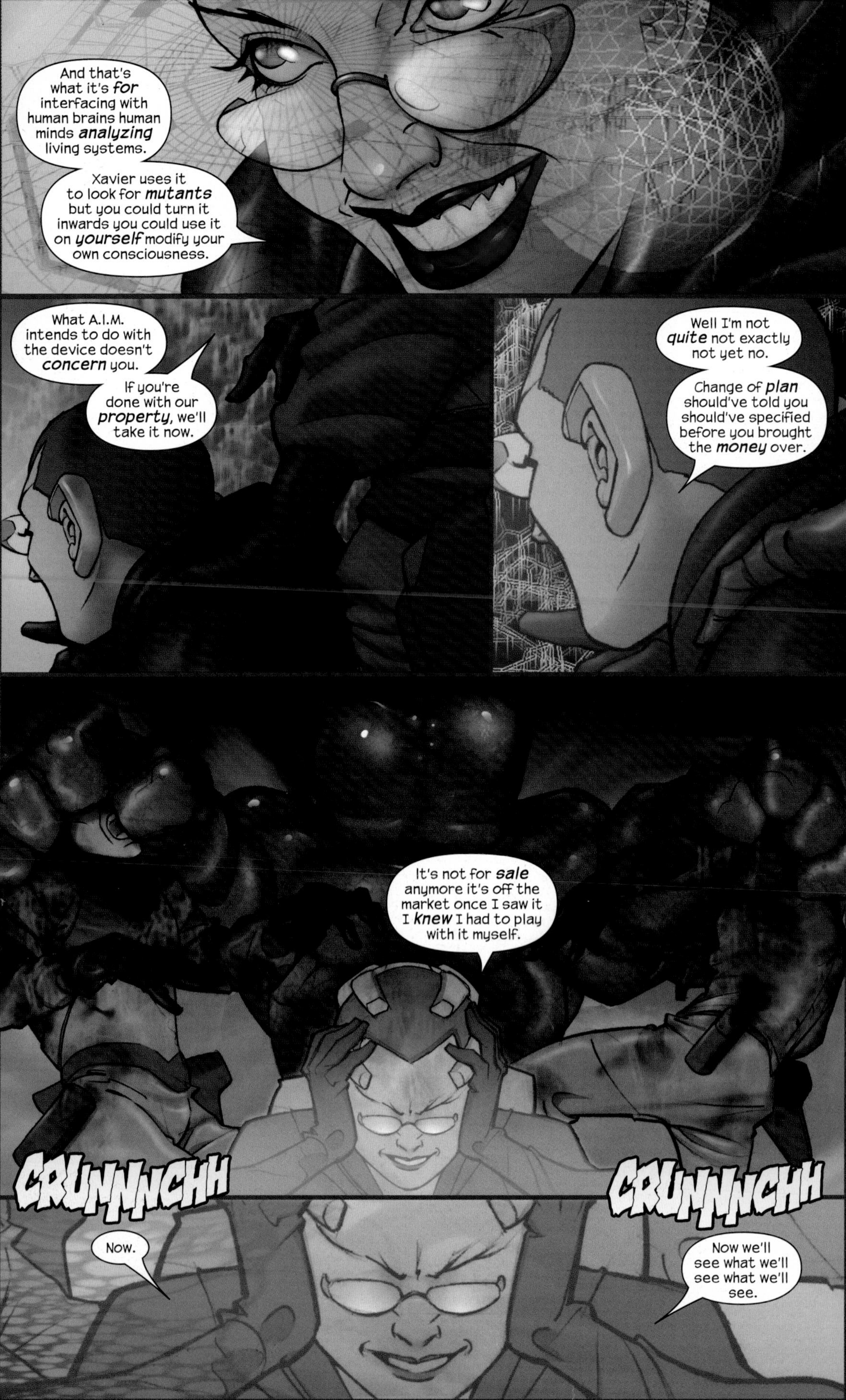

And that's what it's *for* interfacing with human brains human minds ***analyzing*** living systems.
Xavier uses it to look for ***mutants*** but you could turn it inwards you could use it on ***yourself*** modify your own consciousness.
What A.I.M. intends to do with the device doesn't ***concern*** you.
If you're done with our ***property***, we'll take it now.
Well I'm not ***quite*** not exactly not yet no.
Change of ***plan*** should've told you should've specified before you brought the ***money*** over.
It's not for ***sale*** anymore it's off the market once I saw it I ***knew*** I had to play with it myself.
CRUNNNCHH
CRUNNNCHH
Now.
Now we'll see what we'll see what we'll see.

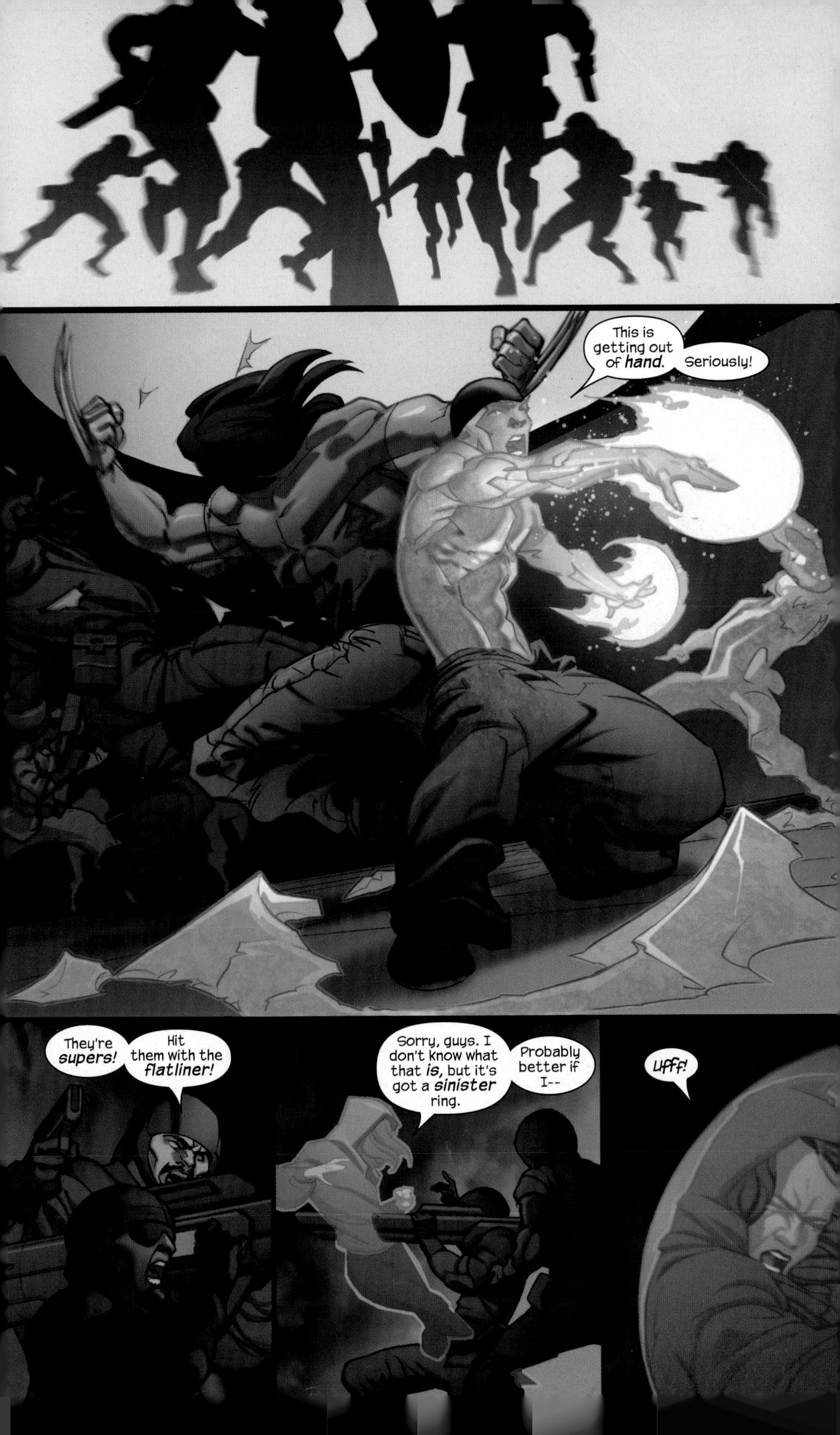
This is getting out of hand.
Seriously!
They're supers!
Hit them with the flatliner!
Sorry, guys. I don't know what that is, but it's got a sinister ring.
Probably better if I--
Uff!

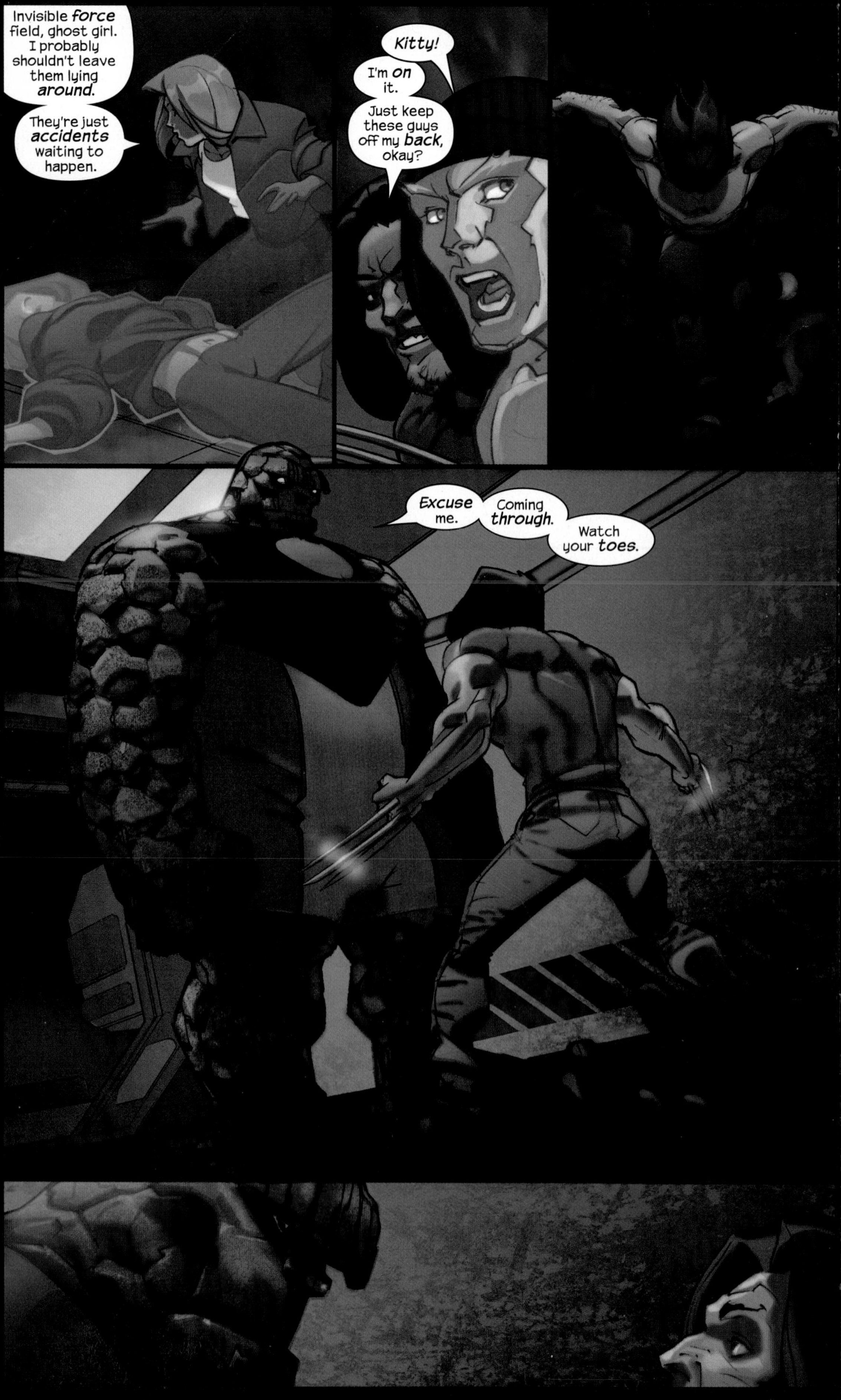
Invisible force field, ghost girl. I probably shouldn't leave them lying around.
They're just accidents waiting to happen.
Kitty!
I'm on it.
Just keep these guys off my back, okay?
Excuse me.
Coming through.
Watch your toes.

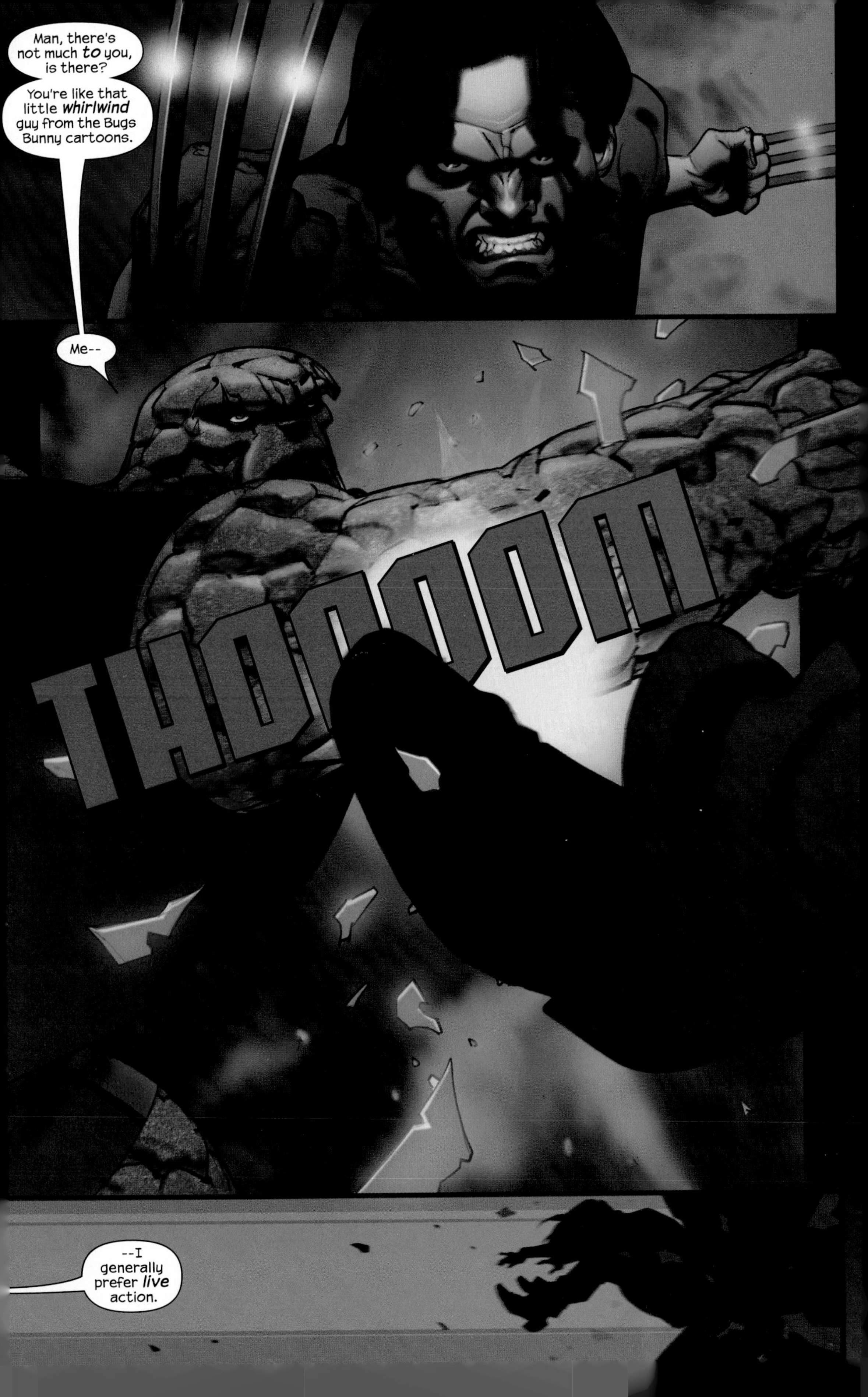
Man, there's not much *to* you, is there?
You're like that little *whirlwind* guy from the Bugs Bunny cartoons.
Me--
THOOOOM
--I generally prefer *live* action.

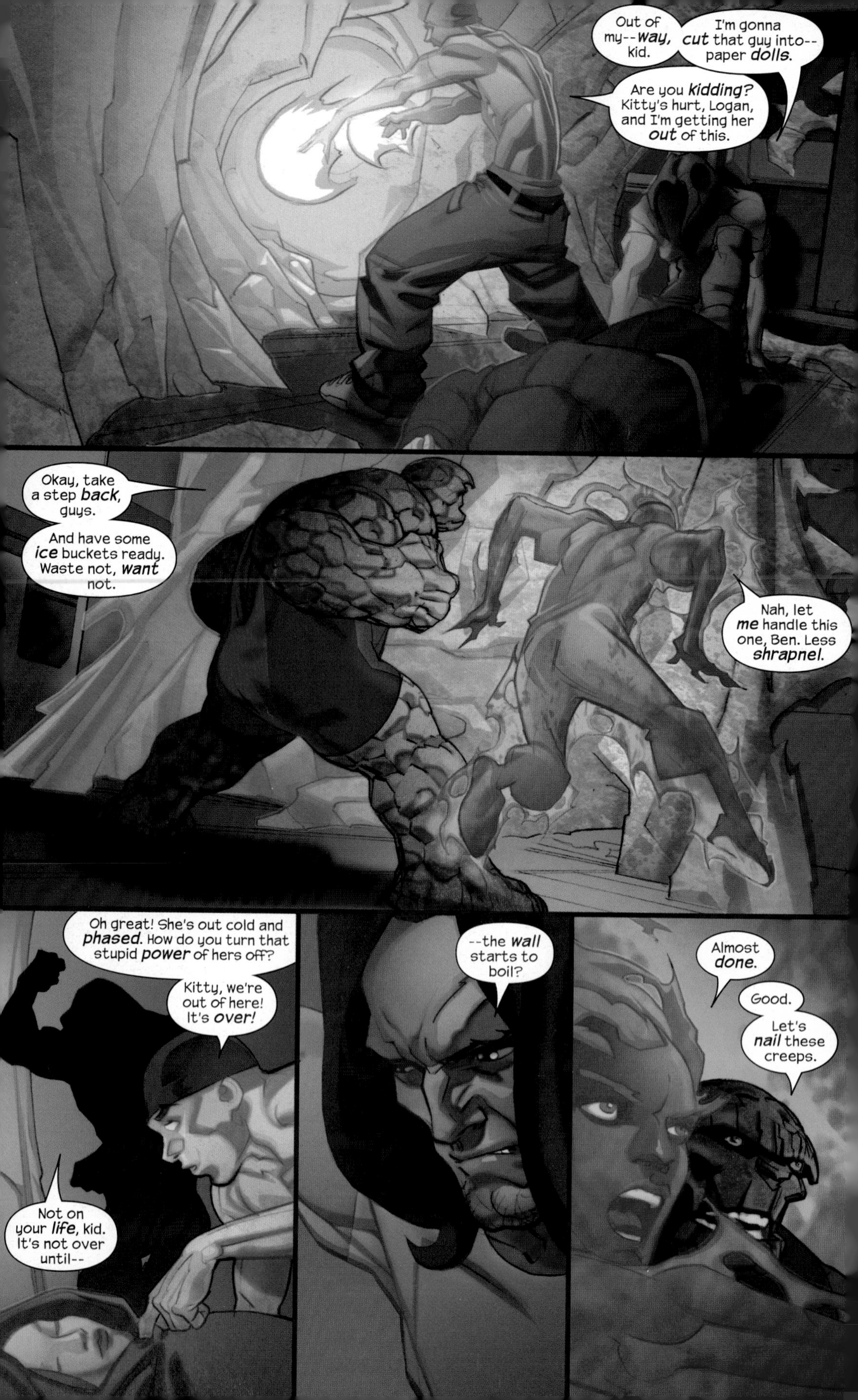
Out of my--way, kid.
I'm gonna cut that guy into--paper dolls.
Are you kidding? Kitty's hurt, Logan, and I'm getting her out of this.
Okay, take a step back, guys.
And have some ice buckets ready. Waste not, want not.
Nah, let me handle this one, Ben. Less shrapnel.
Oh great! She's out cold and phased. How do you turn that stupid power of hers off?
Kitty, we're out of here! It's over!
Not on your life, kid. It's not over until--
--the wall starts to boil?
Almost done.
Good.
Let's nail these creeps.

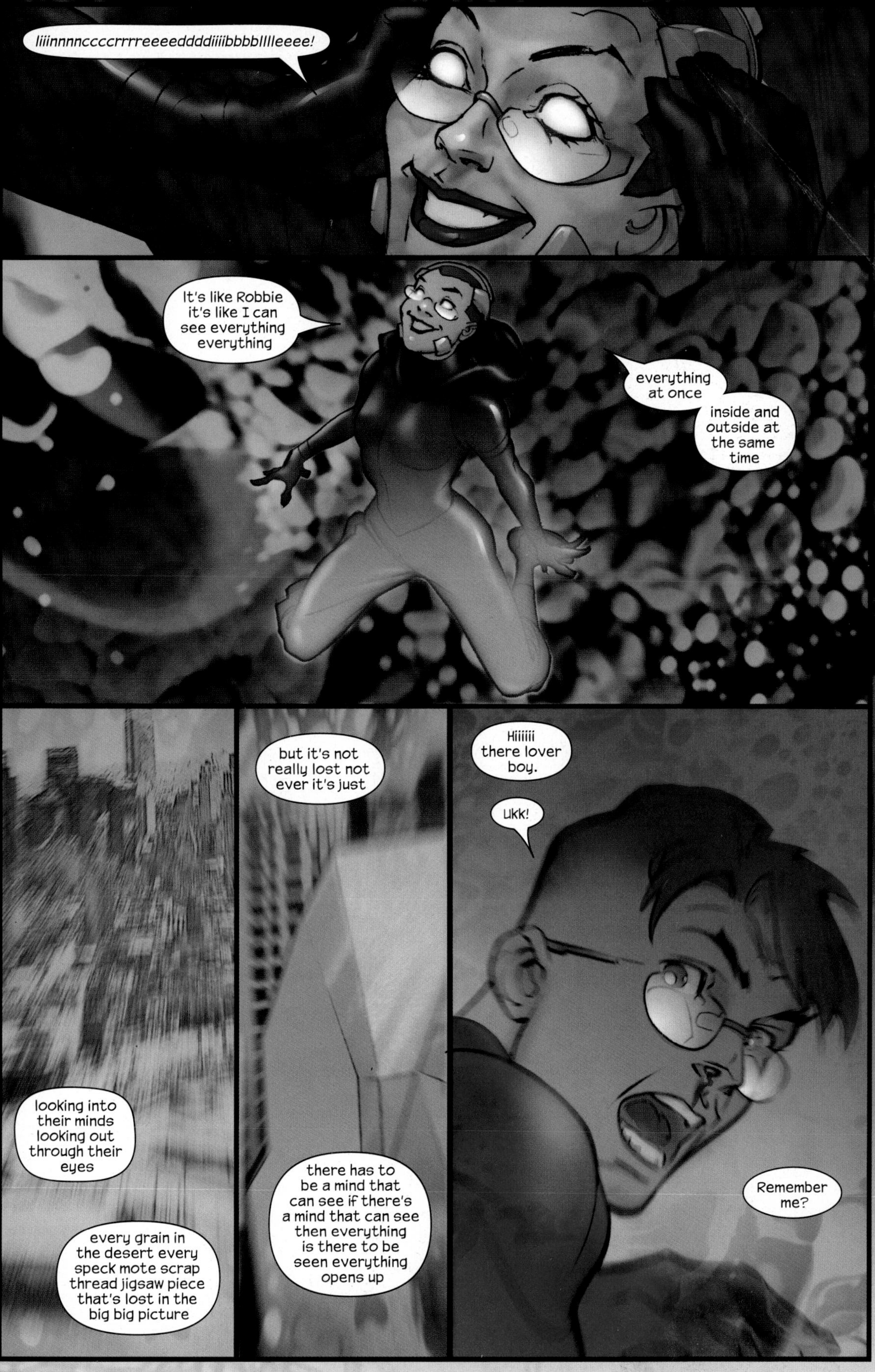

Iiiinnnnccccrrrreeeedddddiiiibbbblllleeee!
It's like Robbie it's like I can see everything everything
everything at once
inside and outside at the same time
looking into their minds looking out through their eyes
every grain in the desert every speck mote scrap thread jigsaw piece that's lost in the big big picture
but it's not really lost not ever it's just
there has to be a mind that can see if there's a mind that can see then everything is there to be seen everything opens up
Hiiiiii there lover boy.
Ukk!
Remember me?

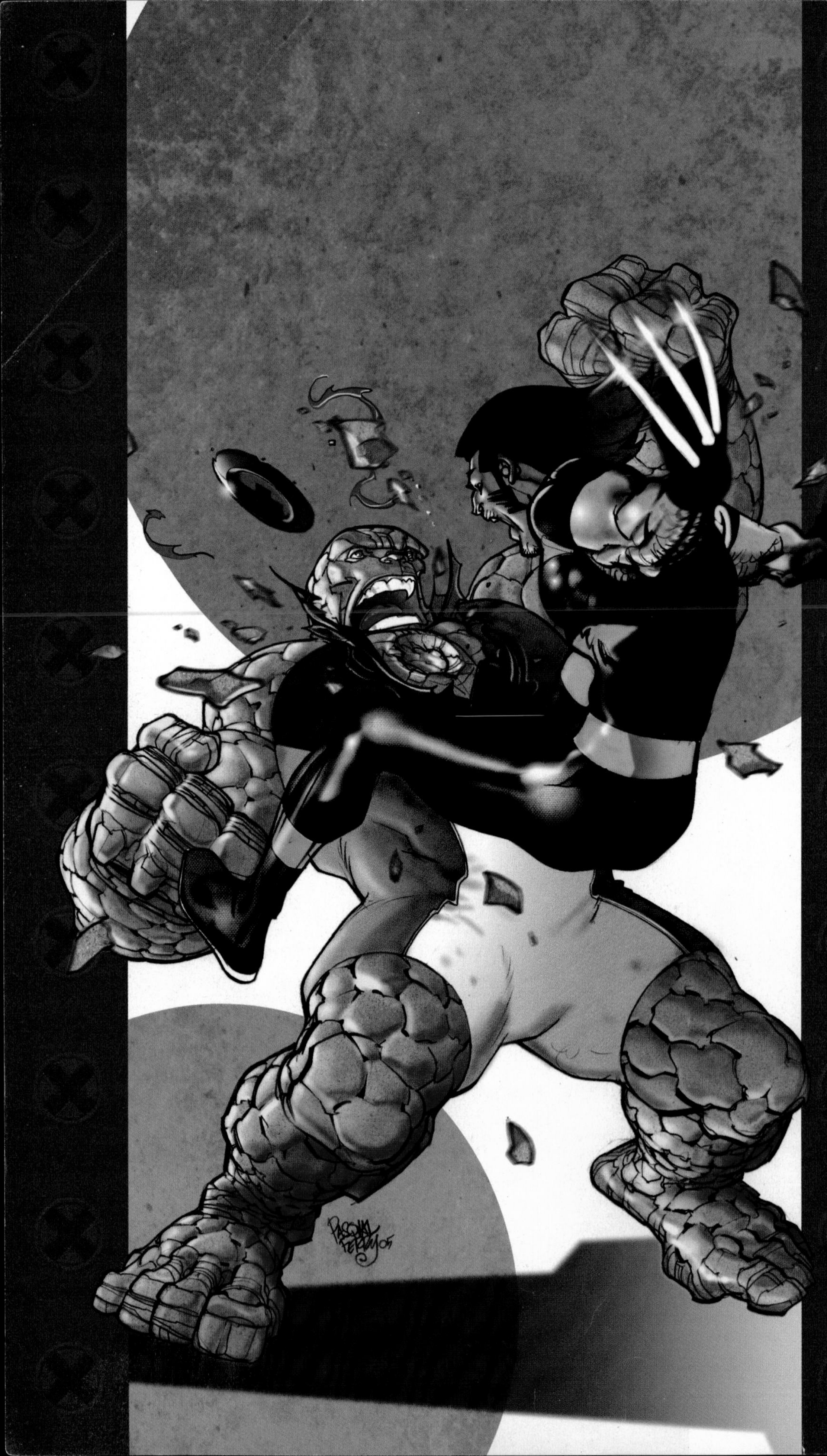

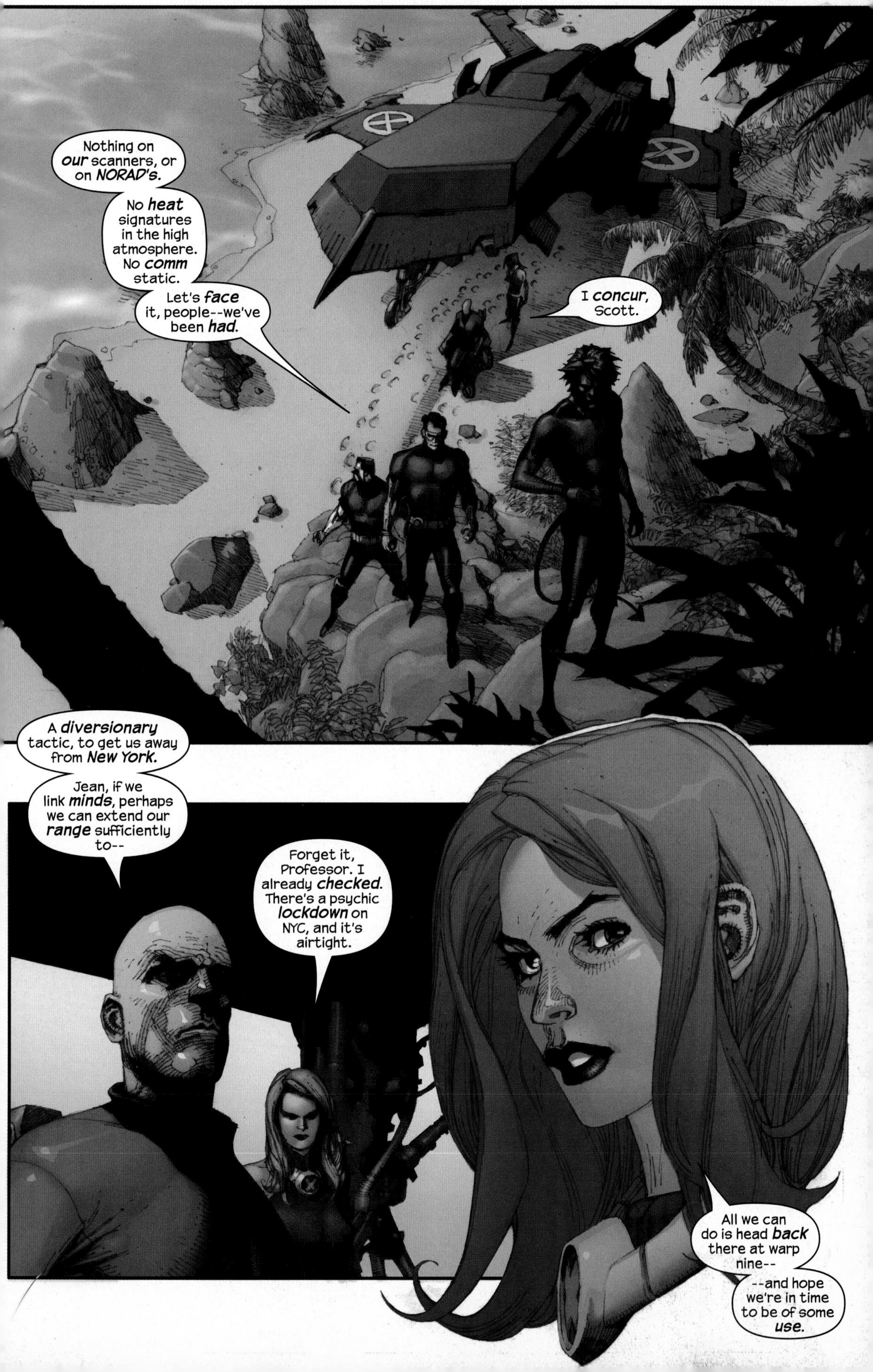
Nothing on our scanners, or on NORAD's.
No heat signatures in the high atmosphere. No comm static.
Let's face it, people--we've been had.
I concur, Scott.
A diversionary tactic, to get us away from New York.
Jean, if we link minds, perhaps we can extend our range sufficiently to--
Forget it, Professor. I already checked. There's a psychic lockdown on NYC, and it's airtight.
All we can do is head back there at warp nine--
--and hope we're in time to be of some use.

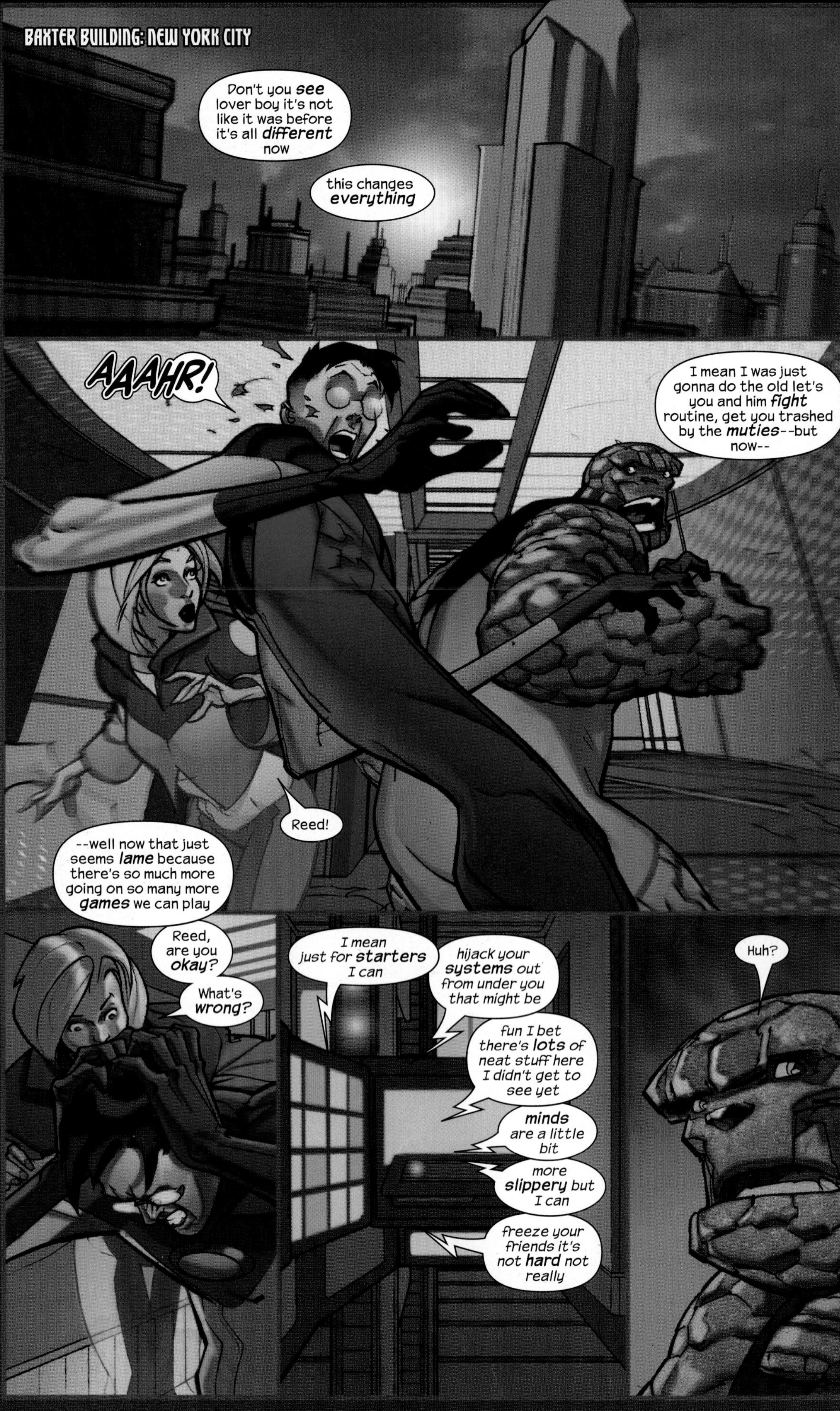

BAXTER BUILDING: NEW YORK CITY
Don't you see lover boy it's not like it was before it's all different now
this changes everything
AAAHR!
I mean I was just gonna do the old let's you and him fight routine, get you trashed by the muties--but now--
Reed!
--well now that just seems lame because there's so much more going on so many more games we can play
Reed, are you okay?
What's wrong?
I mean just for starters I can
hijack your systems out from under you that might be
fun I bet there's lots of neat stuff here I didn't get to see yet
minds are a little bit
more slippery but I can
freeze your friends it's not hard not really
Huh?

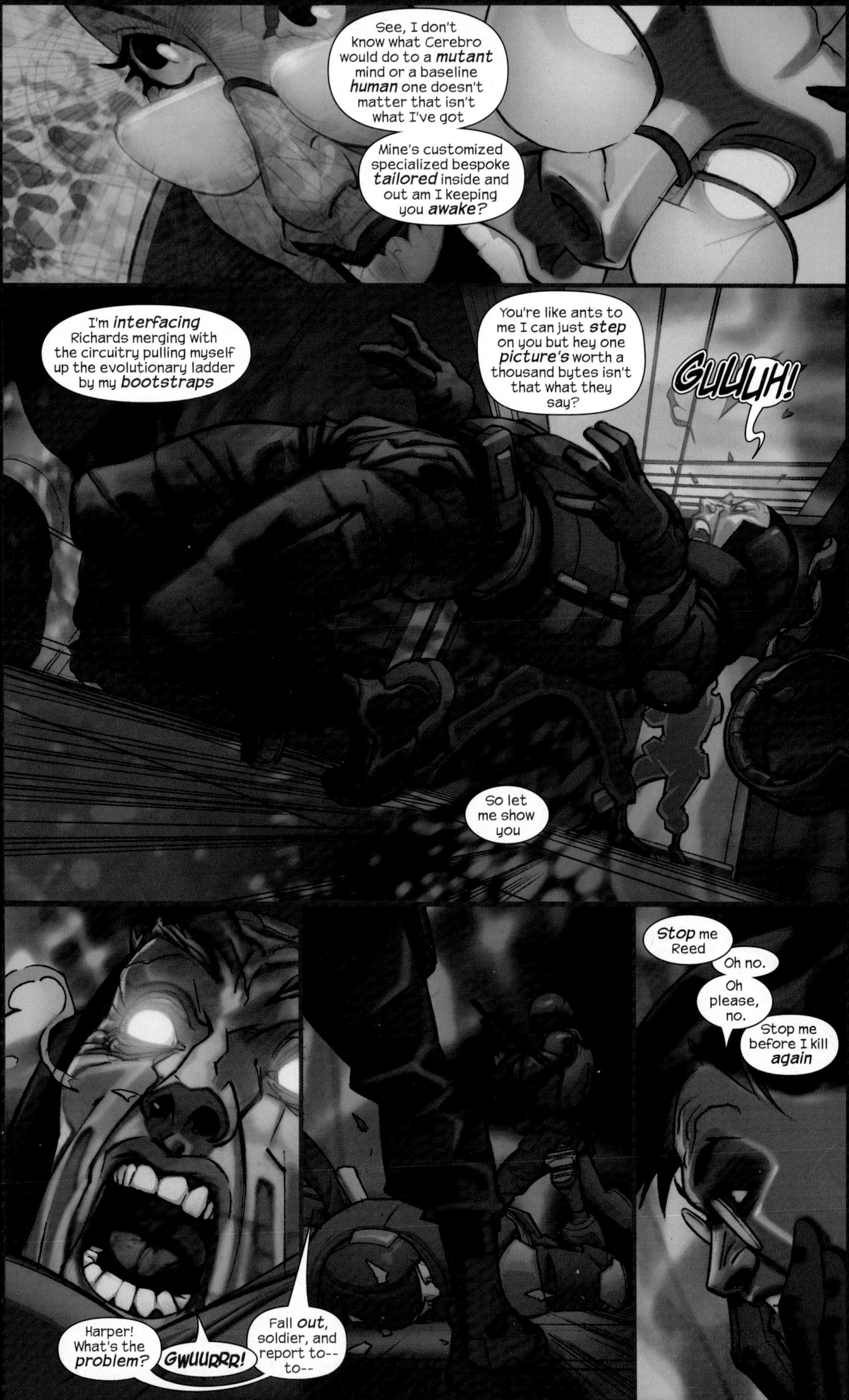

See, I don't know what Cerebro would do to a *mutant* mind or a baseline *human* one doesn't matter that isn't what I've got
Mine's customized specialized bespoke *tailored* inside and out am I keeping you *awake*?
I'm *interfacing* Richards merging with the circuitry pulling myself up the evolutionary ladder by my *bootstraps*
You're like ants to me I can just *step* on you but hey one *picture's* worth a thousand bytes isn't that what they say?
GUUUH!
So let me show you
Harper! What's the *problem*?
GWUURRR!
Fall *out*, soldier, and report to-- to--
Stop me Reed
Oh no.
Oh please, no.
Stop me before I kill *again*

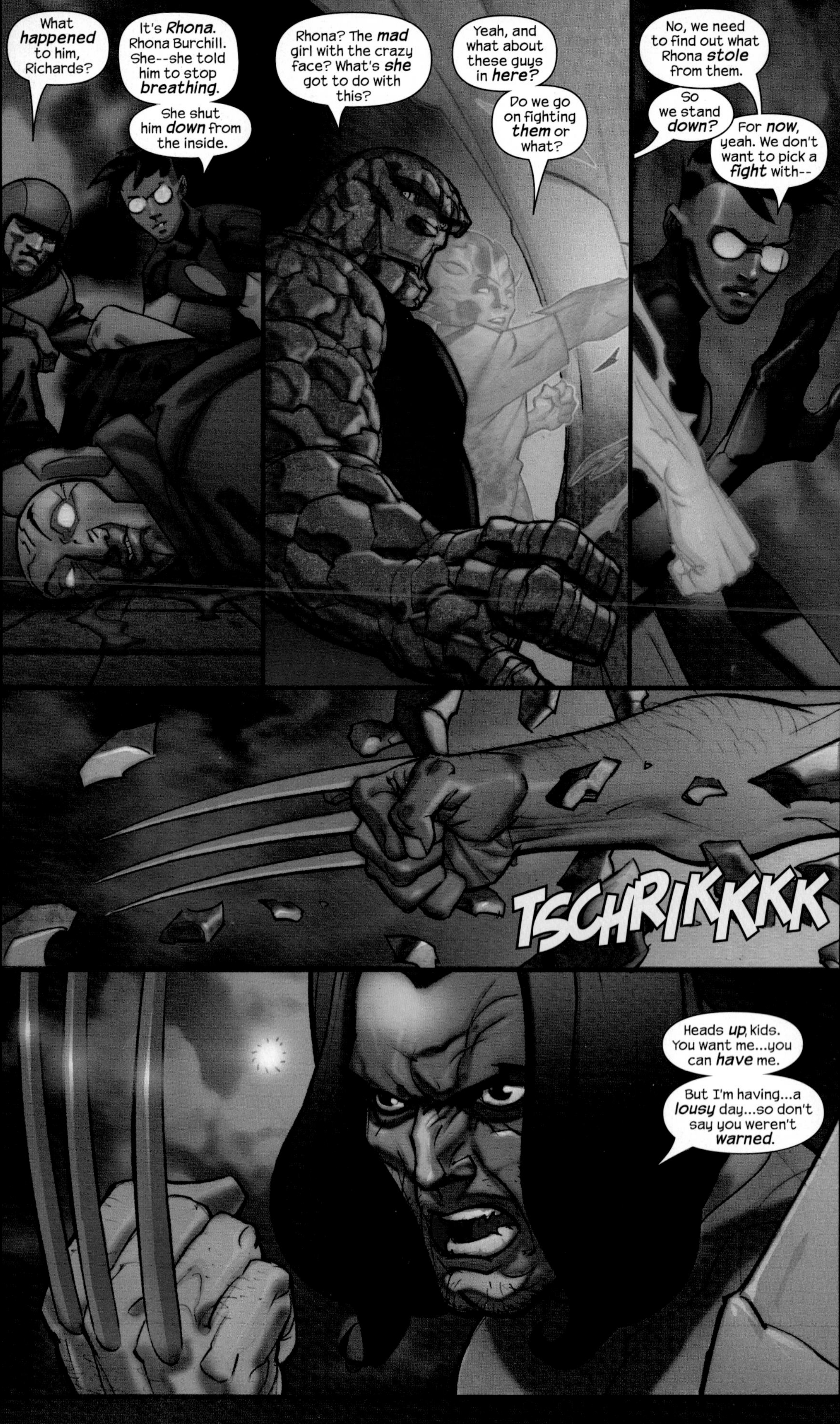
What happened to him, Richards?
It's Rhona. Rhona Burchill. She--she told him to stop breathing.
She shut him down from the inside.
Rhona? The mad girl with the crazy face? What's she got to do with this?
Yeah, and what about these guys in here?
Do we go on fighting them or what?
No, we need to find out what Rhona stole from them.
So we stand down?
For now, yeah. We don't want to pick a fight with--
TSCHRIKKKK
Heads up, kids. You want me...you can have me.
But I'm having...a lousy day...so don't say you weren't warned.

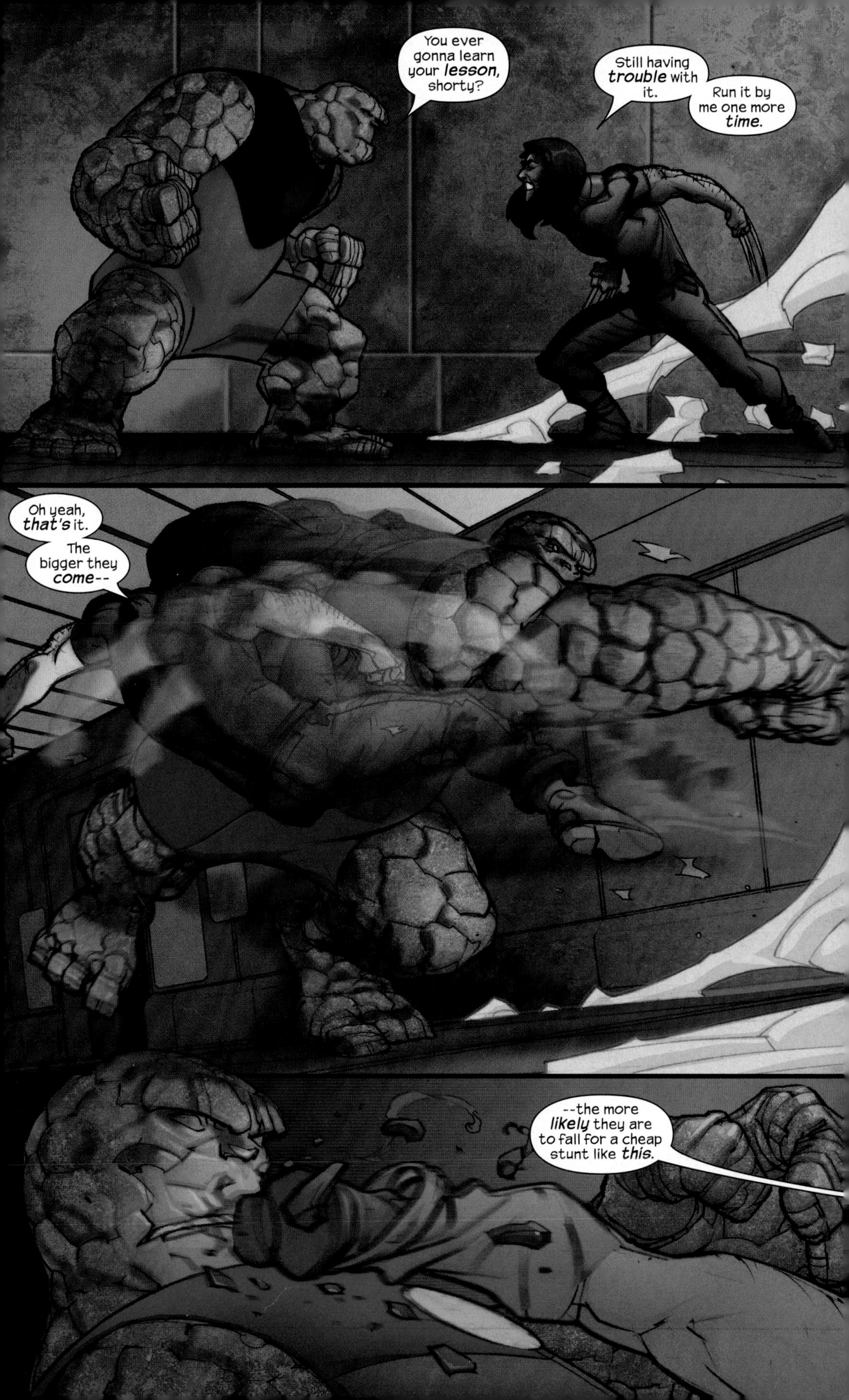
You ever gonna learn your *lesson*, shorty?
Still having *trouble* with it.
Run it by me one more *time*.
Oh yeah, *that's* it.
The bigger they *come*--
--the more *likely* they are to fall for a cheap stunt like *this*.

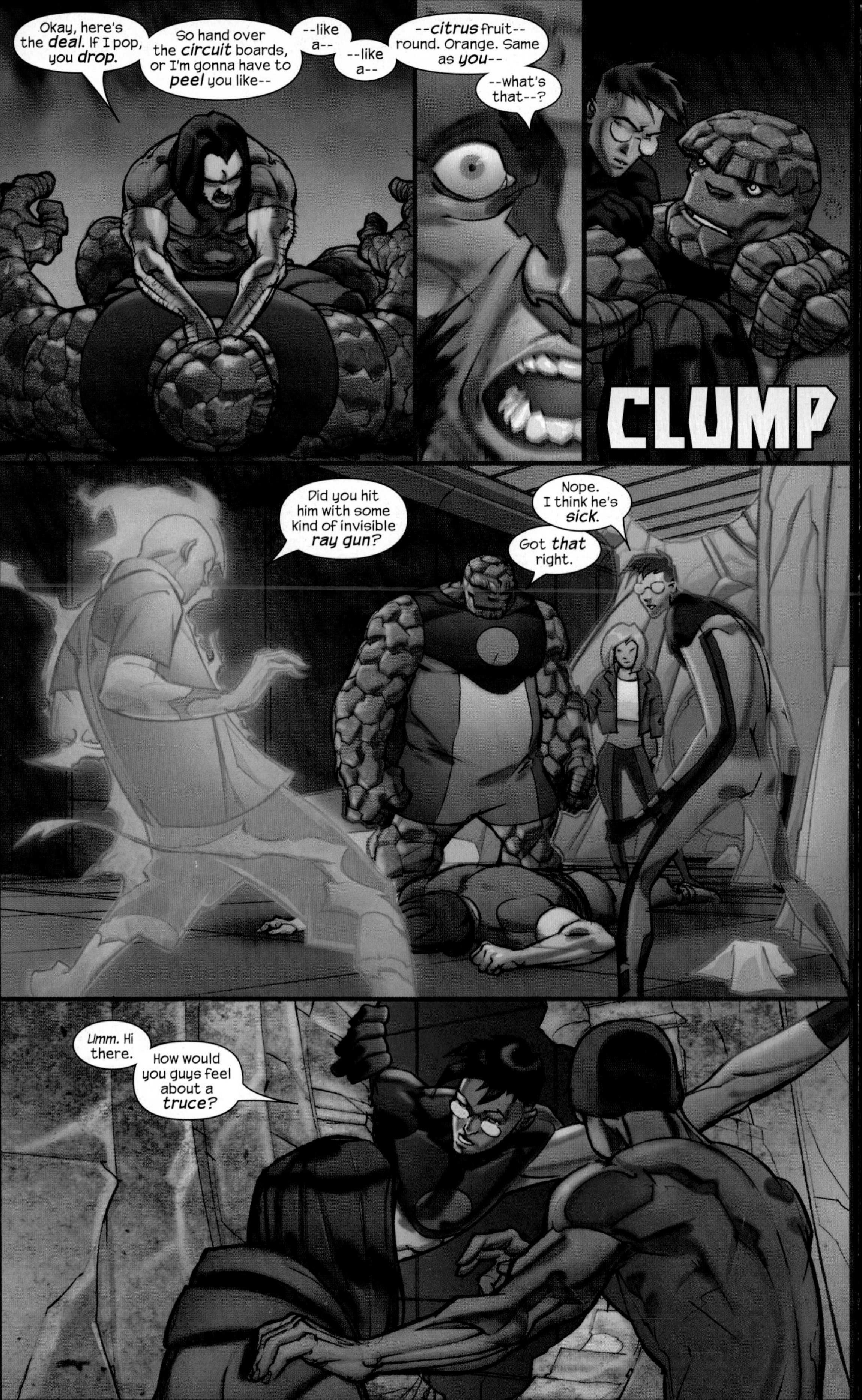

Okay, here's the deal. If I pop, you drop.
So hand over the circuit boards, or I'm gonna have to peel you like--
--like a--
--like a--
--citrus fruit-- round. Orange. Same as you--
--what's that--?
CLUMP
Did you hit him with some kind of invisible ray gun?
Nope. I think he's sick.
Got that right.
Umm. Hi there.
How would you guys feel about a truce?

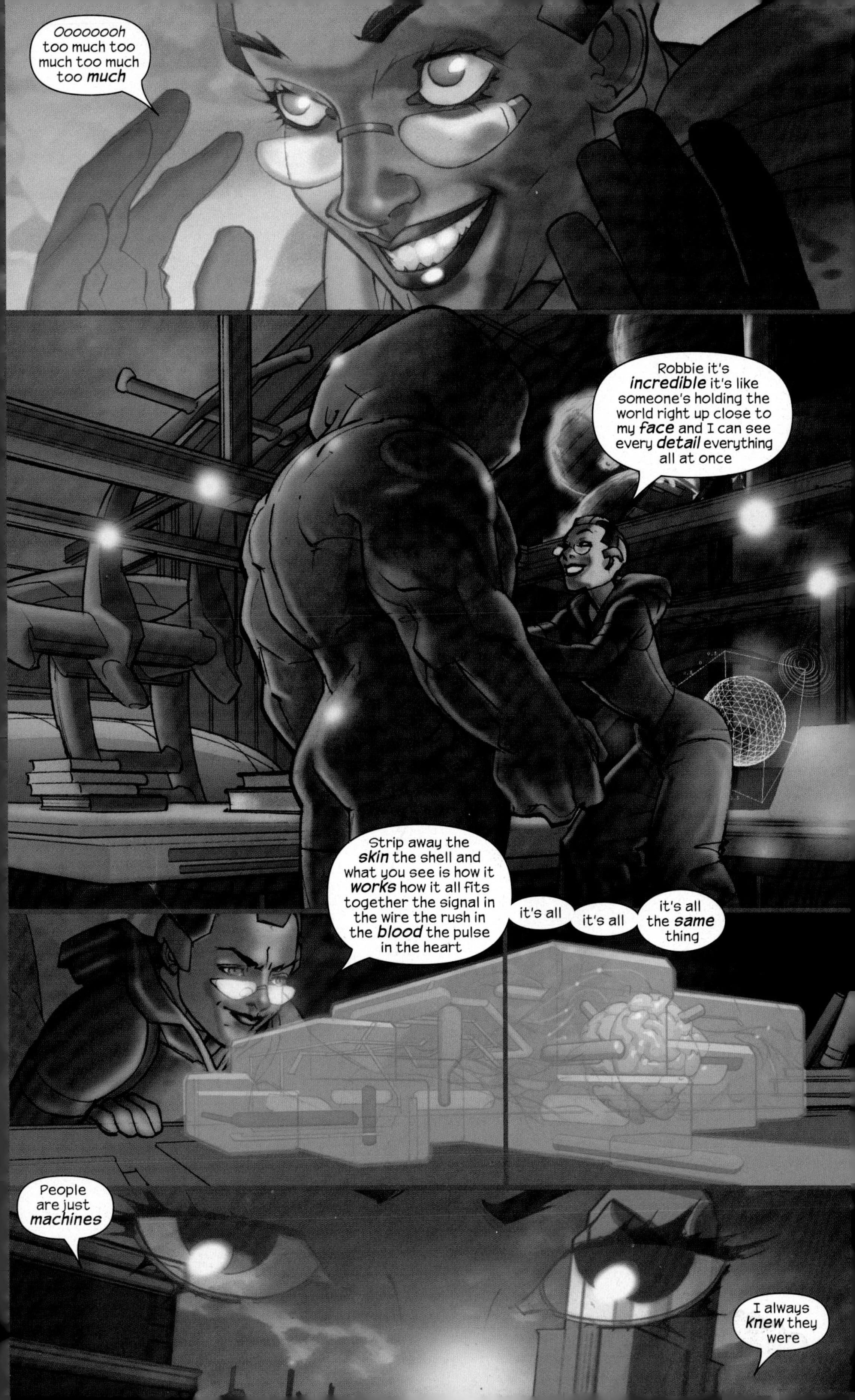
Oooooooh too much too much too much too *much*
Robbie it's *incredible* it's like someone's holding the world right up close to my *face* and I can see every *detail* everything all at once
Strip away the *skin* the shell and what you see is how it *works* how it all fits together the signal in the wire the rush in the *blood* the pulse in the heart
it's all
it's all
it's all the *same* thing
People are just *machines*
I always *knew* they were

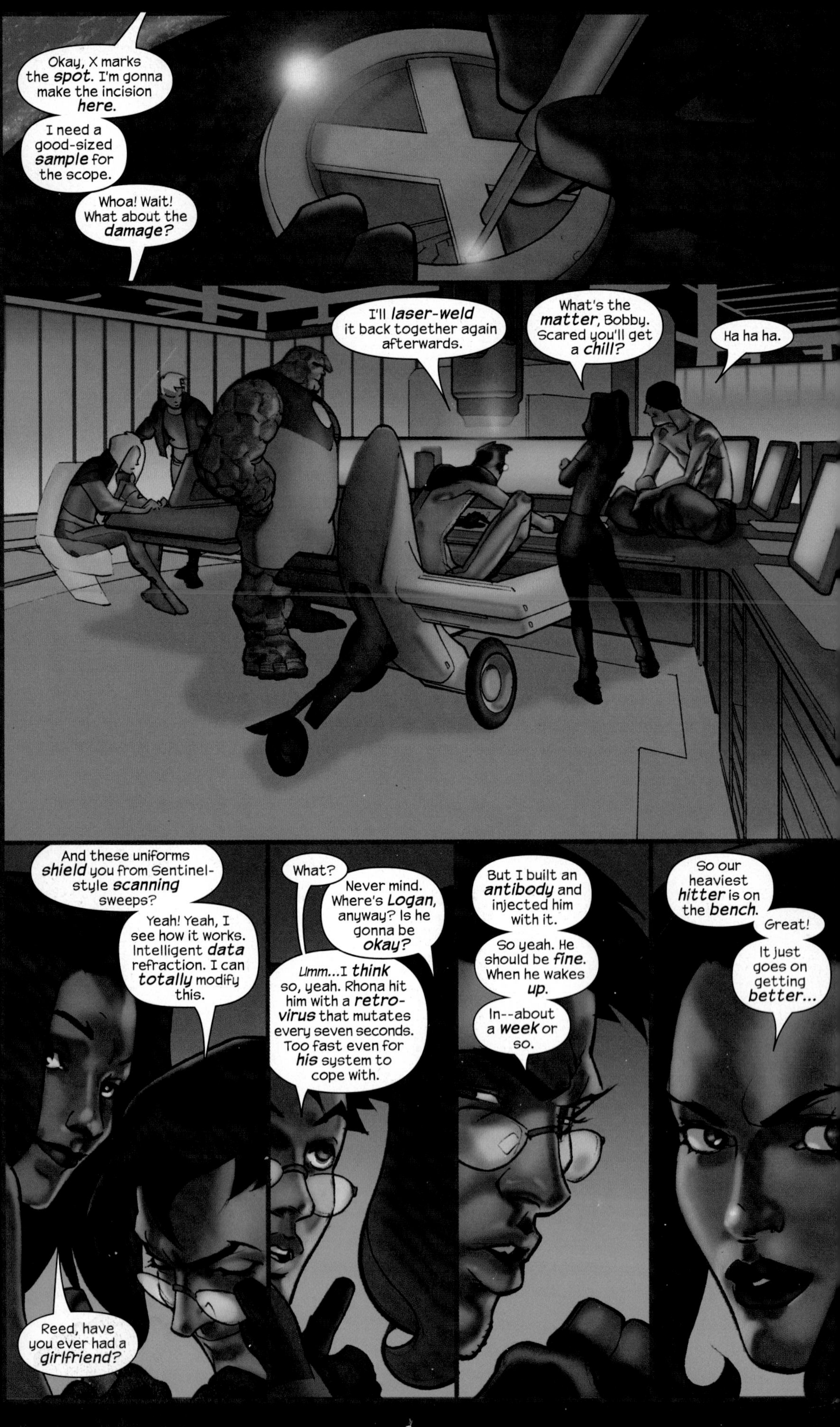
Okay, X marks the spot. I'm gonna make the incision here.
I need a good-sized sample for the scope.
Whoa! Wait! What about the damage?
I'll laser-weld it back together again afterwards.
What's the matter, Bobby. Scared you'll get a chill?
Ha ha ha.
And these uniforms shield you from Sentinel-style scanning sweeps?
Yeah! Yeah, I see how it works. Intelligent data refraction. I can totally modify this.
Reed, have you ever had a girlfriend?
What?
Never mind. Where's Logan, anyway? Is he gonna be okay?
Umm...I think so, yeah. Rhona hit him with a retro-virus that mutates every seven seconds. Too fast even for his system to cope with.
But I built an antibody and injected him with it.
So yeah. He should be fine. When he wakes up.
In--about a week or so.
So our heaviest hitter is on the bench.
Great!
It just goes on getting better...

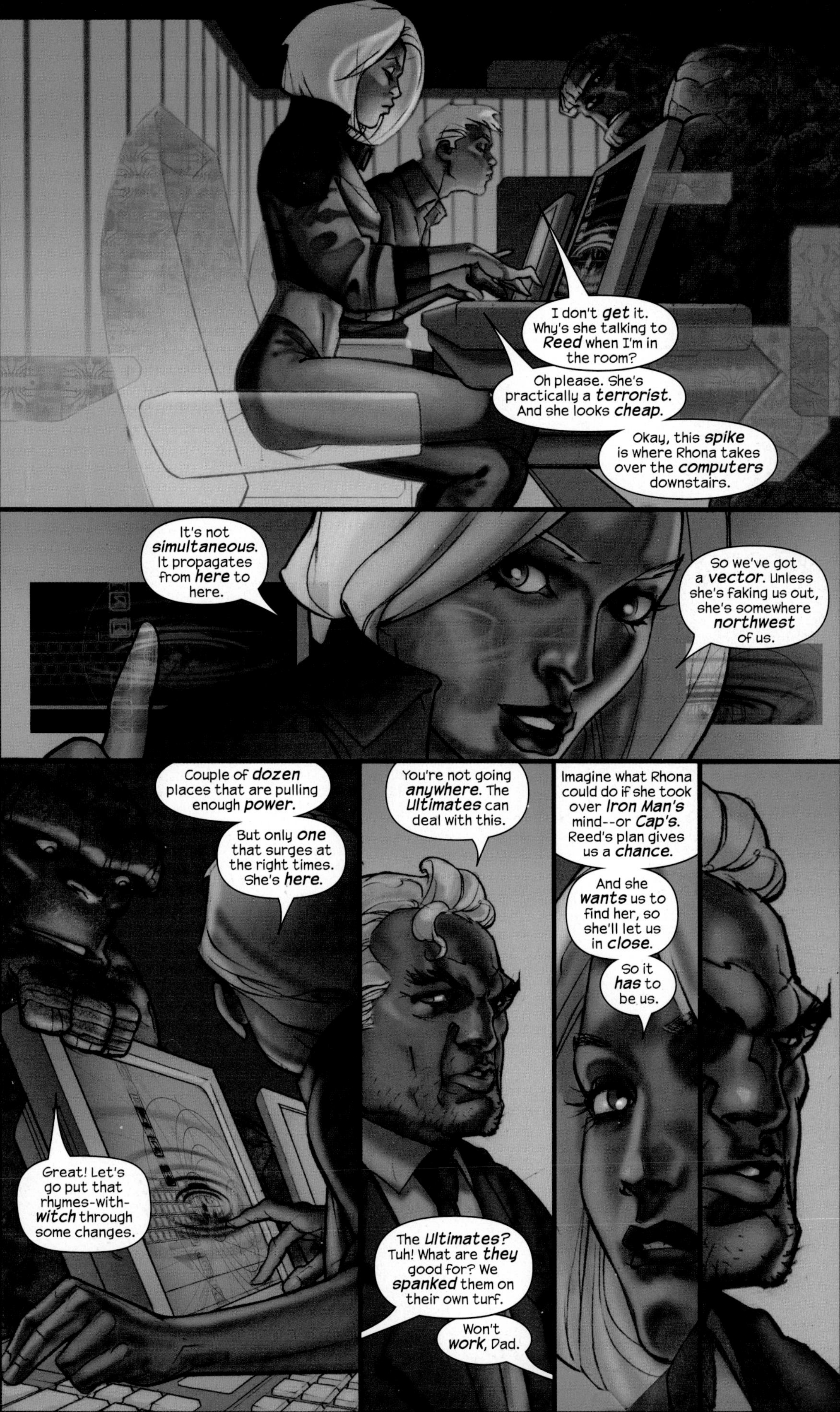
I don't get it. Why's she talking to Reed when I'm in the room?
Oh please. She's practically a terrorist. And she looks cheap.
Okay, this spike is where Rhona takes over the computers downstairs.
It's not simultaneous. It propagates from here to here.
So we've got a vector. Unless she's faking us out, she's somewhere northwest of us.
Couple of dozen places that are pulling enough power.
But only one that surges at the right times. She's here.
Great! Let's go put that rhymes-with-witch through some changes.
You're not going anywhere. The Ultimates can deal with this.
The Ultimates? Tuh! What are they good for? We spanked them on their own turf.
Won't work, Dad.
Imagine what Rhona could do if she took over Iron Man's mind--or Cap's. Reed's plan gives us a chance.
And she wants us to find her, so she'll let us in close.
So it has to be us.

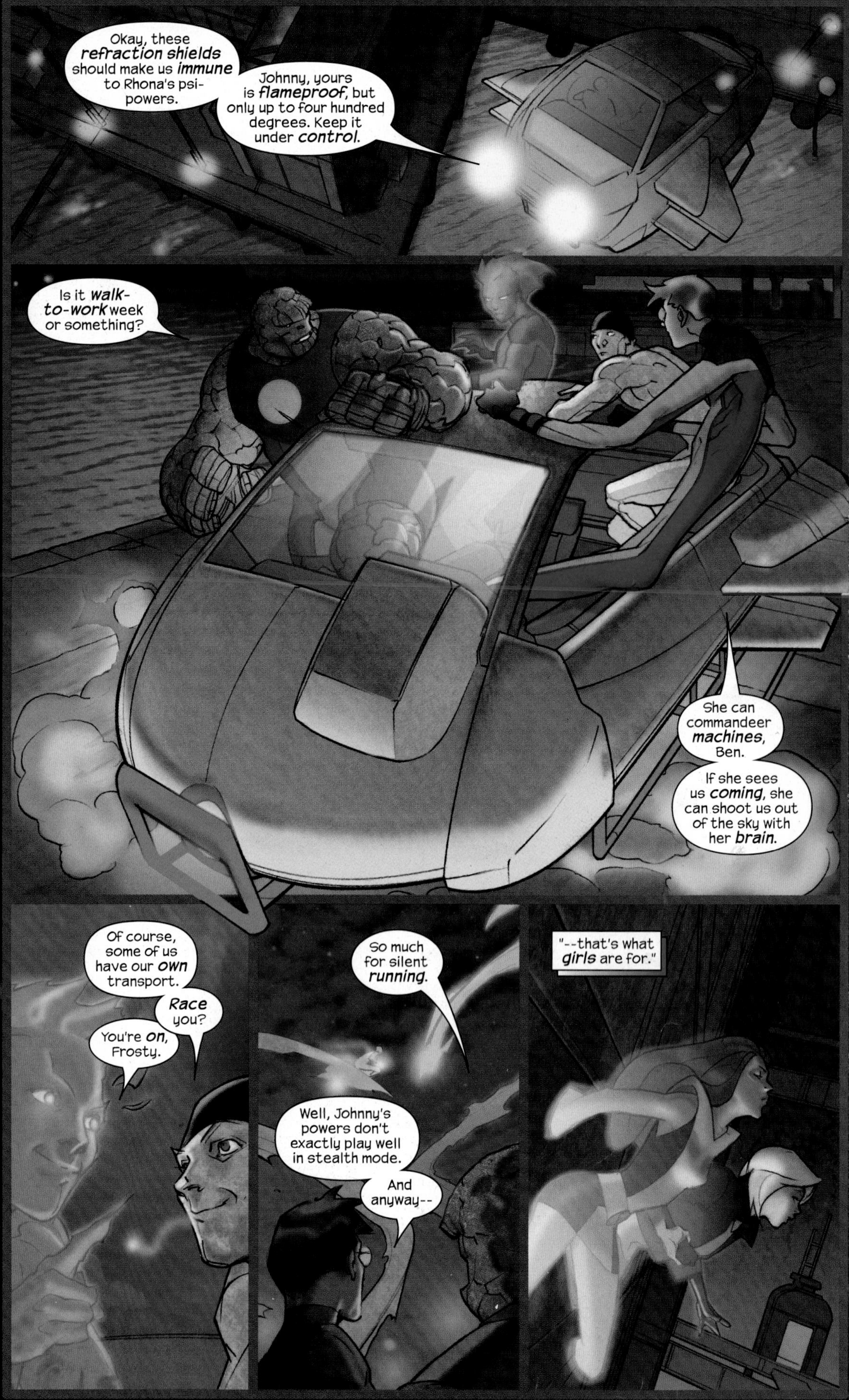
Okay, these refraction shields should make us immune to Rhona's psi-powers.
Johnny, yours is flameproof, but only up to four hundred degrees. Keep it under control.
Is it walk-to-work week or something?
She can commandeer machines, Ben.
If she sees us coming, she can shoot us out of the sky with her brain.
Of course, some of us have our own transport.
Race you?
You're on, Frosty.
So much for silent running.
Well, Johnny's powers don't exactly play well in stealth mode.
And anyway--
"--that's what girls are for."

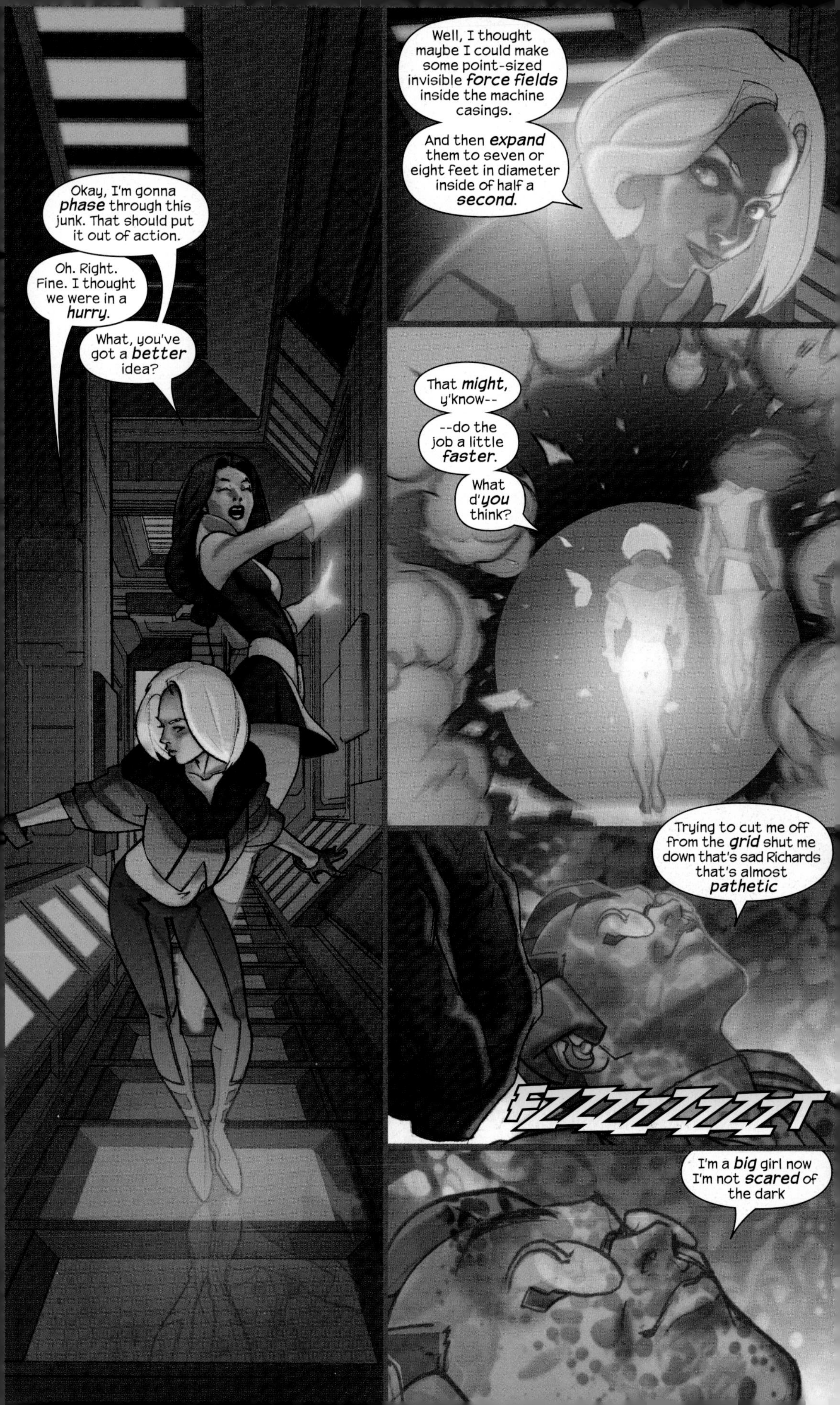

Okay, I'm gonna phase through this junk. That should put it out of action.
Oh. Right. Fine. I thought we were in a hurry.
What, you've got a better idea?
Well, I thought maybe I could make some point-sized invisible force fields inside the machine casings.
And then expand them to seven or eight feet in diameter inside of half a second.
That might, y'know--
--do the job a little faster.
What d'you think?
Trying to cut me off from the grid shut me down that's sad Richards that's almost pathetic
FZZZZZZZZT
I'm a big girl now I'm not scared of the dark

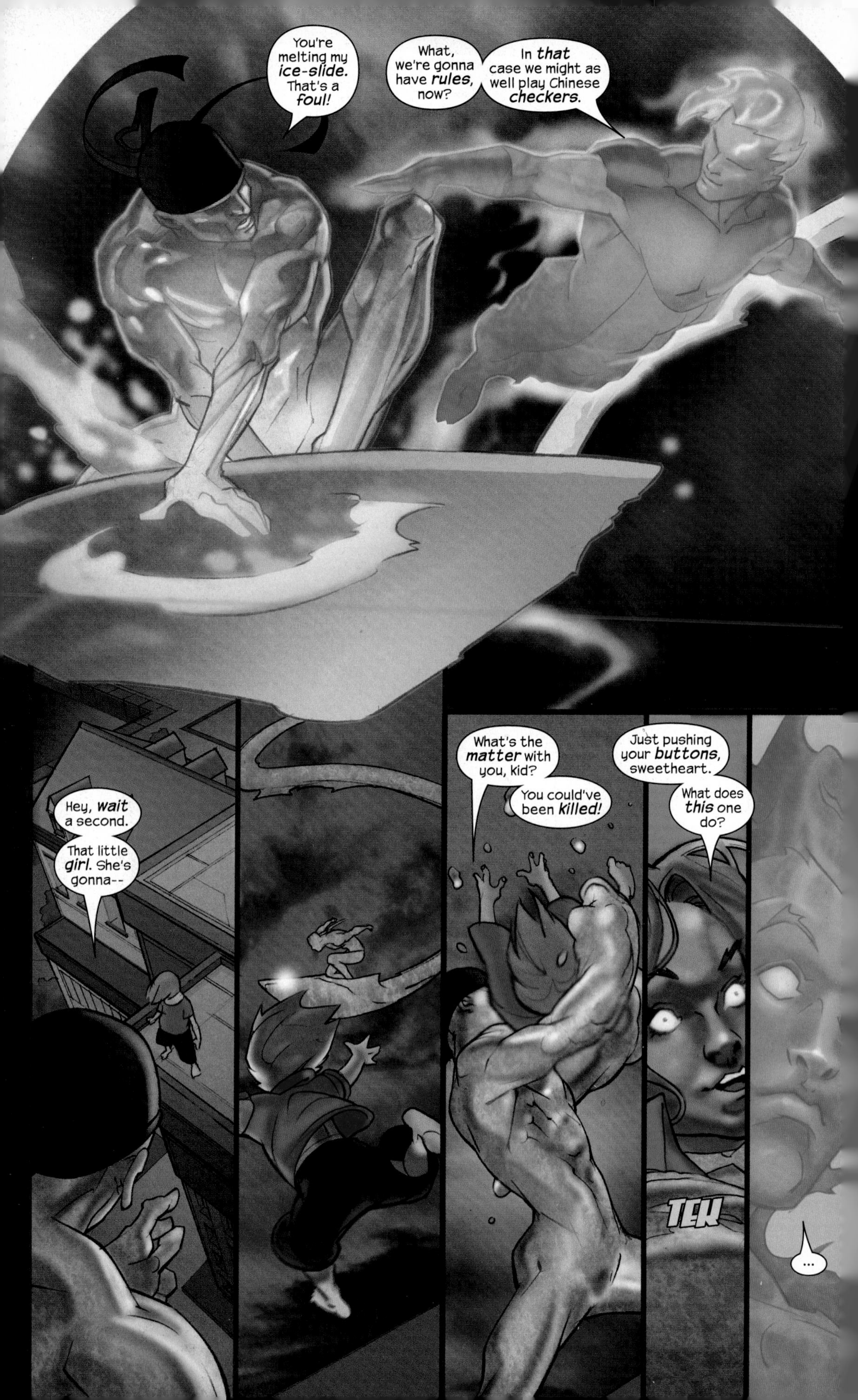

You're melting my *ice-slide.* That's a *foul!*
What, we're gonna have *rules,* now?
In *that* case we might as well play Chinese *checkers.*
Hey, *wait* a second.
That little *girl.* She's gonna--
What's the *matter* with you, kid?
You could've been *killed!*
Just pushing your *buttons,* sweetheart.
What does *this* one do?
TEK
...

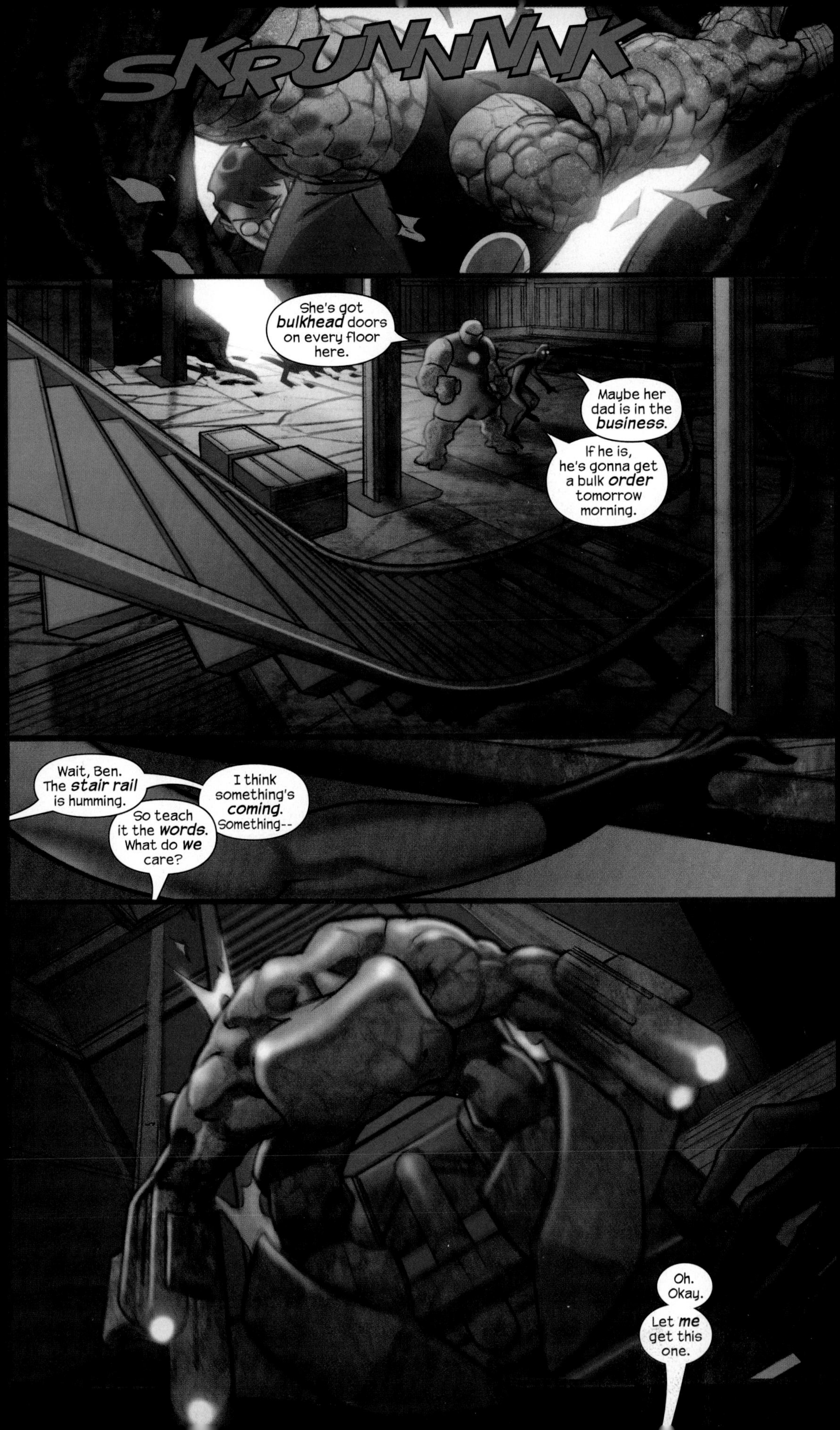
SKRUNNNNK
She's got bulkhead doors on every floor here.
Maybe her dad is in the business.
If he is, he's gonna get a bulk order tomorrow morning.
Wait, Ben. The stair rail is humming.
I think something's coming. Something--
So teach it the words. What do we care?
Oh. Okay.
Let me get this one.

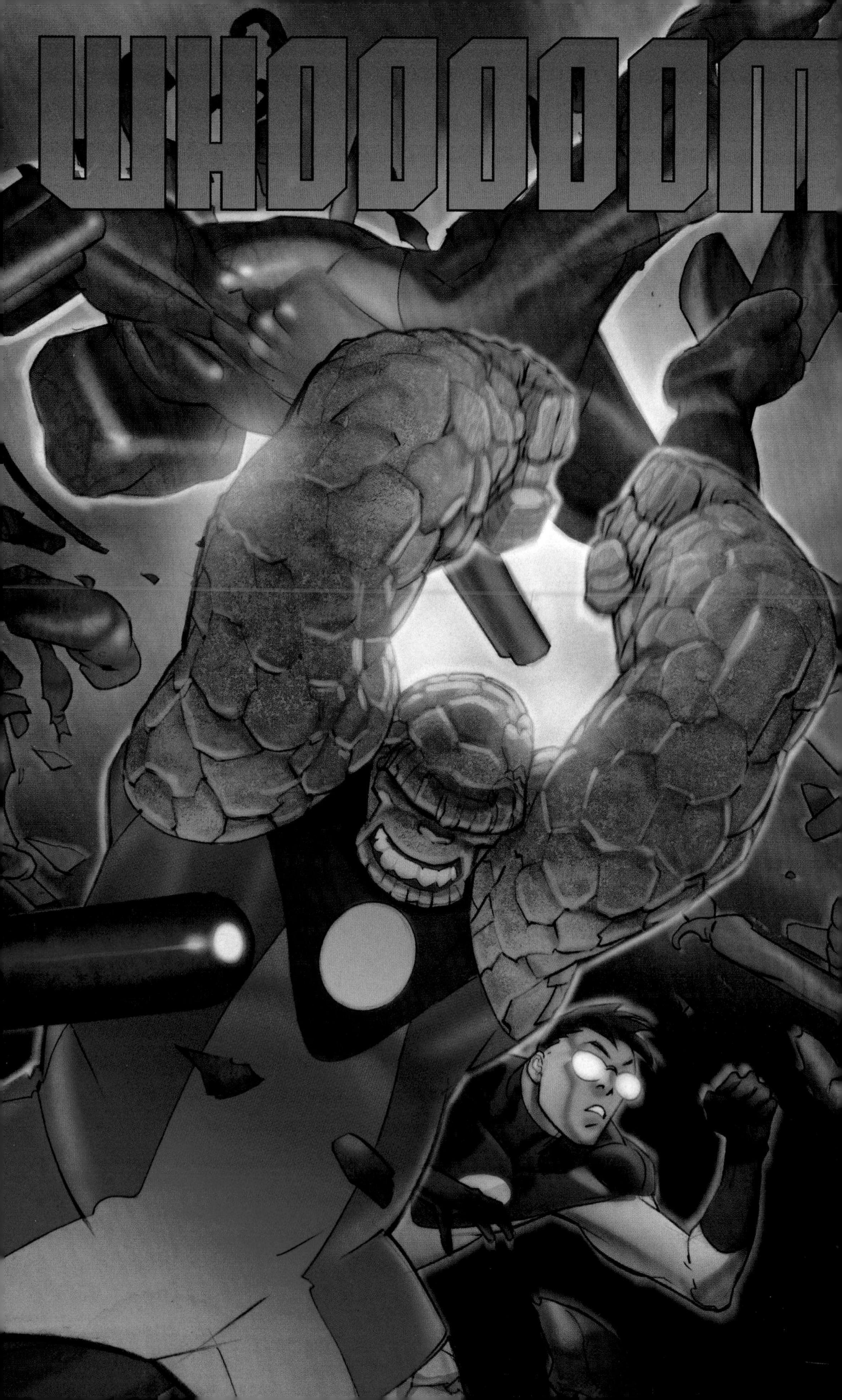
WHOOOOOM

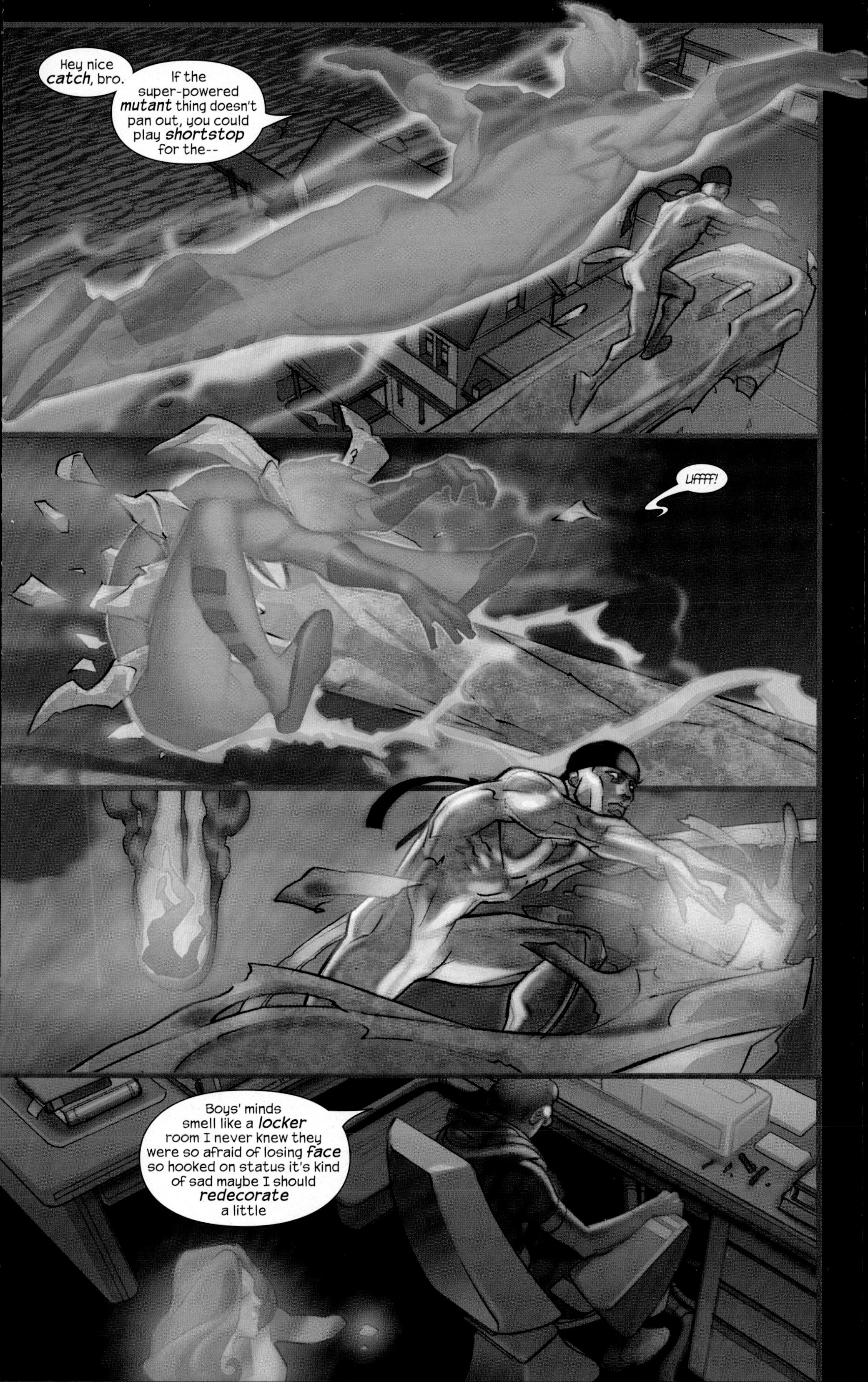
Hey nice catch, bro.
If the super-powered mutant thing doesn't pan out, you could play shortstop for the--
UFFFF!
Boys' minds smell like a locker room I never knew they were so afraid of losing face so hooked on status it's kind of sad maybe I should redecorate a little

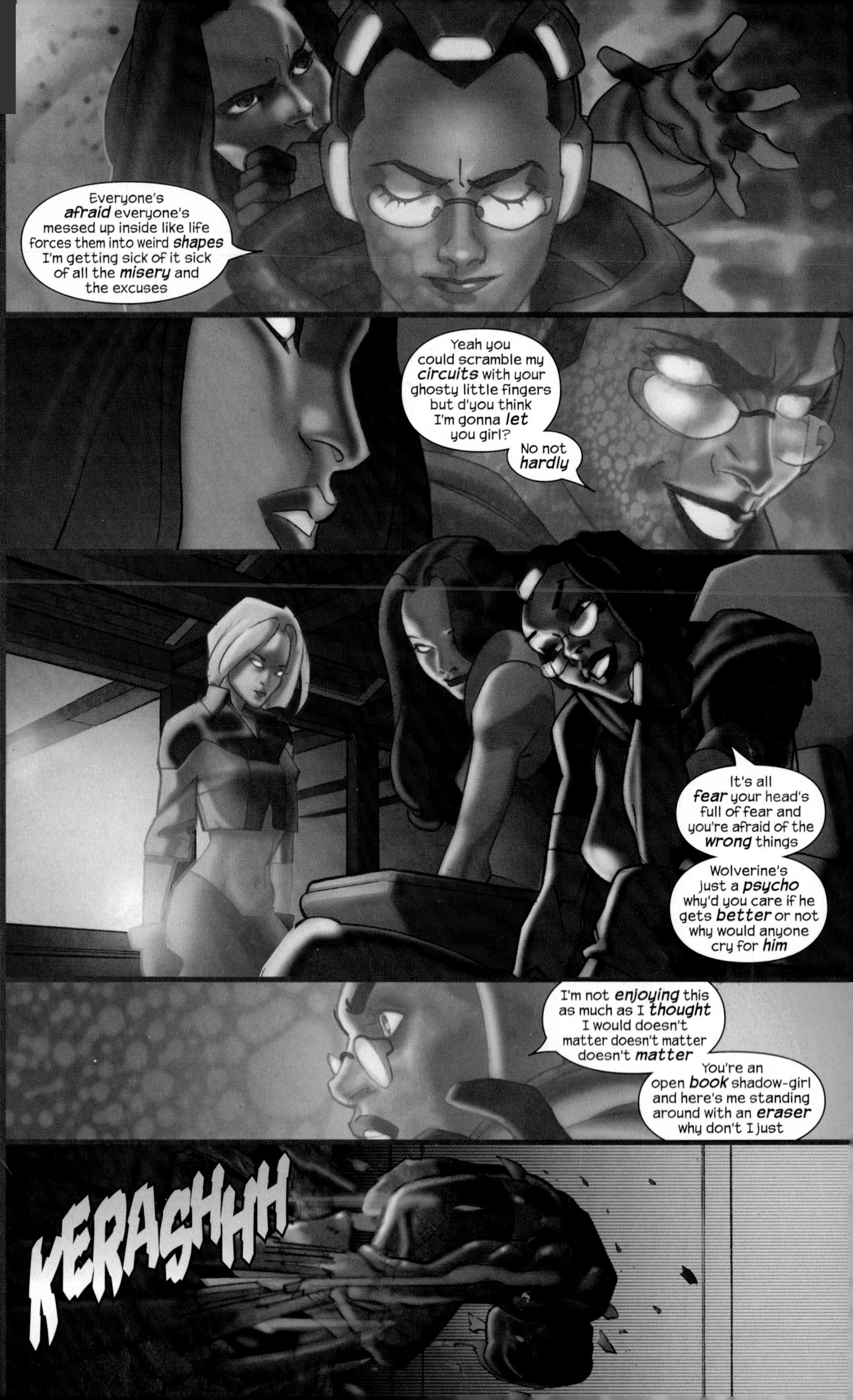
Everyone's afraid everyone's messed up inside like life forces them into weird shapes I'm getting sick of it sick of all the misery and the excuses
Yeah you could scramble my circuits with your ghosty little fingers but d'you think I'm gonna let you girl?
No not hardly
It's all fear your head's full of fear and you're afraid of the wrong things
Wolverine's just a psycho why'd you care if he gets better or not why would anyone cry for him
I'm not enjoying this as much as I thought I would doesn't matter doesn't matter doesn't matter
You're an open book shadow-girl and here's me standing around with an eraser why don't I just
KERASHHH

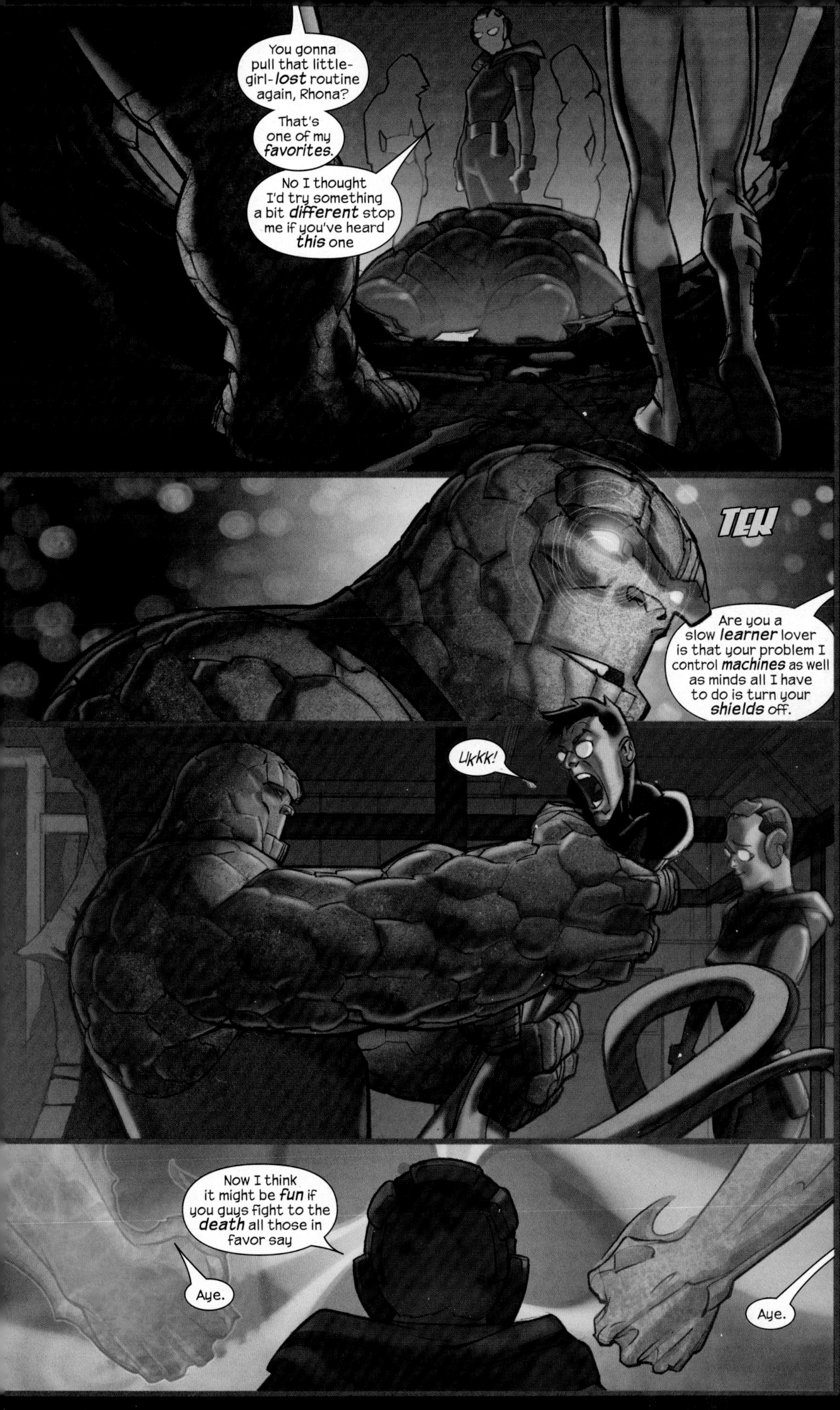
You gonna pull that little-girl-*lost* routine again, Rhona?
That's one of my *favorites*.
No I thought I'd try something a bit *different* stop me if you've heard *this* one
TEK
Are you a slow *learner* lover is that your problem I control *machines* as well as minds all I have to do is turn your *shields* off.
UKKK!
Now I think it might be *fun* if you guys fight to the *death* all those in favor say
Aye.
Aye.

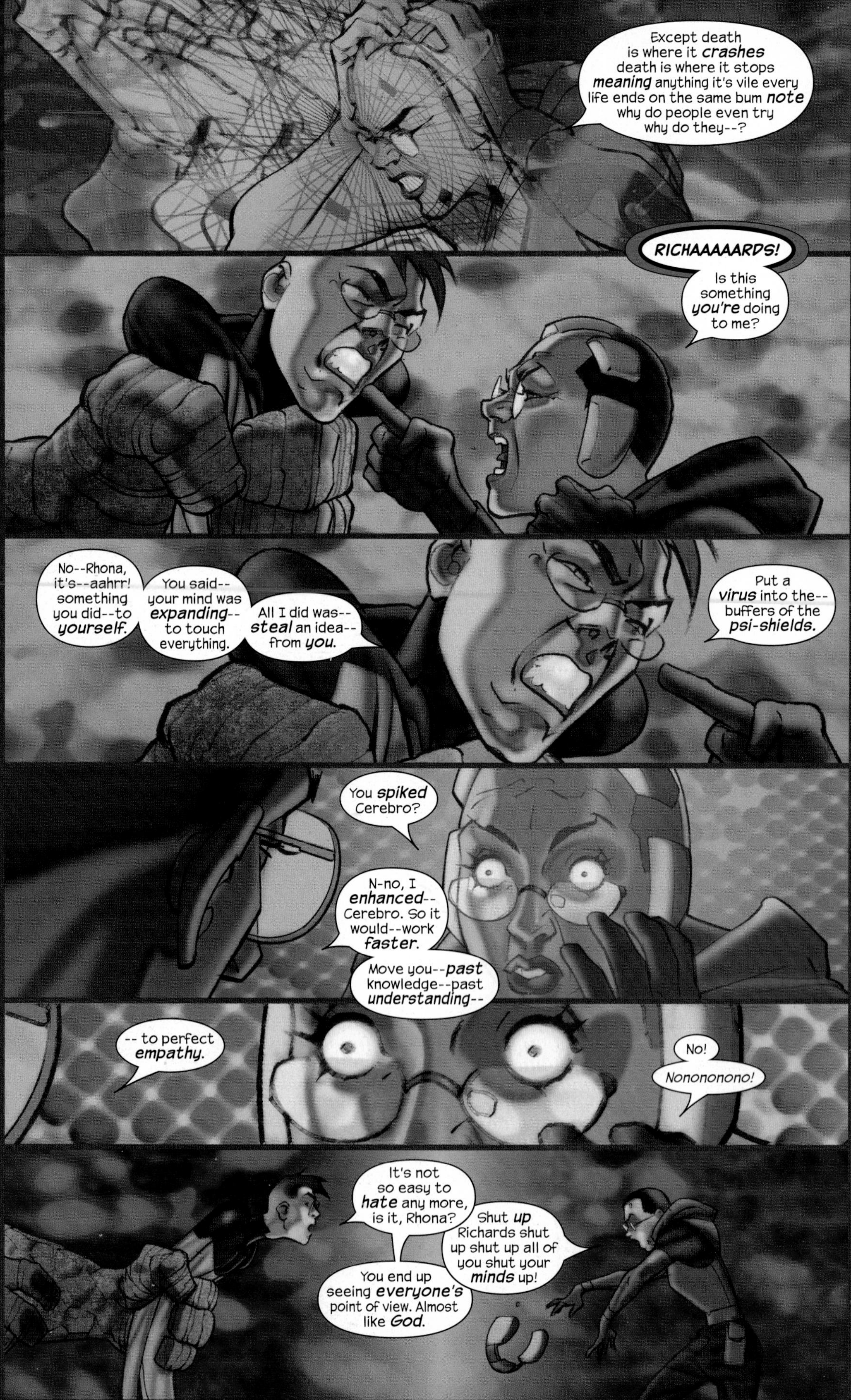
Except death is where it crashes death is where it stops meaning anything it's vile every life ends on the same bum note why do people even try why do they--?
RICHAAAAARDS!
Is this something you're doing to me?
No--Rhona, it's--aahrr! something you did--to yourself.
You said-- your mind was expanding-- to touch everything.
All I did was-- steal an idea-- from you.
Put a virus into the-- buffers of the psi-shields.
You spiked Cerebro?
N-no, I enhanced-- Cerebro. So it would--work faster.
Move you--past knowledge--past understanding--
-- to perfect empathy.
No!
Nonononono!
It's not so easy to hate any more, is it, Rhona?
You end up seeing everyone's point of view. Almost like God.
Shut up Richards shut up shut up all of you shut your minds up!

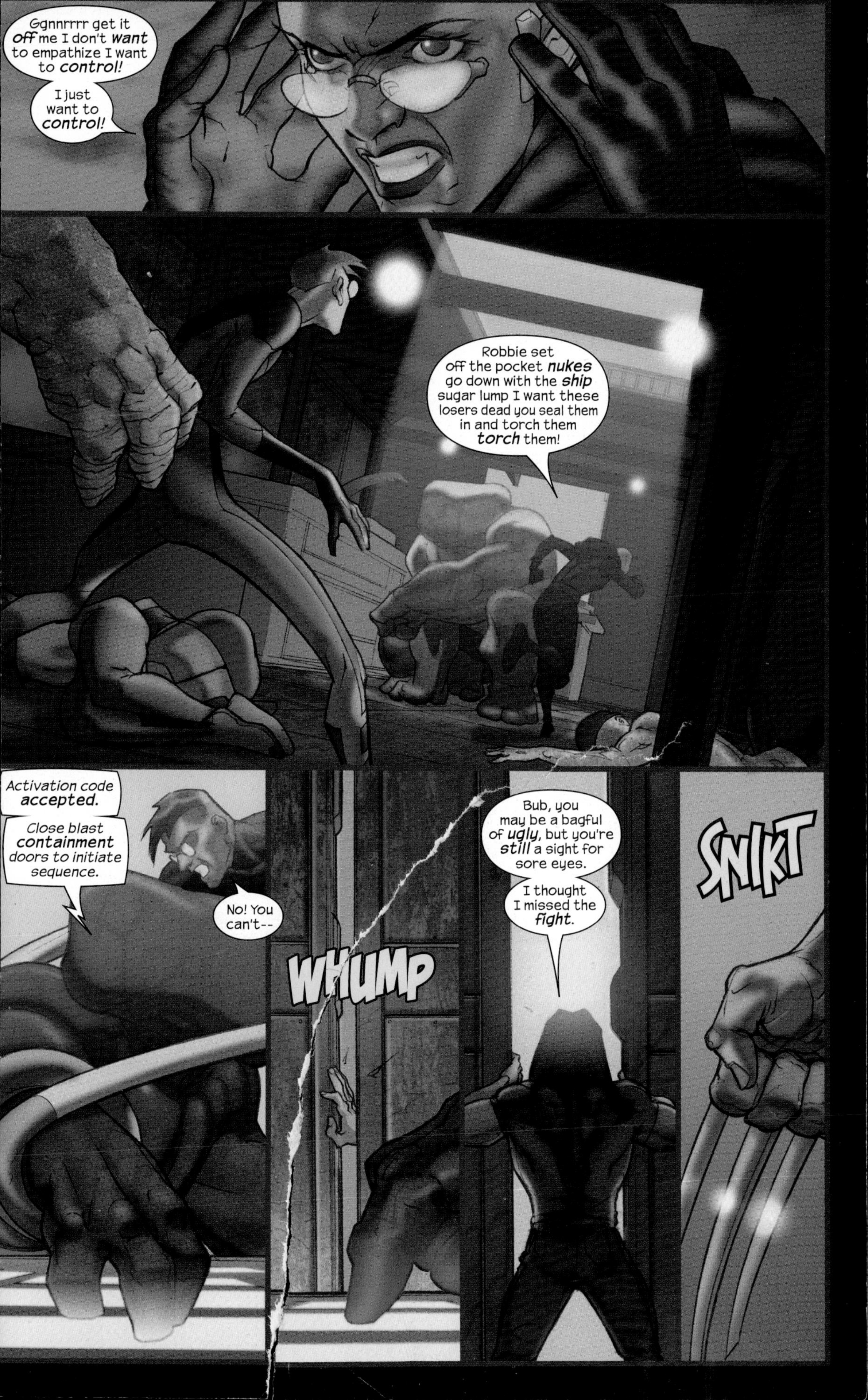
Ggnnrrrr get it off me I don't want to empathize I want to control!
I just want to control!
Robbie set off the pocket nukes go down with the ship sugar lump I want these losers dead you seal them in and torch them torch them!
Activation code accepted.
Close blast containment doors to initiate sequence.
No! You can't--
WHUMP
Bub, you may be a bagful of ugly, but you're still a sight for sore eyes.
I thought I missed the fight.
SNIKT

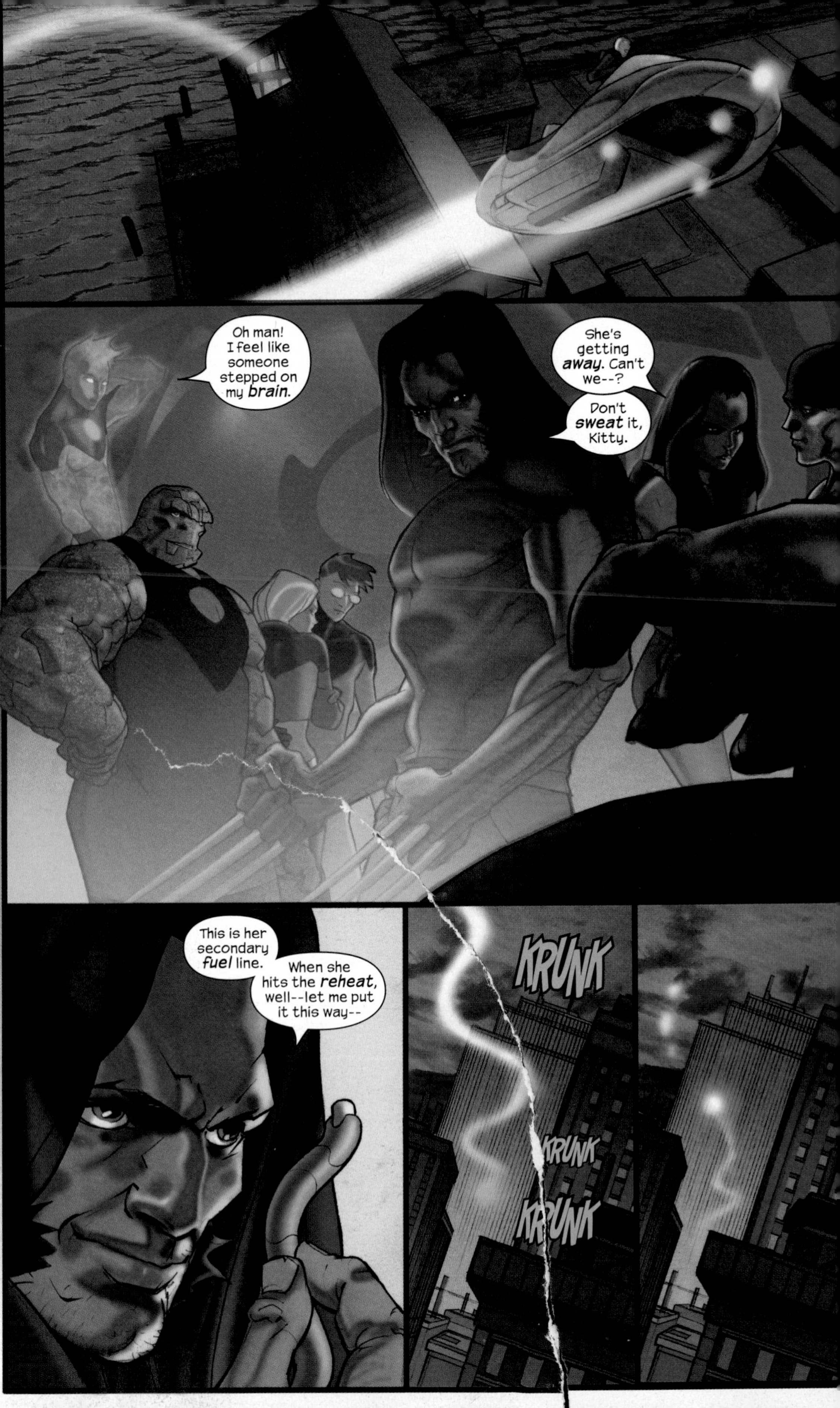
Oh man! I feel like someone stepped on my brain.
She's getting away. Can't we--?
Don't sweat it, Kitty.
This is her secondary fuel line.
When she hits the reheat, well--let me put it this way--
KRUNK
KRUNK
KRUNK

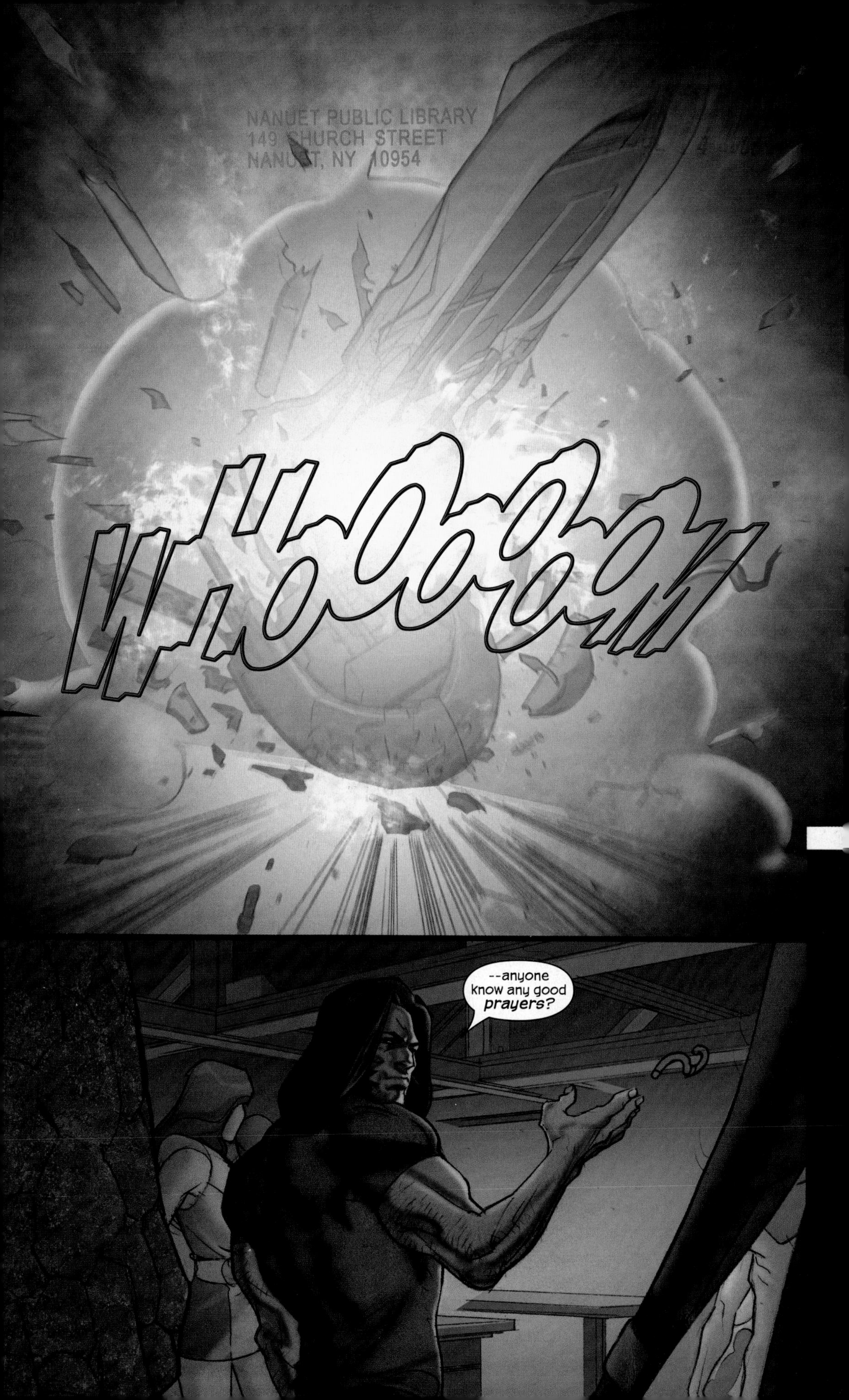
WHOOOOM
--anyone know any good prayers?

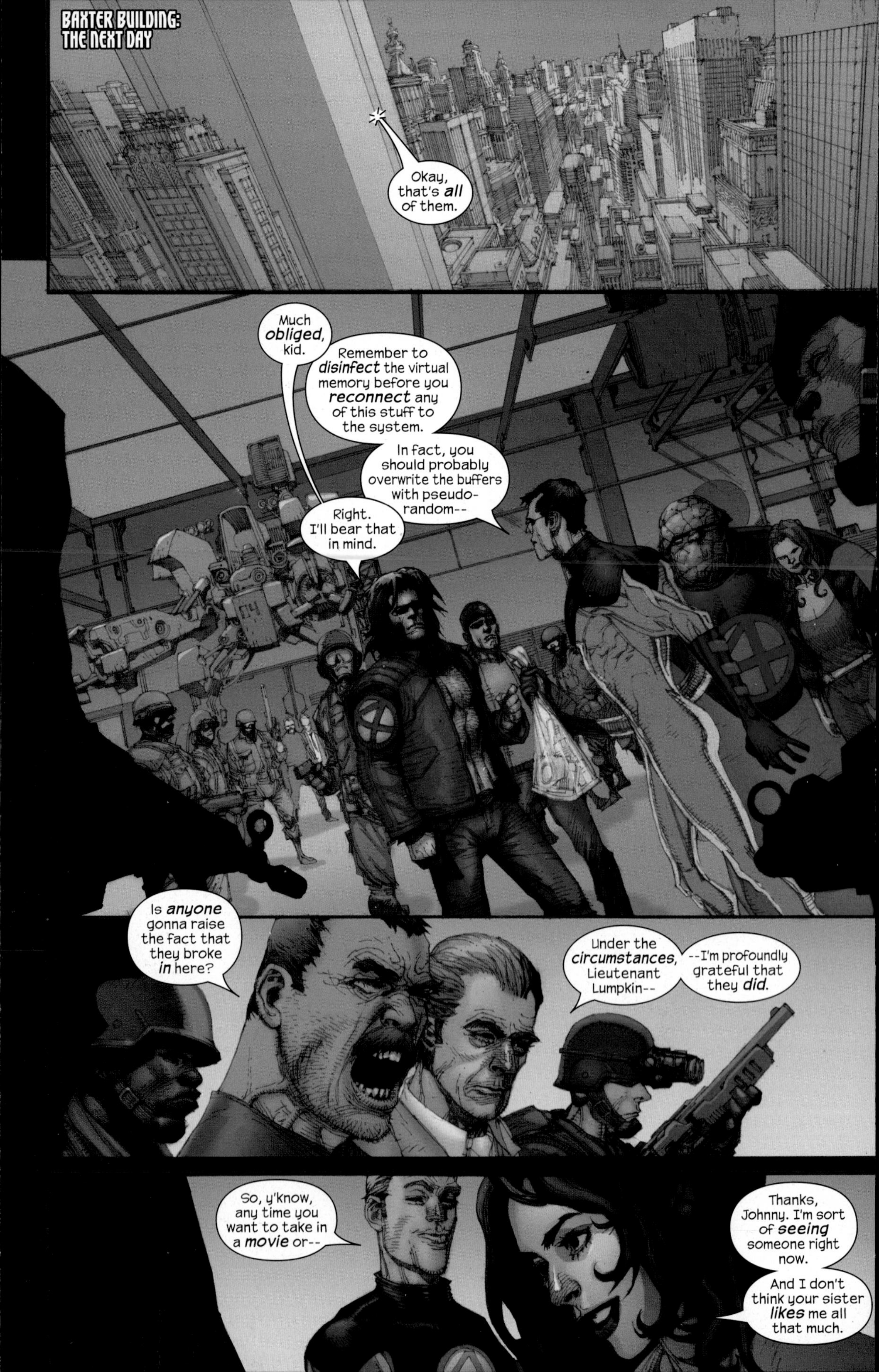
BAXTER BUILDING: THE NEXT DAY
Okay, that's *all* of them.
Much *obliged*, kid.
Remember to *disinfect* the virtual memory before you *reconnect* any of this stuff to the system.
In fact, you should probably overwrite the buffers with pseudo-random--
Right. I'll bear that in mind.
Is *anyone* gonna raise the fact that they broke *in* here?
Under the *circumstances*, Lieutenant Lumpkin--
--I'm profoundly grateful that they *did*.
So, y'know, any time you want to take in a *movie* or--
Thanks, Johnny. I'm sort of *seeing* someone right now.
And I don't think your sister *likes* me all that much.

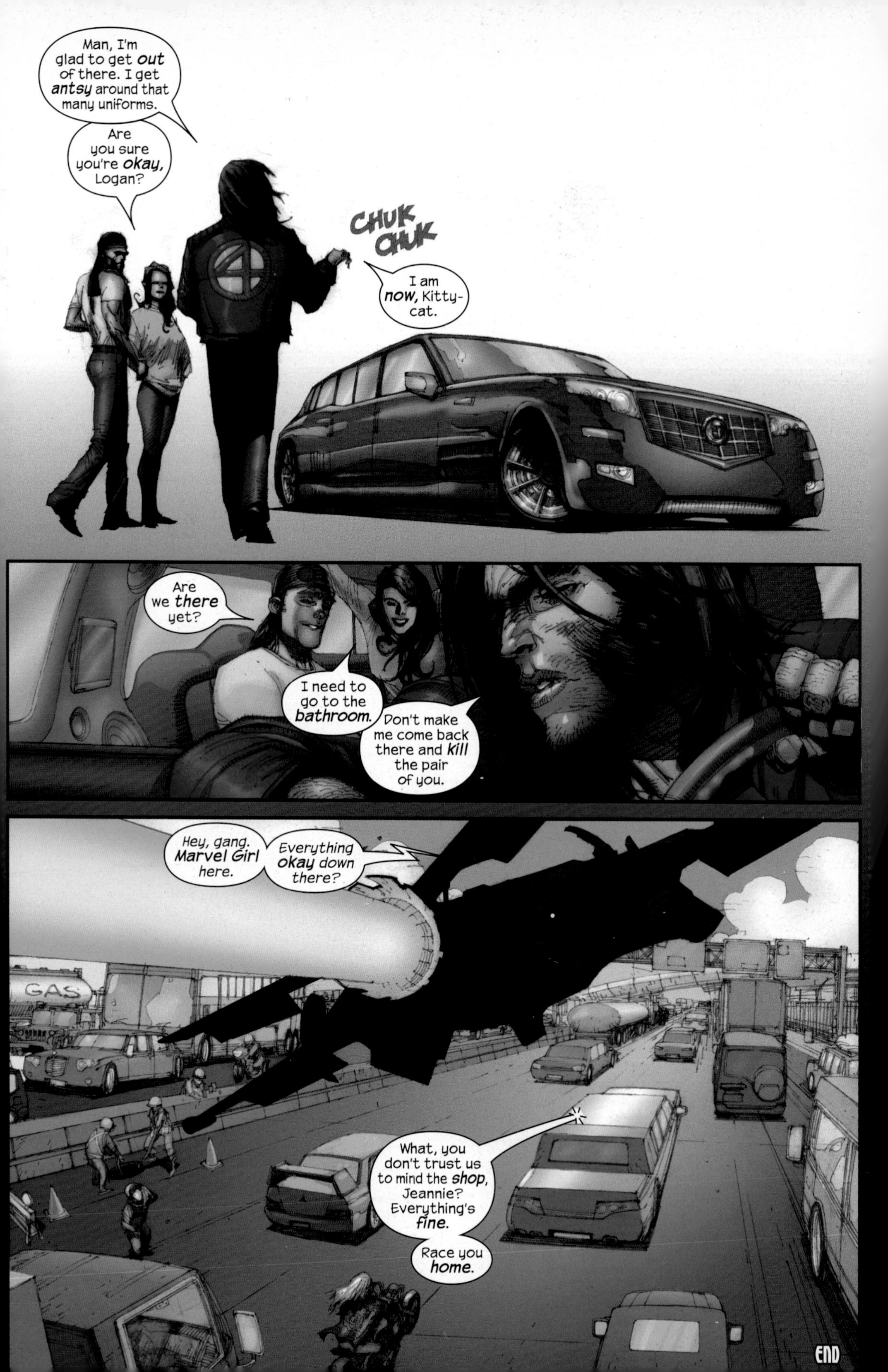
Man, I'm glad to get out of there. I get antsy around that many uniforms.
Are you sure you're okay, Logan?
CHUK CHUK
I am now, Kitty-cat.
Are we there yet?
I need to go to the bathroom.
Don't make me come back there and kill the pair of you.
Hey, gang. Marvel Girl here.
Everything okay down there?
GAS
What, you don't trust us to mind the shop, Jeannie? Everything's fine.
Race you home.
END

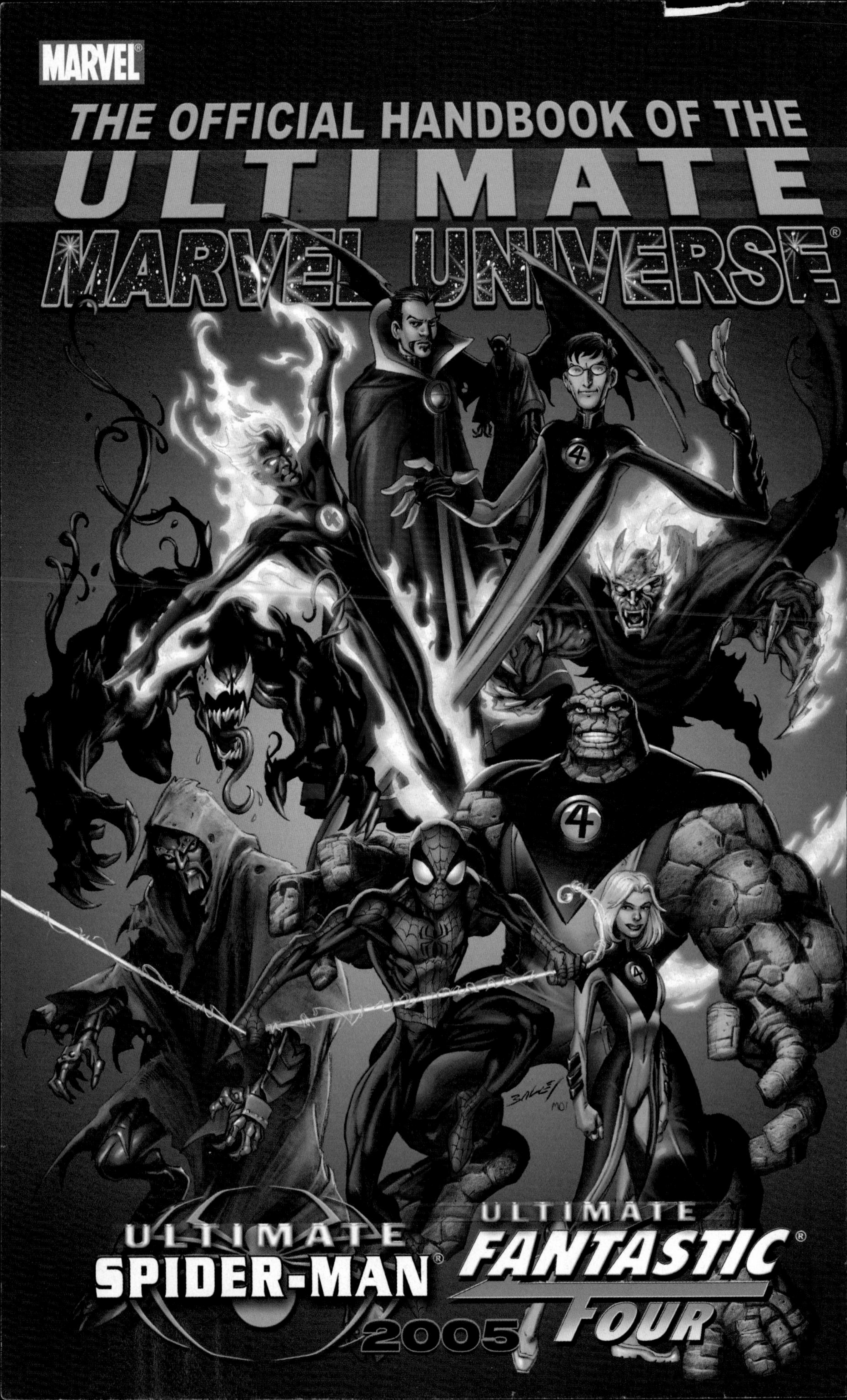
MARVEL
THE OFFICIAL HANDBOOK OF THE
ULTIMATE
MARVEL UNIVERSE
ULTIMATE
SPIDER-MAN
ULTIMATE
FANTASTIC
FOUR
2005

HISTORY: As a young girl, Felicia Hardy saw her cat burglar father sent to prison, where he eventually died. Blaming crime lord Wilson Fisk, the Kingpin of Crime, Felicia vowed to destroy him. Fifteen years later, the adult Felicia became an accountant for Fisk Enterprises, but spent her nights robbing Manhattan's more prominent office buildings as the costumed Black Cat. When Mr. Moore offered to buy his way into the Kingpin's organization with an inscribed stone tablet desired by Fisk, Felicia broke into Moore's building, easily circumventing the security through a combination of skill and incredible luck, and stole the tablet from his office safe. On her way out, she encountered and battled Spider-Man, but despite his slightly greater agility, Spider-Man seemed plagued by bad luck, and she escaped. When video footage of their encounter made the news, police suspected they were partners in crime.

Intrigued, the Cat placed an ad in the Bugle, arranging a meeting with Spider-Man on a rooftop near the site of their battle. She brought Spider-Man wine and cheese and flirted with him, but their romantic reunion was interrupted by Elektra, who had been hired to retrieve the tablet. The Cat and Elektra battled, with the assassin gradually gaining the upper hand. Trying to calm the situation, Spider-Man webbed the Cat while he tried to talk to Elektra, who knocked him off the building. While the others were distracted, the Cat freed herself and made her escape.

Remembering comments the Cat had made to Elektra telling the Kingpin she was not her father, Spider-Man searched Daily Bugle records and figured out her identity. Realizing that if he could work this out, so could the Kingpin, he raced to Felicia's apartment, finding her literally in the crimelord's grasp. Spider-Man's arrival allowed Felicia to break free, and she fled to the roof of her apartment building. As the Kingpin and Elektra arrived in pursuit, she threw the tablet into the harbor. Elektra immediately threw a Sai into Felicia's chest and she fell from the roof into the sea,

REAL NAME: Felicia Hardy
KNOWN ALIASES: The Cat
IDENTITY: Secret
OCCUPATION: Burglar, accountant
CITIZENSHIP: U.S.A.
PLACE OF BIRTH: Unknown
KNOWN RELATIVES: Jack Hardy (father, deceased)
GROUP AFFILIATION: None
EDUCATION: College graduate
FIRST APPEARANCE: Ultimate Spider-Man #50 (2004)

apparently dead. However, several months later, she returned to aid Spider-Man during the inter-gang war between the forces of Kingpin and Hammerhead.

HEIGHT: 5'6"
WEIGHT: 118 lbs.
EYES: Blue
HAIR: Black (wears white wig when in costume)

SUPERHUMAN POWERS: The Black Cat seems to be superhumanly agile. Also, she apparently possesses uncanny luck, resulting in good fortune for her and bad fortune for others around her.

ABILITIES: Felicia is an expert cat burglar with extensive knowledge of security systems.

PARAPHERNALIA: Felicia carries various burglary tools, including a harpoon gun for firing a grappling hook and line; a small spray can for blacking out security cameras; and a mini-computer for unlocking security-coded locks.

POWER GRID	1	2	3	4	5	6	7
INTELLIGENCE							
STRENGTH							
SPEED							
DURABILITY							
ENERGY PROJECTION							
FIGHTING SKILLS							

Art by Mark Bagley

CARNAGE

REAL NAME: Little Ben
KNOWN ALIASES: None
IDENTITY: No dual identity
OCCUPATION: None
CITIZENSHIP: None
PLACE OF BIRTH: Reed Richards Science Center, Empire State University, New York
KNOWN RELATIVES: Peter Parker ("father"), Curt Conners ("father"), Richard Parker ("father")
GROUP AFFILIATIONS: None
EDUCATION: None
FIRST APPEARANCE: Ultimate Spider-Man #61 (2004)

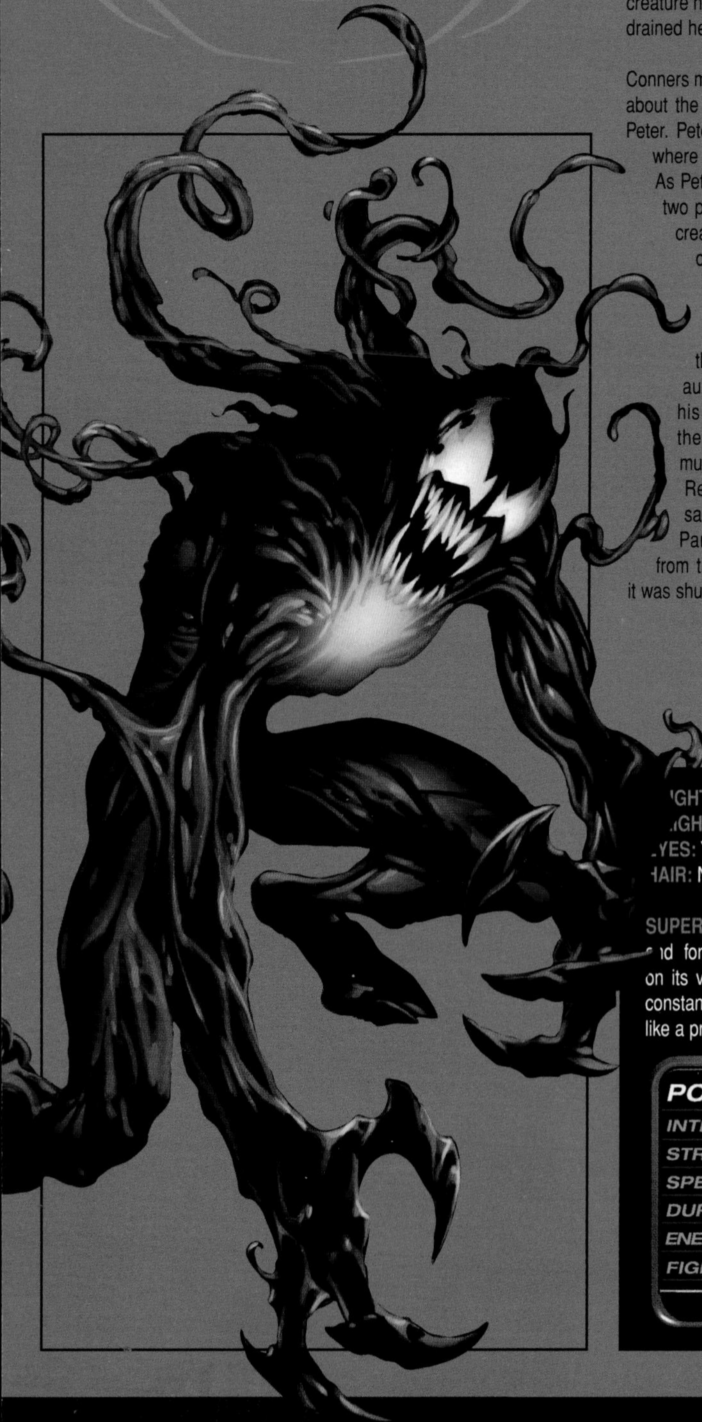

HISTORY: After battling the Gladiator as Spider-Man, Peter Parker was forced to go to Dr. Curt Conners for stitches. Peter told Conners about his accelerated healing, and the doctor decided to study Peter's special blood. Told his DNA might be a cure for cancer, Peter agreed to let Conners run further tests on his blood. Using Richard Parker's notes, Conners spliced his own DNA with Peter's, creating an entirely new organism, whom he dubbed "Little Ben" after his assistant, Ben Reilly. The organism quickly matured and escaped Conners' lab, instinctively draining the first person it stumbled upon, a security guard, killing him. It roamed the streets of New York, feeding off at least one dating couple in the same way it had the guard. Flooded with Peter Parker's memories, the creature headed for Peter's house, where it found Gwen Stacy and drained her, ending her young life.

Conners managed to track the grieving Peter down and came clean about the experiment, but the creature found them and attacked Peter. Peter kept it occupied while Conners returned to his lab, where he hoped to find something that would kill the monster. As Peter and the creature battled through New York, it drained two police officers, nearly completing itself. As Peter saw the creature's true face, he was horrified to see that it wasn't his own but his father's. Enraged, Peter battled the creature into position near the same smokestack he had previously used to destroy his sample of the Suit; he knocked the creature into its superheated core, seemingly destroying the monster. Conners later turned himself over to the authorities for his part in the creature's murders, but Ben Reilly took a sample of Peter Parker's DNA from the lab before it was shut down.

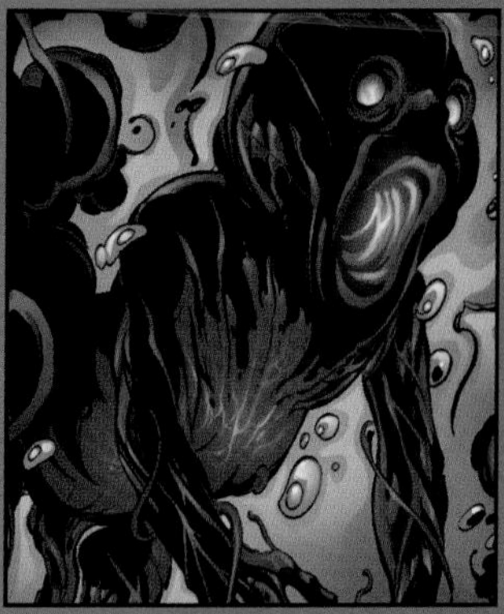

'GHT: Variable
.IGHT: Variable
.YES: Yellow
HAIR: None

SUPERHUMAN POWERS: The creature can alter its shape and form, projecting long tentacles to capture and feed on its victims; it needs to rebuild its damaged DNA matrix constantly by feeding off humans, and does so instinctively, like a predatory animal.

POWER GRID	1	2	3	4	5	6	7
INTELLIGENCE	■						
STRENGTH	■	■	■	■			
SPEED	■	■					
DURABILITY	■	■	■	■			
ENERGY PROJECTION	■	■					
FIGHTING SKILLS	■	■					

Art by Mark Bagley

HISTORY: A noted geneticist who lost his right arm under unrevealed circumstances, Curt Conners dedicated himself to finding a means of restoring lost limbs, studying the regenerative capabilities of reptiles; however, after five years without major breakthroughs, his sponsors were on the verge of cutting his funding. Drowning his disappointment with alcohol, the drunken Conners injected himself with an experimental serum in a desperate attempt to achieve results. The serum regenerated his right arm but also transformed Conners into an inhuman reptilian creature. Seeking refuge in the sewers, he became an urban legend, dubbed "The Lizard" by the press. A sympathetic Spider-Man sought out Conners who attacked the young hero until the Man-Thing happened upon the scene and restored Conners to human form. Conners' restored right arm soon withered and died; however, his DNA remained irreparably damaged, with dormant potential for further transformation, and he cut himself off from his wife and son out of fear for their safety.

Conners turned to research on the experimental biological "Suit" designed by Richard Parker, but his work was undercut when Spider-Man, secretly Richard's son Peter, tested the Suit's capabilities, and one of Conners's students, Eddie Brock, absconded with a second sample, then battled Spider-Man while wearing it. When Spider-Man returned to the lab, he was met by Conners, who had watched reports of the young hero's activities and deduced his identity. Although Conners only vaguely recalled their earlier meeting, he felt that he owed the youth a debt and offered to assist him in any way possible.

Weeks later, haunted by dreams of his reptilian persona, regretting his impulsive separation from his family, and once more facing funding cuts, Conners sought solace in late-night lab work, only to be interrupted by the arrival of Spider-Man, newly injured by the Gladiator. After treating his friend's wounds, Conners studied a sample of Peter's blood and was galvanized by its genetic potential. With Peter's permission, Conners subjected the sample to several experiments over the next two months, earning additional research money and ultimately creating "Little Ben," a rejuvenating organism created by splicing the altered

REAL NAME: Curtis Conners
KNOWN ALIASES: The Lizard
IDENTITY: The general public knows little of Conners' transformation
OCCUPATION: Research scientist, ESU bioengineering instructor
CITIZENSHIP: U.S.A.
PLACE OF BIRTH: Unrevealed
KNOWN RELATIVES: Doris (ex-wife), Timmy (son)
GROUP AFFILIATION: None
EDUCATION: Three doctorates
FIRST APPEARANCE: Ultimate Marvel Team-Up #10 (2002)

DNA of both Conners and Spider-Man with the final sample of Richard Parker's work; however, the creature escaped the laboratory and killed several people. After Spider-Man seemingly destroyed it, Conners, devastated at having once more wreaked havoc via reckless experimentation, confessed his involvement in the deaths and surrendered himself to the police. How his life will next touch Spider-Man's remains to be seen.

HEIGHT: 5'10"
WEIGHT: 196 lbs.
EYES: Brown (as reptilian, yellow)
HAIR: Brown (as reptilian, none)

SUPERHUMAN POWERS: In reptilian form, Conners possessed superhuman strength and speed, as well as claws useful for both clinging to walls and fighting. His reptilian persona was distinct from his human identity and was capable of only the most rudimentary speech.

ABILITIES: Conners is a brilliant geneticist, albeit hindered by depression and alcoholism.

POWER GRID	1	2	3	4	5	6	7
INTELLIGENCE							
STRENGTH							
SPEED							
DURABILITY							
ENERGY PROJECTION							
FIGHTING SKILLS							

*GREEN BARS INDICATE LIZARD RATINGS.

DAREDEVIL

REAL NAME: Matthew "Matt" Murdock
KNOWN ALIASES: None
IDENTITY: Secret
OCCUPATION: Lawyer
CITIZENSHIP: U.S.A.
PLACE OF BIRTH: Unknown
KNOWN RELATIVES: Unnamed father (deceased)
GROUP AFFILIATION: Partner in Nelson & Murdock Law Firm
EDUCATION: Columbia University (undergraduate); unidentified law school
FIRST APPEARANCE: (mentioned) Ultimate Marvel Team-Up #6 (2001); (appeared) Ultimate Marvel Team-Up #7 (2001)

HISTORY: Blinded in his youth but somehow secretly gifted with enhanced non-visual senses, Matt Murdock also lost his father, murdered for refusing to go along with a fixed fight. At university, Matt dated Elektra Natchios, whose friend Mel was raped. When the rapist, Trey, went free because of his father's connections, Elektra threatened Trey and he hired thugs to burn down her father's business. Matt forced the thugs to confess, implicating Trey; but Trey went free again and attacked Mel. Elektra trapped him, intending to kill him, but Matt intervened. Matt removed his mask to show that he trusted her, but Elektra told him it was too late. She cut Trey's femoral artery and gave Matt a choice; save Trey from bleeding to death, or go with her. Matt chose the former.

Matt and his friend Foggy Nelson interned at the firm of Summers and Lyall, where gunmen tried to kill Cullen, a mob bookkeeper turning States' evidence. Matt switched off the lights and easily overcame them. Later, he learned that Cullen worked for Leander Natchios, cousin of Elektra's father Dimitris, who was an unwilling part of Leander's money laundering schemes. When Dimitris was wrongly arrested for Cullen's murder, Matt worked with Elektra to learn the true killer was assassin Benjamin Poindexter, who had been sent by the Kingpin. Poindexter next targeted William Savage, Cullen's attorney, who had been blackmailing the Kingpin with a copy of Cullen's ledger. Matt and Elektra drove Poindexter off, but not before he killed Savage; however, he left behind the ledger. Elektra sucker-punched Matt and traded the ledger to the Kingpin for her father's freedom. Matt later confronted her with information showing that her father would have been cleared anyway.

Matt formed a law partnership with Foggy in Hell's Kitchen and protected the area as the costumed Daredevil, encountering Spider-Man while pursuing the killer vigilante known as the Punisher. Daredevil dismissed Spider-Man as too immature to be a crime-fighter. Months later, Daredevil reluctantly teamed with Wolverine and Spider-Man to protect Hell's Kitchen from rogue Weapon X agents.

HEIGHT: 6'
WEIGHT: 200 lbs.
EYES: Blue
HAIR: Red

SUPERHUMAN POWERS: Daredevil's senses of touch, hearing, taste and smell are enhanced to superhuman levels. Combined, they form a "radar sense" replacing his sight.

ABILITIES: An accomplished acrobat and fighter, Daredevil is an Olympic-level athlete and gymnast. He is also a skilled attorney.

PARAPHERNALIA: Daredevil carries a Billy Club, disguised as a cane in civilian garb.

POWER GRID	1	2	3	4	5	6	7
INTELLIGENCE							
STRENGTH							
SPEED							
DURABILITY							
ENERGY PROJECTION							
FIGHTING SKILLS							

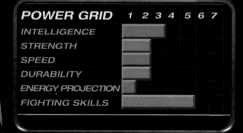

Art by David Finch with Salvador Larroca (inset)

DOCTOR OCTOPUS

HISTORY: Respected scientist Otto Octavius was working for Osborn Industries on a S.H.I.E.L.D.-funded U.S. government project to create a super-soldier serum, the Oz Compound; he was also an industrial spy for Osborn's rival, Justin Hammer. After the Compound accidentally mutated teenager Peter Parker, Otto's employer Norman Osborn decided to test a sample on himself. He had Otto supervise the procedure, but an explosion destroyed the lab, and the mechanical arms Otto wore for delicate experiments were fused to his skin. Otto eventually awoke in government custody, his mechanical arms still attached so their grafting could be studied; he went berserk, escaped, and slew the new occupant of his old home. Irrationally blaming Hammer for his condition, Otto attacked Hammer's "Big Apple Energy Dome" facility, soundly defeating Spider-Man in the process. Days later, Otto attacked Hammer's secret, illegal New Jersey genetics facility, murdering its scientists, calling in the press to observe, and terrorizing Hammer until he suffered a heart attack. Before he could do any further damage, Spider-Man arrived. Better prepared this time, the arachnid hero turned Octopus's own electrical attack against him, pounded Octopus into unconsciousness and ripped out one of the villain's tentacles.

S.H.I.E.L.D. captured Otto, removed his tentacles, and incarcerated him alongside other genetically enhanced criminals (including Osborn) for study and interrogation. Otto seemingly co-operated until he remotely activated his arms, killed his captors and freed his fellow inmates. As de facto head of the escapees, Osborn had Otto breach SHIELD security and deactivate the defences of their Triskelion HQ. They kidnapped Spider-Man and blackmailed him into joining their attack on the White House, but the Ultimates recaptured them and Wasp defeated Doctor Octopus. Once more stripped of his arms, he was incarcerated in the super-prison known as The Raft.

REAL NAME: Otto Octavius
KNOWN ALIASES: Ock, Doc Ock
IDENTITY: Public
OCCUPATION: Scientist, criminal
CITIZENSHIP: U.S.A.
PLACE OF BIRTH: Unknown
KNOWN RELATIVES: Roselita Octavius (ex-wife)
GROUP AFFILIATION: Norman Osborn's "Six"
EDUCATION: Ph.D in various sciences
FIRST APPEARANCE: (as Octavius) Ultimate Spider-Man #2 (2000); (as Doctor Octopus) Ultimate Spider-Man #14 (2001)

Learning of plans to make a Spider-Man movie featuring him as a villain, Otto remote-controlled his arms into freeing him and attacked the film shoot, again battling Spider-Man. Subduing Spider-Man and abducting him to Brazil, Otto was soon defeated and taken into custody in the States, where Nick Fury melted his mechanical arms down into molten slag.

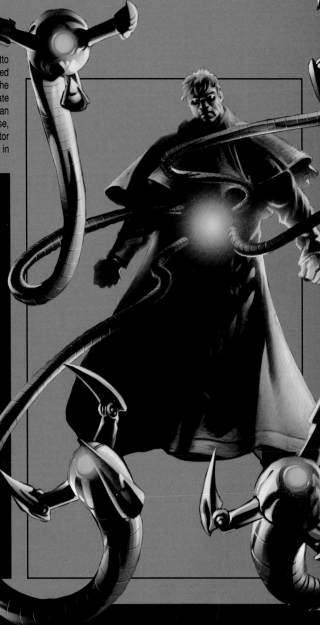

HEIGHT: 5'10"
WEIGHT: 170 lbs.
EYES: Gray
HAIR: Brown

SUPERHUMAN POWERS: Octopus can mentally control his mechanical arms, even when they are miles away.

ABILITIES: Scientific genius.

PARAPHERNALIA: Otto's four mechanical arms, initially fused to his skin, were later surgically removed. They house a variety of built-in tools. The arms can extrude claws for grasping or cutting, act as bludgeons, move at incredible speeds, or release electrical charges. They can carry Octopus and additional weights along at high speed, climbing over obstacles and around buildings, and are strong enough to throw cars and rip Spider-Man's webbing. Otto wears special glasses to protect his damaged eyes.

POWER GRID	1	2	3	4	5	6	7
INTELLIGENCE							
STRENGTH							
SPEED							
DURABILITY							
ENERGY PROJECTION							
FIGHTING SKILLS							

Art by Mark Bagley

DOCTOR STRANGE

REAL NAME: Stephen Strange, Jr.
KNOWN ALIASES: Sorcerer to the Stars
IDENTITY: Publicly known
OCCUPATION: Sorcerer
CITIZENSHIP: U.S.A.
PLACE OF BIRTH: Unknown
KNOWN RELATIVES: Stephen Strange (Dr. Strange, father), Clea Strange (mother)
GROUP AFFILIATION: None
EDUCATION: College dropout
FIRST APPEARANCE: Ultimate Marvel Team-Up #12 (2002)

HISTORY: Stephen Strange Jr. is the son of Earth's undisputed master of the mystic arts. The elder Stephen Strange was a brilliant but arrogant surgeon until his drunk driving killed his wife and unborn child; the accident also injured his hands, ending his surgical career. Searching the world for a cure, he followed rumors to the Himalayan home of the Ancient One, who taught him both sorcery and humility, and Strange became the Earth dimension's most powerful sorcerer. Returning to civilization after the Ancient One's time on Earth ended, Strange settled in New York. He took on a servant, Wong (part of a long family line who served Masters of the Mystic arts), and a disciple, Clea, who later became Strange's wife. When Strange suddenly vanished, the pregnant Clea searched for him; she eventually gave up hope, abandoning magic and raising her son to believe his father had died in a car accident. When that son turned 21, though, Wong told him the truth about his father. Wong tutored the new Dr. Strange in the mystic arts, using the Ancient One's texts; he displayed a natural aptitude, mastering the basics within a year.

The mage Xandu sought the Wand of Watoomb and learned it was in Strange's house. He bewitched Spider-Man, who smashed through Strange's attic window, breaking the house's seal of magical defenses. Strange halted Spider-Man's attack, freed him from Xandu's control and questioned him. Xandu soon entered the house and overpowered the novice Strange, but was subdued by Spider-Man. The youthful hero then departed, and Strange cast a spell removing his visitor's memories of the encounter.

Months later, Dr. Strange went public as the celebrity "Sorcerer to the Stars". The Daily Bugle sent Ben Urich and Peter Parker to interview him, but they arrived just as he was attacked by a nightmare being from a dimensions of dreams while meditating. Wong sent the visitors away, but a suspicious Parker returned as Spider-Man and witnessed Wong's attempts to wake his master. Mistaking these efforts for an attack, Spider-Man again smashed through the window, once more shattering the mansion's mystic wards. When the nightmare manipulator shifted its focus to the unshielded Spider-Man, Strange awoke and entered Spider-Man's dreamscape to save him from the entity. The dream creature confronted Strange with a vision of his father, but this merely angered Strange, who dispelled it, allowing both men to awaken.

HEIGHT: 5'10"
WEIGHT: 150 lbs.
EYES: Blue
HAIR: Black

SUPERHUMAN POWERS: Strange is a sorcerer who can open dimensional portals, fire mystic energy bolts, remove bonds and perform various other feats.

PARAPHERNALIA: Strange possesses various mystic artifacts and tomes.

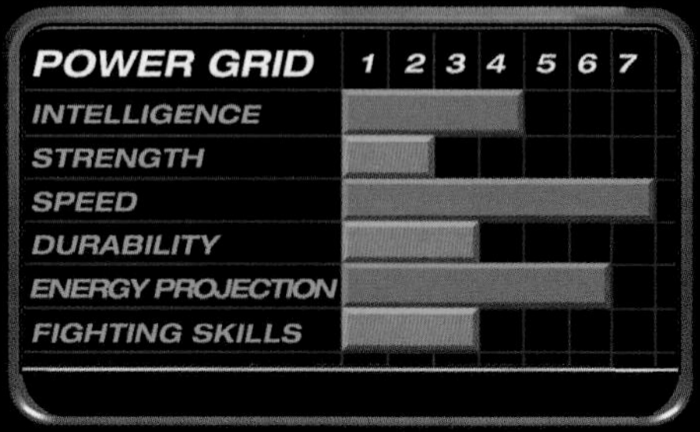

POWER GRID	1	2	3	4	5	6	7
INTELLIGENCE							
STRENGTH							
SPEED							
DURABILITY							
ENERGY PROJECTION							
FIGHTING SKILLS							

HISTORY: Dillon was a criminal who underwent illegal genetic experiments carried out by Dr. John Skrtic on behalf of industrialist Justin Hammer, who was competing with Osborn Industries to win a lucrative government contract to create a super-soldier serum. Developing electrical powers and calling himself Electro, Dillon was sold into the service of the Kingpin of Crime, Wilson Fisk, in return for construction contracts for another of Hammer's projects. As Fisk's willing enforcer, Electro defeated Spider-Man after the hero broke into Fisk Tower. Electro later watched Kingpin murder Frederick Foswell, the underboss known as Mr. Big, for having supplied Spider-Man with information. When Spider-Man returned to the Tower a few days later to steal surveillance footage of Foswell's murder, Electro and the Enforcers opposed him, but Spider-Man tricked Electro into stunning the Enforcer Ox, took down the other two Enforcers, and caused Electro to short out violently by dousing him with water from a broken pipe.

When a hospitalized Electro awoke weeks later, the Kingpin had fled the country and F.B.I. agents were waiting to question Dillon. Electro killed everyone in the room and fled, but he was swiftly recaptured by Captain America, Iron Man and the Black Widow. He was imprisoned in a secure S.H.I.E.L.D. facility alongside other genetically modified criminals (Doctor Octopus, Kraven, Norman Osborn and Sandman), his powers blocked by a high-tech control collar, to be studied and interrogated by Hank Pym (Giant Man). Months later, Dr. Octopus engineered a breakout and the group slaughtered their way to freedom, killing 35 S.H.I.E.L.D. agents on their way out. They then assaulted S.H.I.E.L.D.'s Triskelion main base in search of Spider-Man, who had been moved there for his own protection. Octopus breached computer security to shut down the base's defenses, Electro overloaded the generators, and the criminals managed to capture Spider-Man and escape.

Spider-Man was coerced into joining their attack on the White House itself. Conventional forces fell before them in seconds, but their progress was halted on the front lawn outside the Oval Office

REAL NAME: Max Dillon
KNOWN ALIASES: None
IDENTITY: Known to the authorities
OCCUPATION: Criminal
CITIZENSHIP: U.S.A. with criminal record
PLACE OF BIRTH: Unknown
KNOWN RELATIVES: Unnamed mother
GROUP AFFILIATION: Norman Osborn's "Six"
EDUCATION: Unknown
FIRST APPEARANCE: Ultimate Spider-Man #10 (2001)

by the arrival of the Ultimates. Electro attacked Thor, and their battle raged into the air; but Electro's powers proved no match for the alleged God of Lightning, and along with his teammates, Electro was soon returned to custody.

HEIGHT: 5'9"
WEIGHT: 140 lbs.
EYES: Blue
HAIR: Blond (shaved bald)

DISTINGUISHING FEATURES: Electro has lightning-shaped tattoos on his head. He lacks fingerprints.

SUPERHUMAN POWERS: Electro can generate electricity, throw lightning bolts and fly by riding on electrical currents. Without his containment suit, he tends to turn into a being of pure electricity when he uses his powers.

PARAPHERNALIA: Electro formerly wore a containment suit that helped him control and focus his powers.

POWER GRID	1	2	3	4	5	6	7
INTELLIGENCE							
STRENGTH							
SPEED							
DURABILITY							
ENERGY PROJECTION							
FIGHTING SKILLS							

ELEKTRA

REAL NAME: Elektra Natchios
KNOWN ALIASES: El
IDENTITY: No dual identity
OCCUPATION: Assassin for hire
CITIZENSHIP: U.S.A.
PLACE OF BIRTH: Unknown
KNOWN RELATIVES: Unnamed mother (deceased), Dimitris Natchios (father), Irene (aunt), Paul Natchios (second cousin), Leander Natchios (second cousin)
GROUP AFFILIATION: None
EDUCATION: Columbia University undergraduate
FIRST APPEARANCE: Ultimate Spider-Man Super-Special #1 (2002)

HISTORY: Elektra Natchios began studying martial arts under Master Stone when she was six, soon after her mother died from breast cancer. After finishing school, she attended Columbia University, where she dated blind classmate Matt Murdock. When Elektra's friend Mel was raped by a boy called Trey, the charges were dropped thanks to Trey's influential father. After Elektra threatened Trey, his hired thugs firebombed her father's dry cleaning business. Matt forced the thugs to confess, but again Trey was freed, and Elektra began to fear Matt was lying to her since she suspected he was not truly blind. After Trey attacked Mel again, Elektra ambushed him, planning to kill him. Trying to stop her, Matt showed he trusted her by sharing his secret: though he was blind, his other senses were superhumanly enhanced. Unmoved, Elektra cut Trey's femoral artery and gave Matt a choice; save Trey from bleeding to death or be with her. Matt chose the former.

Elektra quit school and moved back in with her father, whose cousins Paul and Leander paid to rebuild his business but then used the store for money laundering. Elektra agreed to settle her father's debts by stealing the ledger of their bookkeeper Cullen, who was about to testify against the cousins. She found the ledger, but Cullen was slain by the professional assassin Poindexter, who then tried to kill her. Elektra escaped, but Poindexter framed Elektra's father for Cullen's murder. Seeking to clear him, Elektra teamed with Matt and learned that Poindexter was hired by the Kingpin, who also sought the ledger. The duo failed to prevent Poindexter from killing Cullen's lawyer, William Savage, who had another copy of the book, but Poindexter failed to retrieve the ledger. Sucker-punching Matt, Elektra traded the ledger to the Kingpin for Poindexter and clearing her father. She fought Poindexter and won, impressing the Kingpin, who offered to employ her. Later, Matt revealed there had been evidence that would have cleared her father without Kingpin's aid.

Elektra became a freelance assassin, though Spider-Man stopped her from killing a Latverian General. The Kingpin hired her to retrieve a stolen stone tablet, bringing her into conflict with the Black Cat and Spider-Man; when the Cat threw the tablet into the river, Elektra impaled her on a thrown Sai, seemingly killing her. Recently, Elektra has started working for the Kingpin again, after Hammerhead began a gang war challenging his rule of the underworld.

HEIGHT: 5'9"
WEIGHT: 130 lbs.
EYES: Brown
HAIR: Black

ABILITIES: Elektra is an accomplished martial artist trained in ninja arts, an Olympic-level athlete and gymnast, and an expert with the Sai and other weaponry.

PARAPHERNALIA: Elektra usually wields twin Sais and shuriken.

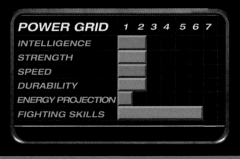

POWER GRID	1	2	3	4	5	6	7
INTELLIGENCE							
STRENGTH							
SPEED							
DURABILITY							
ENERGY PROJECTION							
FIGHTING SKILLS							

Art by Salvador Larroca

ENFORCERS

HISTORY: A criminal trio who act as muscle for New York crime lords, the Enforcers consist of "Fancy" Dan, a diminutive gunman; Montana, a whip expert who generally wears a cowboy hat and trench coat; and Ox, a gigantic strongman. Having seen a photograph of the trio accompanied by his uncle's killer, Spider-Man tracked them down as a possible lead to the Kingpin, but when he tried to question them, a fight began. At first the hero underestimated them; Ox shrugged off a punch to the gut, then Montana managed to wrap his whip round Spider-Man's neck. Breaking loose, he swiftly webbed the group up, but his interrogation efforts were interrupted by their employer, Mr. Big, who gladly told Spider-Man where to find the Kingpin. Further discussion was prevented by the arrival of the F.B.I., whose surveillance operation had been disrupted by Spider-Man's actions; the wall-crawler speedily departed, leaving the Enforcers to the Feds.

Three nights later, the Kingpin confronted Mr. Big and forced the Enforcers to pick a side, ordering Montana and Ox to hold Mr. Big while he placed Spider-Man's captured mask over Mr. Big's head, then crushed his skull. Ox considered becoming a federal witness for his part in Mr. Big's death, feeling he was not a true man because he gave in to his fear of the Kingpin. Montana concurred, because they had broken an oath, but Fancy Dan felt it was foolish even to consider crossing the Kingpin. When Spider-Man again broke into the Kingpin's building, the Enforcers confronted him alongside Electro. Though outnumbered, Spider-Man prevailed —he tricked Electro into stunning Ox, webbed Dan's guns to his hands, causing a backfire, and knocked Montana out. Before departing, Spider-Man tried to convince the barely conscious Ox to confess to the police about the Kingpin's activities.

CURRENT MEMBERS: Fancy Dan (Dan Rubenstein, a.k.a. Dan Crenshaw); Montana Bale (a.k.a. Montana Stern), Ox (Bruno Sanchez)
BASE OF OPERATIONS: New York City
FIRST APPEARANCE: (photo of group) Ultimate Spider-Man #8 (2001); (in person) Ultimate Spider-Man #9 (2001)

Months later, the Kingpin sent the Enforcers after his rebellious subordinate, Julio, who was gambling with Kingpin's money. Spider-Man arrived in time to stop Fancy Dan from shooting Julio, and the Enforcers were soon webbed up once again and left for the police. Once the Kingpin's lawyer had them released, they were warned that another failure would earn the Kingpin's wrath.

When the Daily Bugle stopped supporting Sam Bullit's campaign to become D.A. after learning of his ties to Kingpin, the Enforcers were sent to intimidate editor J. Jonah Jameson into reversing that stance. Spider-Man intervened, webbing up both Dan and Montana and beating a wounded Ox until Dan managed to fire a shot through the webbing and wing him; Ox then smashed Spider-Man against a car, knocking him out. The delay had allowed Jameson to recover his composure, and he stunned the trio by trying to interview them about their ties to Kingpin and Bullit, distracting them long enough for Spider-Man to revive and subdue the criminals. As security arrived, a web-bound Dan said he intended to break the team up; but the Enforcers later returned, battling Spider-Man, Black Cat, Shang-Chi and Danny Rand alongside their new employer, Kingpin's rival, Hammerhead.

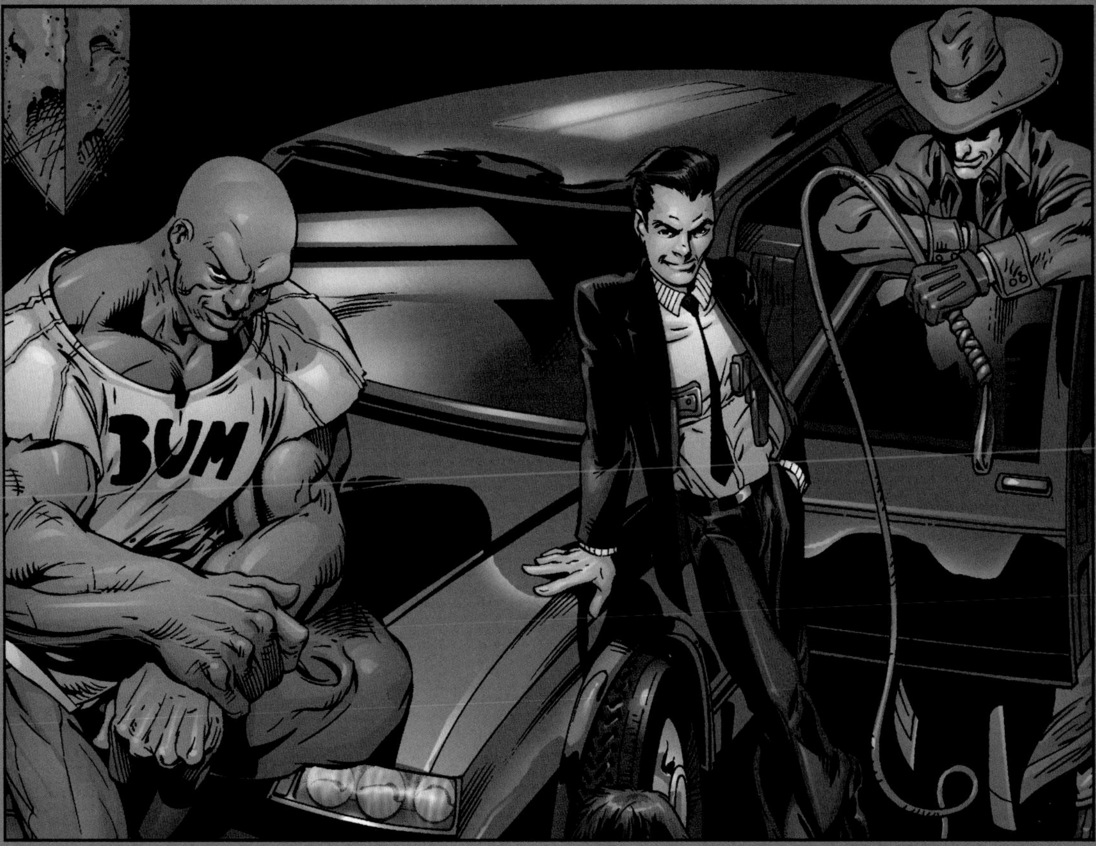
BUM

Art by Mark Bagley

FANTASTIC FOUR

CURRENT MEMBERS: Human Torch (Johnny Storm), Invisible Woman (Susan Storm), Mr. Fantastic (Reed Richards), Thing (Ben Grimm)
BASE OF OPERATIONS: Baxter Building, Manhattan

HISTORY: Over a decade ago, the U.S. government, under the auspices of the Director of Mainland Technology Development, began gathering international child prodigies at a Manhattan laboratory facility in the Baxter Building, giving them the best resources and teachers the project could afford. Headed by scientist Franklin Storm and the U.S. military's General Ross, the project discovered the N-Zone, an otherdimensional space which paralleled our own. When 11-year-old Reed Richards independently accessed this zone and began sending small toys into it, the project recruited him to join their work. Over the following ten years, Reed Richards, Victor Van Damme, and other students and instructors worked on the project before the government ultimately constructed its N-Zone teleportational gate in the Nevada desert, intending to teleport an apple to a receptor in Guantanamo Bay, Cuba.

Unbeknownst to the others, Victor Van Damme altered the device settings and, upon its activation, the five people on its steps vanished into Unbeknownst to the others, Victor Van Damme altered the device settings and, upon its activation, the five people on its steps vanished into interdimensional space, returning altered. Reed Richards returned to the same spot, transformed into a mass of pliable cells. Ben Grimm, Reed's childhood friend, was transported to Mexico and transformed into the rockish Thing; Johnny Storm was transported to Paris, his skin converted to flame-emitting cells; Victor Van Damme was transported to an unrevealed location and acquired a mechanized skin; while Sue Storm was transported into the Nevada desert, acquiring invisibility powers.

Arthur Molekevic, a fired Baxter Building instructor who had covertly observed the experiment and its transformed subjects, sent his artificial ani-men after the five. Initially retrieving Susan while the government gathered Reed, Ben, and Johnny at the Baxter Building, Molekevic then sent what seemed to be an enormous monster after them. Defeating [it,] they followed it to Molekevic's underground laboratories and retrieved Susan, inadvertently destroying the underground chambers in the process and apparently burying Molekevic. The government relocated the remaining Baxter Building students to a secondary facility in Oregon, and dedicated the Manhattan facility to the quiet study of the altered four. When Van Damme attacked the Baxter Building some months later, Reed tracked him to Copenhagen. Refused permission to go to Denmark by the government, the quartet went anyway in Reed's childhood "Fantasti-Car," knowing they needed Victor's knowledge to restore themselves. Battling Van Damme, they were unable to defeat him before the government arrived and were forced by international law to set him free.

The four used a reconstructed N-Zone transporter to pilot a decommissioned U.S. Space Shuttle, heavily modified by Reed Richards and awkwardly christened the "Awesome" by Johnny Storm, to explore the N-Zone itself. The quartet made contact there with the being known as Nihil, who tried to kill them and followed them back to Earth, where both ships crashed in Las Vegas. The Fantastic Four were officially "outed" as super-human on the Sunset Strip while defeating Nihil and his alien crew. Returning to the Baxter Building, they were briefly attacked by a rejected Baxter thinker named Rhona Burchill who was jealous of Reed's status, and subsequently aided the Ultimates, with Ben and Johnny fighting beside Nick Fury, Carol Danvers, and the Ultimates' Thor and Black Widow against the Kree, while Reed and Sue went into space with Iron Man to investigate Gah Lak Tus. The quartet also investigated the mystery of a secret race known as the Inhumans, then pursued a group of Chrono-Bandits across time after they duplicated a time machine which Reed and Sue had co-created. Recently Reed made interdimensional-contact with another universe's version of the Fantastic Four, bringing the team into conflict with an alien world afflicted with a zombie-creating-virus.

GELDOFF

HISTORY: A Latverian orphan who was experimented on in the womb, Geldoff was born a mutant; unaware of this, he grew up fearing mutants as the "devil's children". Adopted and brought to America as a teenager, he eagerly embraced American culture, especially football. While drunk at a party, Geldoff showed off by blowing up random cars with his mutant powers. The next day, the principal suspended half the football team for their involvement in the destructive party; Geldoff demanded the team be reinstated. When the principal refused, Geldoff blew up the principal's car, and then a car belonging to another teacher who called him a name (presumably "mutant"). Aware of Geldoff's rampages, Spider-Man confronted the youth, denounced his irresponsible behavior, and tried to contain Geldoff's powers with webbing; however, Geldoff simply exploded the webbing. When the police arrived, Spider-Man made to leave, and Geldoff begged to go with him, realizing he had overstepped himself. Spider-Man refused, but Geldoff clung on to the back of his costume as Spidey swung away; he lost his grip high in the air, and Spider-Man rescued him.

Taking Geldoff to a nearby rooftop, Spider-Man again tried to make Geldoff realize how irresponsible he had been. They also discussed the nature of Geldoff's powers, but the mutant-phobic Geldoff insisted he was a "magic man" rather than a mutant. Spider-Man tried to convince him to use his abilities to help people, but Geldoff couldn't see why. When Spider-Man paused to foil a robbery in a shop below, Geldoff blew up a vehicle outside the shop, injuring those inside indiscriminately. Geldoff believed he had performed a good deed, and was shocked when an enraged Spider-Man attacked him. Geldoff angrily threatened to use his powers directly on the hero, but was interrupted by the arrival of the X-Men. Confronted by actual mutants who told him he was a mutant, too, Geldoff fainted...twice.

Geldoff was loaded onto the X-Men's jet, to be taken back to their mansion for examination. Awakening in a panic en route, Geldoff blew out the side of the plane. He and Spider-Man were sucked out, but Jean Grey rescued them while Storm saved the plane. Later, at the mansion, Professor Xavier telepathically sedated Geldoff and determined his experimental origins. Horrified, Xavier decided to present Geldoff to scientific organizations and the U.N. as proof of immoral and illegal genetic research. Spider-Man headed home, but not before the woozy Geldoff apologized for threatening him.

HEIGHT: 5'11"
WEIGHT: 145 lbs.
EYES: Blue
HAIR: Light brown

SUPERHUMAN POWERS: Geldoff can generate and discharge explosive energy balls. How this power affects living tissue is unknown, as he has yet to use it on anything organic; Geldoff himself seems immune to the energy.

POWER GRID	1	2	3	4	5	6	7
INTELLIGENCE	■	■					
STRENGTH	■	■					
SPEED	■	■					
DURABILITY	■	■					
ENERGY PROJECTION	■	■	■	■			
FIGHTING SKILLS	■	■					

REAL NAME: Geldoff (full name unrevealed)
KNOWN ALIASES: None
IDENTITY: No dual identity
OCCUPATION: Student
CITIZENSHIP: Latveria
PLACE OF BIRTH: Latveria
KNOWN RELATIVES: Unnamed adoptive parents
GROUP AFFILIATION: None
EDUCATION: High school student (not yet graduated)
FIRST APPEARANCE: Ultimate Spider-Man #40 (2003)

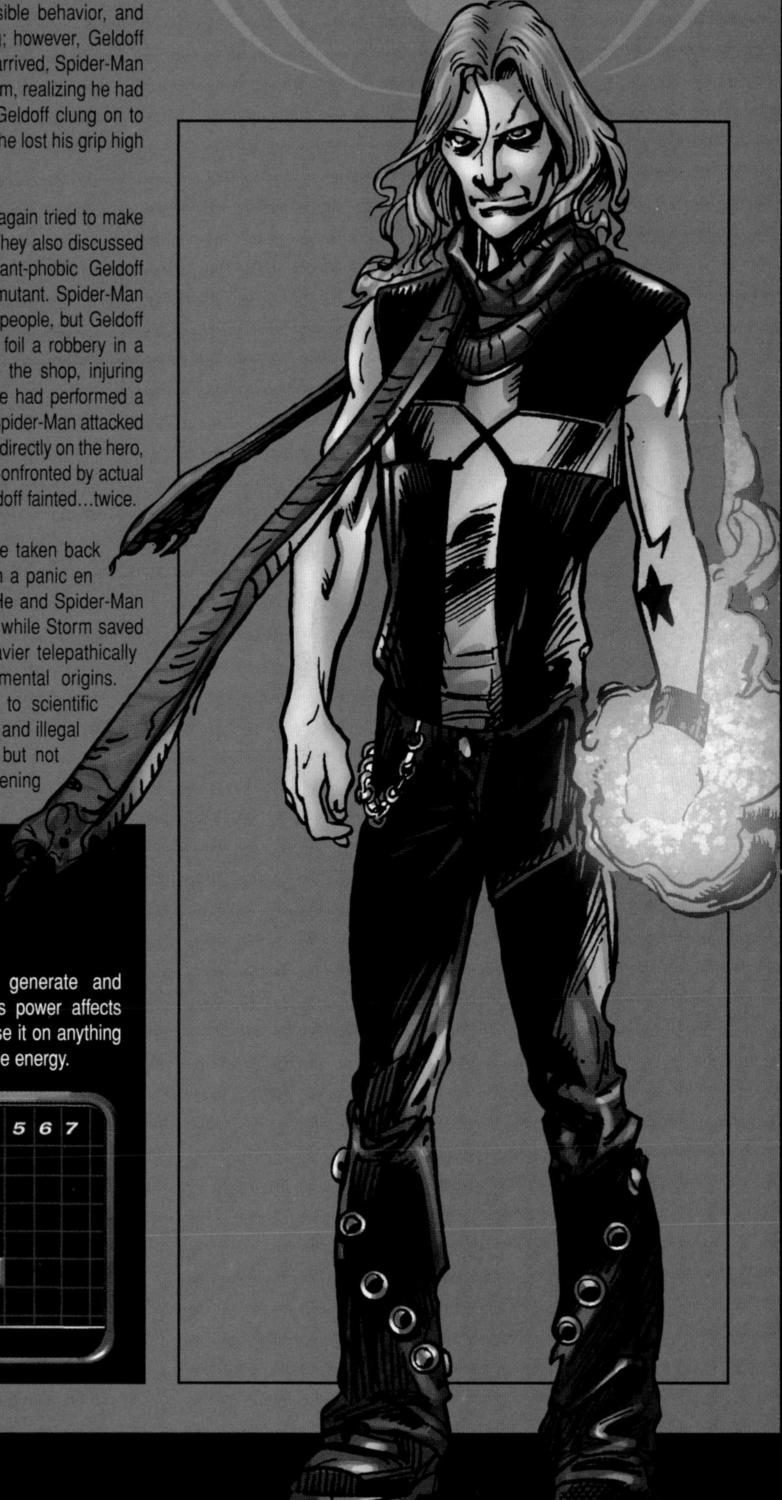

Art by Mark Bagley

GREEN GOBLIN

REAL NAME: Norman Osborn
KNOWN ALIASES: None
IDENTITY: Known to the authorities
OCCUPATION: Criminal; formerly CEO and founder of Oscorp (Osborn Industries, Inc.); scientist
CITIZENSHIP: U.S.A. with criminal record
PLACE OF BIRTH: Unknown
KNOWN RELATIVES: Cher Osborn (half-sister), Harry Osborn (son), unnamed wife (deceased), Amberson (father), unnamed brother or brother-in-law
GROUP AFFILIATION: Osborn's unnamed "Six"
EDUCATION: Ph.D in various sciences
FIRST APPEARANCE: (as Norman) Ultimate Spider-Man #1 (2000); (as Goblin) Ultimate Spider-Man #4

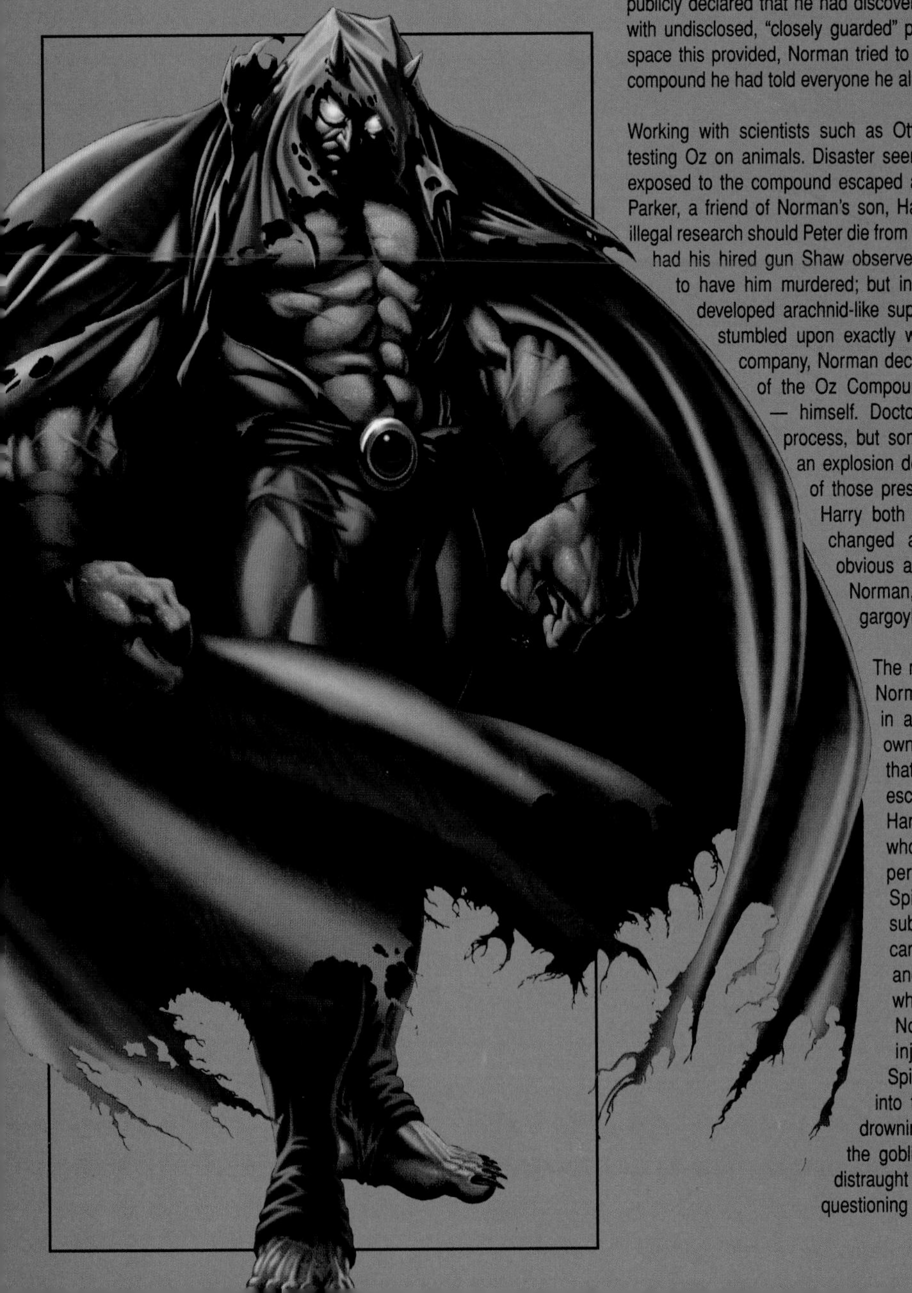

HISTORY: Norman Osborn was a scientific genius who founded his own company, Oscorp, over thirty years ago. It developed new technologies and innovative materials for the manufacturing, construction, automotive and chemical-processing industries, among others. Osborn also liked to keep his company at the forefront of new sciences, such as bioengineering. When Colonel Nick Fury made it quietly known that S.H.I.E.L.D. wanted to tender contracts to the private sector to develop new "Super Soldier Serums," Oscorp took on competitors such as Hammer Industries to win the corporate bidding war; however, it rapidly became clear that Norman had misled S.H.I.E.L.D. as to how ready his company was to produce results. They had rushed the research process to win the bid, their formulae were messy, and their presentation had been largely "smoke and mirrors." After two and a half years without results, Fury severed ties between S.H.I.E.L.D. and Oscorp. Losing the contract left Oscorp shaky; to bolster their reputation and share price, Norman publicly declared that he had discovered a miracle compound, Oz, with undisclosed, "closely guarded" properties. With the breathing space this provided, Norman tried to rush the development of the compound he had told everyone he already had.

Working with scientists such as Otto Octavius, Norman began testing Oz on animals. Disaster seemed to strike when a spider exposed to the compound escaped and bit visiting student Peter Parker, a friend of Norman's son, Harry. Fearing exposure of his illegal research should Peter die from the effects of the bite, Osborn had his hired gun Shaw observe the boy, and was prepared to have him murdered; but instead of becoming ill, Peter developed arachnid-like super-powers. Believing he had stumbled upon exactly what he needed to save his company, Norman decided to test direct application of the Oz Compound on a human guinea pig — himself. Doctor Octavius supervised this process, but something went horribly wrong; an explosion destroyed the lab, killing most of those present. Octavius and bystander Harry both survived, though both were changed as a result; but the most obvious and immediate effect was on Norman, who was transformed into a gargoyle-like strongman.

The monstrous, mentally muddled Norman wandered the streets in a haze before destroying his own mansion home in a fireball that killed his wife; Harry barely escaped. Norman next attacked Harry's school, hunting for Peter, who had adopted the costumed persona of Spider-Man. As Spider-Man, Parker tried to subdue the monster, their fight carrying them towards the city and climaxing atop a bridge, where police marksmen riddled Norman with gunfire. Badly injured, Norman lunged at Spider-Man, missed, and plunged into the waters below, apparently drowning. Informing the police that the goblin was his mutated father, a distraught Harry was taken away for questioning and his own protection.

Norman survived, regaining human form. Using injections of Oz to transform again, Norman gradually gained full use of his speech and mental faculties in his monstrous form. Continued exposure to the drug also drove him insane, and he began to see tiny creatures that would provide him with conflicting advice on what to do. He remained in hiding at first, using his connections to recover Harry from protective custody and have the investigations into the lab explosion and his mansion fire dropped. He hired a psychiatrist, Doctor Warren, who hypnotized Harry into believing his father had not been the creature he had seen.

When Norman's old rival, Justin Hammer, was slain by an equally insane Otto Octavius (now calling himself Doctor Octopus), Norman decided to come out of hiding. He concocted a cover story claiming Hammer had been behind the attacks, acts of sabotage which had forced Norman to go into seclusion to protect his son, and which had now ended with Hammer's demise. Not believing this for a second, Nick Fury had S.H.I.E.L.D. illegally spy on Norman. Harry returned to school, inviting Peter Parker to visit him and his father; not knowing what else to do, the terrified youth reluctantly accepted. As soon as Peter and Norman were alone, Norman assumed his goblin form and told Parker that he would work for Norman or see his loved ones suffer. At school the next day, Fury confided in Peter, explaining that S.H.I.E.L.D. knew of Norman's threats but could do nothing until Osborn made a public move.

That night, Norman tried to tighten his hold on Peter by inviting Peter's Aunt May to his skyscraper; angrily, Peter went alone to confront him. Norman met him on the roof in his goblin form, and when Peter refused to meet his demands, Norman snatched the arriving Mary Jane Watson, Peter's girlfriend, who had likewise been lured to the building. Osborn carried the terrified girl to the Queensboro Bridge, then threw her off. As Spider-Man leapt to her rescue, S.H.I.E.L.D. attack helicopters moved in. Attacked by both Peter and the gunships, Norman fled back to his skyscraper, intending to inject himself with even more Oz. When Harry interrupted, Norman used a post-hypnotic suggestion to render him unconscious, then took more of the serum, mutating further. Spider-Man arrived seconds later, but was swiftly overpowered. Harry awoke to see his father strangling the unmasked hero, backlit by the lights of the approaching attack copters. Peter managed to kick free and bury Norman under a heavy stone desk, which Norman shrugged off, throwing it out the window. Spider-Man grabbed it with his webbing to stop it from smashing down into the busy street below, but left himself exposed; as Norman tried to rip his head off, Harry rammed a large piece of jagged metal through his father's back. Norman turned on his son, and seeing an opening, the S.H.I.E.L.D. choppers opened fire. Injured beyond the limits of his endurance, Norman collapsed and reverted to a comatose human form.

Norman was taken into S.H.I.E.L.D. custody and stored alongside other genetically mutated criminals in a secure research facility, where he was studied and interrogated by Dr. Hank Pym (Giant Man). Fury said they would remain imprisoned until they either cooperated or died. When Pym asked Norman in a group session why he had destroyed his life by deliberately mutating himself, Norman accused him of simply wanting to steal the secret of the Oz formula. Enraged to learn that S.H.I.E.L.D. already had the formula, as they had confiscated everything he owned, Norman began to transform, proving he no longer needed injections of Oz, before security measures brought him down.

A few months later, fellow inmate Doctor Octopus engineered a breakout, and the criminals slaughtered their way out the facility, hiding out together. Norman became de facto leader of

their group, which included Doctor Octopus, Electro, Kraven and Sandman. Osborn called the White House, demanding amnesty, one hundred million dollars, his company and his son back, and that Fury be fired; otherwise, he would make public the story of their illegal imprisonment and bring the President down. Fixated on the idea that Peter Parker was his son, Norman had Octopus hack into S.H.I.E.L.D. systems and shut down security at its main base, the Triskelion, allowing the escaped villains to kidnap Spider-Man, who had been taken into protective custody there. With a blackmailed Spider-Man increasing their numbers to six, the group assaulted the White House, but was intercepted on the front lawn by S.H.I.E.L.D. and the Ultimates. Norman battled both Captain America and Spider-Man (who had learned his loved ones were safe in S.H.I.E.L.D. custody), but was then confronted by Harry, who had been brought in by Fury. As his son pleaded with him to stop, Norman began to revert to human form until Iron Man shot him from behind, deliberately overloading his genetic sequence; Norman's transformation went out of control and he collapsed, stuck midway between forms. Fury had the unconscious villain cryogenically frozen and removed for further tests; however, it seems inevitable that he will break free someday and return to plague Fury and Spider-Man again.

HEIGHT: 5'9" (as Osborn); variable, usually 7' (as Goblin)
WEIGHT: 150 lbs. (as Osborn); variable, usually 1000 lbs. (as Goblin)
EYES: Blue (as Osborn); green (as Goblin)
HAIR: Brown (as Osborn); none (as Goblin)

DISTINGUISHING FEATURES: Green skin and gargoyle-like appearance in goblin form.

SUPERHUMAN POWERS: Norman's goblin form is superhumanly strong, and can leap hundreds of feet at a time; as the Goblin, he also possesses clawed hands that facilitate climbing, durable (but not bulletproof) skin, and accelerated healing. He can generate fiery bolts of energy from his hands.

ABILITIES: Norman is a scientific genius, especially versed in genetics.

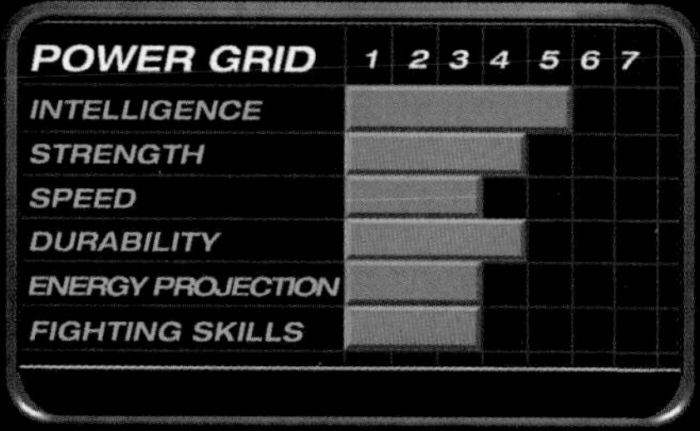

POWER GRID	1	2	3	4	5	6	7
INTELLIGENCE							
STRENGTH							
SPEED							
DURABILITY							
ENERGY PROJECTION							
FIGHTING SKILLS							

JUSTIN HAMMER

REAL NAME: Justin Hammer
KNOWN ALIASES: None
IDENTITY: Publicly known
OCCUPATION: CEO of Hammer Industries, owner of Hammer Towers and Hammer Casino
CITIZENSHIP: U.S.A.
PLACE OF BIRTH: Unknown
KNOWN RELATIVES: Unnamed father (deceased)
GROUP AFFILIATION: None
EDUCATION: College graduate
FIRST APPEARANCE: Ultimate Spider-Man #16 (2002)

HISTORY: The son of a self-made millionaire, Justin Hammer succeeded his father as CEO of Hammer Industries, parlaying his wealth into other successful ventures such as Hammer Towers and Hammer Casino. Powerful and influential, Hammer gained an audience with the President and complained about the recent outbreak of mutants, claiming it was bad for business. During this meeting, Hammer first met S.H.I.E.L.D. agents Woo and Carter. One of Oscorp's top competitors for government-sponsored super-soldier programs, Hammer Industries would often perform illegal genetic enhancements on criminals and the mentally unstable. An early success that became known as Electro was traded to crime lord Wilson Fisk in exchange for the construction permits for Hammer's dream, the Big Apple Energy Dome. Hammer paid Dr. Otto Octavius to act as a corporate spy inside Oscorp, which blew up in his face after a lab accident transformed Otto into the criminally insane Dr. Octopus, who blamed Hammer for the accident. After Doc Ock destroyed Hammer's office, S.H.I.E.L.D. agents Woo and Carter questioned Hammer while Spider-Man eavesdropped on their conversation.

Desperate for protection from Dr. Octopus, Hammer called Dr. John Skrtic, the head of his bioengineering program, who claimed none of their current experiments were ready. Hammer and his bodyguards were horrified when Skrtic showed them the current status of Flint Marko, the subject of the Sandman Project, who was having trouble adjusting to his powers. At the opening of the Big Apple Energy Dome, Hammer's big moment was ruined by Dr. Octopus, who attacked the dome during the press conference. Spider-Man arrived and battled Dr. Octopus, but was defeated and later blamed by Hammer for the attack.

Spider-Man confronted Hammer in his office over the accusations and Hammer attempted to bribe him, offering $50,000 to act as protection against Dr. Octopus. Spider-Man rejected the offer and left. Mere seconds after Spider-Man departed, Hammer received a call from Dr. Skrtic, but Dr. Octopus revealed that he had killed Skrtic and was destroying Hammer's genetics lab in New Jersey. Hammer agreed to meet Dr. Octopus and pay him off, but when Hammer arrived, he saw that Doc Ock had called the media as well. Hammer's chauffeur attempted to drive away, but Dr. Octopus hoisted the limousine off the ground. As Spider-Man intervened and battled Dr. Octopus, Hammer suffered a fatal heart attack in the commotion. Too terrified to emerge, several lab techs stayed behind in his partially destroyed genetics lab, where they watched over the Sandman Project until S.H.I.E.L.D. took them into custody.

HEIGHT: 5'6"
WEIGHT: 150 lbs.
EYES: Brown
HAIR: Gray

POWER GRID	1	2	3	4	5	6	7
INTELLIGENCE							
STRENGTH							
SPEED							
DURABILITY							
ENERGY PROJECTION							
FIGHTING SKILLS							

HAWK-OWL

HISTORY: Jack Danner's older brother Joe knocked his own brains out when he stepped on a rake; then, when Jack was five, his father's drunken driving killed his parents. Neither tragedy turned him into a tortured, vengeful soul. Jack spent the next seven years in St. Frederick's Orphanage, cared for by Father Joe. When he was twelve, his Aunt Ruth returned from Europe, taking custody of Jack and his best friend Daniel Tolliver, housing them in Danner Manor. Unable to cope with their delinquent ways, Ruth soon accepted an offer from groundskeeper Kwi Chi to raise them alongside his own son, Lee Chi. He taught all three discipline and the martial arts. One night, Jack witnessed a hawk attacking an owl in the woods, and he raced to the rescue; afterwards, Kwi stated that Jack was now both the hawk and the owl.

The boys grew up strong and inseparable. Together they won martial arts tournaments, served in the military, and went to university. Jack traveled the world, training under the best fighting teachers. Back in Chicago, Jack decided to do something about the soaring crime rate and became the vigilante Hawk-Owl, operating out of the Owl's Nest, a hidden base atop the Manor.

Jack began to consider adopting a child, imagining fighting alongside a son as Hawk-Owl and "Woody"; he even had a costume made for the latter. When robbers broke into St. Frederick's to hide from the police and took children hostage, Hawk-Owl captured them with the assistance of orphan Hank Kipple. Impressed by Kipple, Jack arranged to adopt him. The cynical Hank viewed his new father with open contempt, unwilling to trust anyone after being alone for so long. Even when he discovered the Nest and Jack's alter-ego, Hank rejected him. To prove he was serious about being a father, Jack offered to quit being Hawk-Owl; once Hank realized he wasn't bluffing, they finally began to bond. Soon after, the Ultimates tried to draft Hawk-Owl into their ranks; unimpressed by their arrogance, Hawk-Owl came to blows with Captain America and Giant-Man until Thor ended the fight, and the Ultimates departed.

When Hank's school principal Morgan Jones became the criminally insane Principal and put Jack in a coma, Hank tried to stop Jones as Woody, placing himself in peril before the awakened Hawk-Owl came to his rescue. The duo continue to protect Chicago, dedicated to making the windy city a little safer.

REAL NAME: Jack Danner
KNOWN ALIASES: None
IDENTITY: Known to authorities
OCCUPATION: Vigilante
CITIZENSHIP: U.S.A.
PLACE OF BIRTH: Unknown
KNOWN RELATIVES: Ruth Danner (aunt), Joe Danner Sr (father, deceased), unnamed mother (deceased), Joe Jr. (brother, deceased), Hank Kipple (adopted son)
GROUP AFFILIATION: Partner of Woody
EDUCATION: University graduate
FIRST APPEARANCE: Ultimate Adventures #1 (2002)

HEIGHT: 6'1"
WEIGHT: 190 lbs.
EYES: Blue
HAIR: Black

ABILITIES: Hawk-Owl is a highly trained fighter, extremely agile and acrobatic, and very accurate with thrown weapons.

PARAPHERNALIA: Jack wears an armored costume with night vision lenses in its helmet. He carries bolas, throwing discs and customized handcuffs, as well as a device that makes owls attack on command. He usually travels using a flying car.

POWER GRID	1	2	3	4	5	6	7
INTELLIGENCE	■	■	■				
STRENGTH	■	■	■				
SPEED	■	■					
DURABILITY	■	■					
ENERGY PROJECTION	■						
FIGHTING SKILLS	■	■	■	■	■	■	

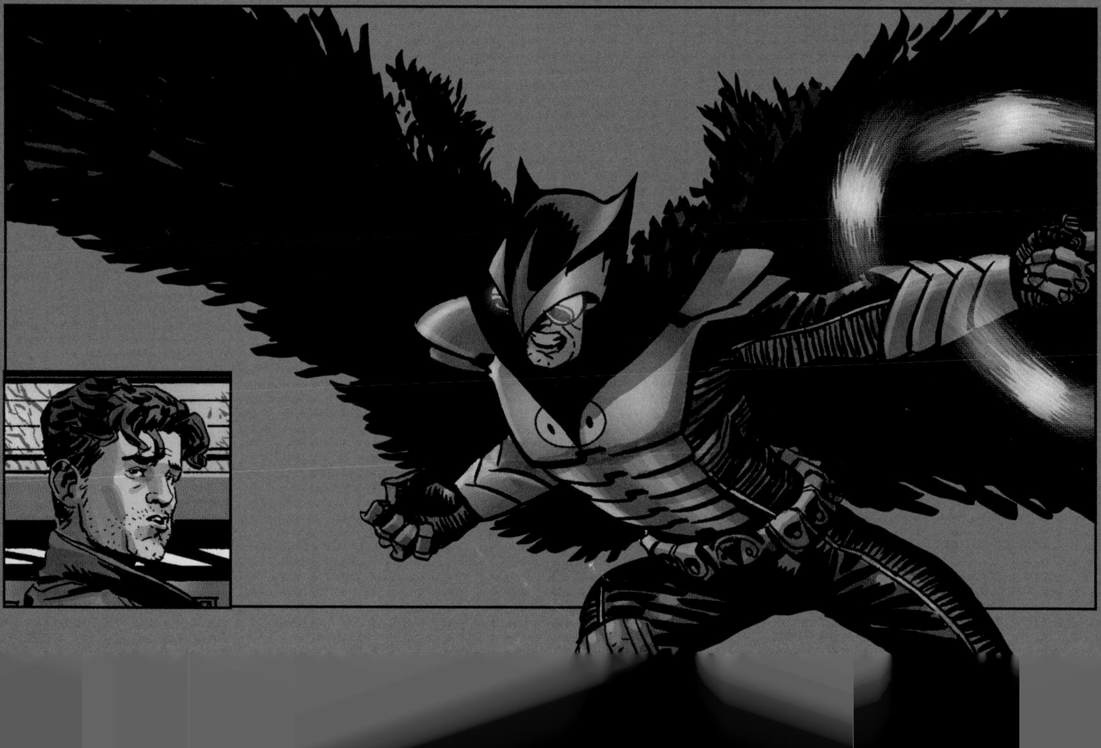

HUMAN TORCH

REAL NAME: Johnny Storm
KNOWN ALIASES: None
IDENTITY: Secret
OCCUPATION: Adventurer
CITIZENSHIP: U.S.A.
PLACE OF BIRTH: Unrevealed
KNOWN RELATIVES: Franklin Storm (father), Mary Storm (mother, deceased), Susan Storm (sister)
GROUP AFFILIATION: Fantastic Four
EDUCATION: High school student (not yet graduated)
FIRST APPEARANCE: Ultimate Fantastic Four #1 (2004)

HISTORY: Johnny Storm, the youngest child of scientist Franklin Storm, failed to inherit the genius shared by his father and older sister, Sue. Educated through public schooling, Johnny attended high school at P.S. 440. He spent his formative years at the Baxter Building labs; but despite his access to its high-tech resources, he rebelliously resisted taking advantage of this opportunity to learn.

Johnny attended the test of Reed Richards' Nevada desert N-Zone teleportational device and was transported by its malfunction to France. Waking in a hospital bed there, he briefly burst into flame with no harm to himself. Taken to the Baxter Building, he continually inadvertently burst into flame, slowly learning to control his combustion by reciting "Flame On" and "Flame Off." When the Baxter Building was attacked by Arthur Molekevic's genetically constructed monster, Johnny accidentally burned through a window and fell from the skyscraper, discovering he could fly while aflame.

Alone among the foursome, Johnny dreamed of using his powers to be a super hero like the Ultimates; however, his father insisted Johnny finish high school, which he was coerced into attending. He registered at a school in Queens, and made friends quickly, meeting Liz Allen, Mary Jane Watson, and Peter Parker (secretly Spider-Man), among others. When Johnny accidentally caught fire at a beach bonfire, he fled, returning only briefly to ask Liz Allen to meet with him so he could explain. Though Allen didn't show, Spider-Man did, and the two talked before cooperating to save people trapped in a burning building. Johnny's spirit was renewed by Spider-Man's contention that the drawbacks of super-powers are outweighed by the good they can do, and he shared with Spider-Man the name he would use when the team went public: the Human Torch. The Fantastic Four were forced to go public while battling the alien Nihil on the Las Vegas Sunset Strip; Johnny has since reveled in fame and the Fantastic Four's adventures.

HEIGHT: 5'10"
WEIGHT: 160 lbs.
EYES: Blue
HAIR: Blond

SUPERHUMAN POWERS: Johnny's external surface, including his skin, nails, hair, and eyes, is covered with a microscopic layer of transparent fireproofing plates, making him fully immune to fire damage. His cells generate plasma jets through clean nuclear fusion, allowing Johnny to emit flame from part or all of his skin, and even to fly. Johnny powers this fusion internally, so if he does not consume enough energy to generate new protective cells regularly, he runs the risk of literally burning himself up. He can also control flame outside of himself, though this has yet to be explained.

PARAPHERNALIA: Johnny wears a specially constructed impact suit which is flameproof yet permeable enough to allow his flame to pass through it.

POWER GRID	1	2	3	4	5	6	7
INTELLIGENCE							
STRENGTH							
SPEED							
DURABILITY							
ENERGY PROJECTION							
FIGHTING SKILLS							

HISTORY: The eldest child of renowned scientist Franklin Storm, Sue Storm inherited her father's genius. Since early childhood, she has been one of the prodigies studying and working at the Baxter Building, a midtown Manhattan government research lab. Following her father into physics, at age eight she built a sugar-powered rocket and accidentally destroyed her father's car, after which she changed her focus to "inner space" biology. Romancing brilliant Baxter Building classmate Reed Richards, Sue became a formidable scientist in her own right, earning four doctorates in bio-chemical sciences. Attending the Nevada desert testing of Reed's N-Zone dimensional teleporter, Sue was transported a mere three miles into the desert by the device's malfunction. She was retrieved by former Baxter Building instructor Dr. Arthur Molekevic, who took her to his underground facilities below Manhattan, calmed her, and helped her to gain control of her new abilities, while he sent a "monster" to the Baxter Building to retrieve three others who had been transformed by the N-Zone experiment. In the company of those three, Susan fled Molekevic and used her invisible protective force field to take them all back to the surface.

Making the study of herself and her three partners her new life's work, Sue spent months investigating their abilities and charting their powers while improving her own understanding of herself. She has deduced the nature of both Reed and Johnny's changes, though her own powers remain unexplained and she is unable to penetrate Ben's skin with any more detail than determining his internal fluid pressure. Susan continues to develop her force fields, though there are physical side effects to extreme usage. When Van Damme attacked the Baxter Building with a squad of flying insects, Susan contained and compacted a squad of them within a force field, developing a nosebleed in doing so, and later caught a crashing helicopter in her force field, suffering severe physical stress.

Susan has proven capable of standing on her own, and after the team went public she assumed the codename "Invisible Woman." Her force fields have been the Four's ace in the hole, saving their lives when Nihil dumped Reed and Ben into the near-vacuum of the N-Zone and single-handedly stopping the time-traveling Chrono-

REAL NAME: Susan "Sue" Storm
KNOWN ALIASES: None
IDENTITY: Secret
OCCUPATION: Scientist
CITIZENSHIP: U.S.A.
PLACE OF BIRTH: Unrevealed
KNOWN RELATIVES: Franklin Storm (father), Mary Storm (mother, deceased), Johnny Storm (brother)
GROUP AFFILIATION: Fantastic Four
EDUCATION: Multiple advanced degrees
FIRST APPEARANCE: Ultimate Fantastic Four #1 (2004)

Bandits. She co-created the chrono-tunnel with Reed Richards, and has conducted biological studies of the Kree alien Mahr Vehl and extra-dimensional life in the N-Zone. Though her newfound fame has brought her unsought attention from the likes of billionaire playboy Tony Stark, she remains romantically attached to Reed Richards despite her concerns about his overdevotion to science.

HEIGHT: 5'6"
WEIGHT: 110 lbs.
EYES: Blue
HAIR: Blonde

SUPERHUMAN POWERS: Susan can make herself and her clothing invisible to all wavelengths of light. She can project invisible force fields of an unknown nature, and has used these force fields to enclose and smash items, and to protect and lift herself and others.

ABILITIES: Storm is a scientific genius, holding advanced degrees in four biochemical fields.

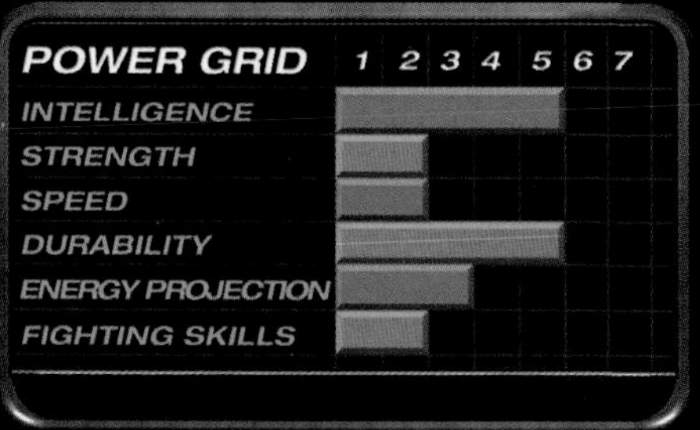

POWER GRID	1	2	3	4	5	6	7
INTELLIGENCE							
STRENGTH							
SPEED							
DURABILITY							
ENERGY PROJECTION							
FIGHTING SKILLS							

Art by Stuart Immonen

J. JONAH JAMESON

REAL NAME: J. Jonah Jameson
KNOWN ALIASES: None
IDENTITY: No dual identity
OCCUPATION: Publisher of the Daily Bugle, editor, reporter
CITIZENSHIP: U.S.A.
PLACE OF BIRTH: Unrevealed, probably New York City
KNOWN RELATIVES: Unnamed wife; unnamed son (believed deceased)
GROUP AFFILIATION: None
EDUCATION: Unrevealed, presumed journalism degree
FIRST APPEARANCE: Ultimate Spider-Man #6 (2001)

HISTORY: J. Jonah Jameson began his journalism career as a teen copy boy at the Daily Bugle; at 18 his editor let him accompany reporters on assignment to learn more about the newspaper business, experience that nurtured Jameson's love of the news industry and New York. He rose rapidly through the Bugle's ranks, eventually becoming editor-in-chief and hiring editor Robbie Robertson as his right-hand man; co-workers for twenty years, Jameson values Robertson's expertise, but he also recognizes that Robertson's legendary cool-headedness can often be a vital foil for his own impulsiveness. In recent years, Jameson, now Bugle publisher, was horrified when his astronaut son was lost during a mission on the space shuttle Orion; the authorities had few answers for Jameson, citing only "technical malfunction" and unable to even provide him a body to bury. Grief weighed heavily on Jameson, and when, some months later, the adventurer Spider-Man debuted, Jameson bitterly resented the costumed cut-up for winning instant recognition and, among some, dedication, while his son lay dead and forgotten. Nevertheless, news was news, and Jameson offered a high price for anyone who could bring the Bugle a photograph of the mysterious Spider-Man; the call was answered by teenage Peter Parker, who provided Jameson with the sought-after photo; impressed by the boy's technical know how, the publisher hired him as a part-time web designer, unaware Parker was in fact Spider-Man. Robertson and top reporter Ben Urich grew concerned over Jameson's growing obsession with "debunking" Spider-Man's heroic reputation, although hardly as concerned as Parker.

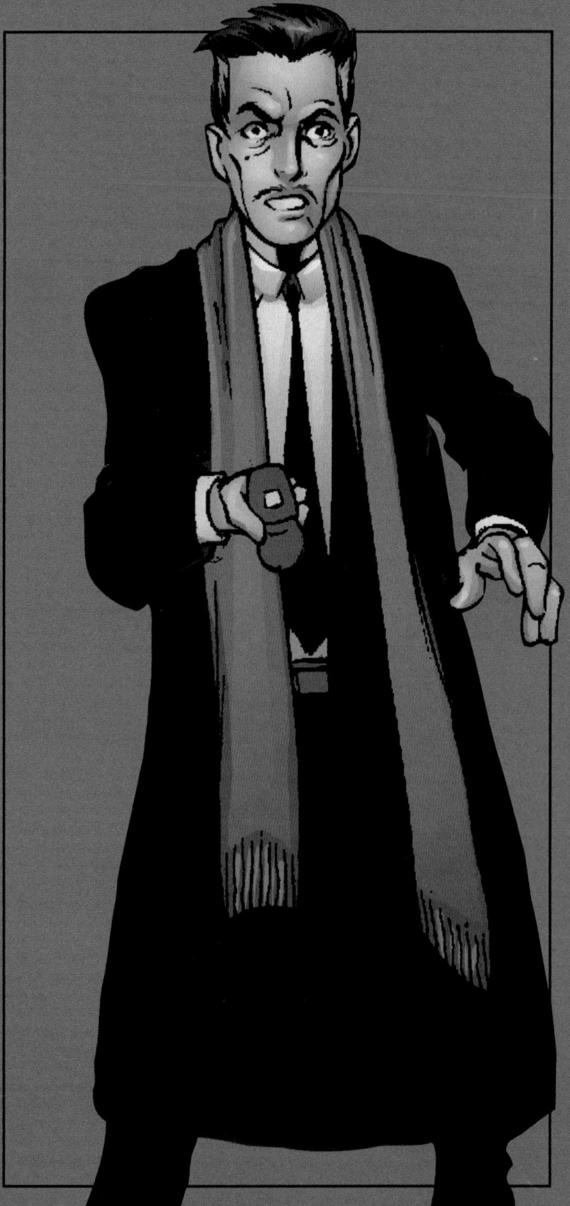

When attorney Sam Bullit, a frequent associate of Wilson Fisk, the so-called Kingpin of Crime, ran for District Attorney on an anti-Spider-Man platform, Jameson pledged the Bugle's support despite Robertson's reservations. When Parker, appalled that Fisk had evaded imprisonment after being caught in the act of murder, questioned the publisher's policies, Jameson, perhaps subconsciously recognizing the untenability of his position, fired Parker on the spot. However, when Urich interviewed Bullit, it became plain that the candidate's criminal ties could not be ignored, and Jameson swallowed his pride and wrote an expose on Bullit, with one of the Kingpin himself in the works. For his efforts, he found himself accosted by the Kingpin's Enforcers, only to be rescued by his nemesis Spider-Man. Jameson proved he had not lost all of his professionalism by attempting to interview not only his rescuer but also his attackers, although neither attempt panned out. In the wake of the encounter, Jameson admitted to himself that grief over his son's mysterious and unrecognized death had colored his judgment about the adventurer in the "creepy mask," and he resolved to address this blind spot that so jaundiced his newsman's eye. Jameson has taken little interest in Spider-Man since, but whether his continued distrust of costumed heroes will overcome his determination remains to be seen.

HEIGHT: 5' 11"
WEIGHT: 183 lbs.
EYES: Brown
HAIR: Brown with white temples

ABILITIES: J. Jonah Jameson is an accomplished journalist and business executive whose wealth can provide him with ready resources in case of emergency.

POWER GRID	1	2	3	4	5	6	7
INTELLIGENCE	■	■	■				
STRENGTH	■	■					
SPEED	■	■					
DURABILITY	■	■					
ENERGY PROJECTION	■						
FIGHTING SKILLS	■	■					

Art by Mark Bagley

KINGPIN

HISTORY: For more than fifteen years, Wilson Fisk has been New York's Kingpin of Crime, the city's leading crimelord. He rose to power with ruthless determination, squeezing out his predecessor, Silvio Manfredi (a.k.a. Silvermane) in the process. Though his true vocation is known to the police and press, he has never been successfully convicted for his activities, though the authorities have come close on occasion — for instance, when Cullen, a bookkeeper employed by the Natchios brothers, Fisk subordinates, turned State's evidence many years ago. Though the brothers promised their superior that Cullen was unaware of their link to him, the accountant actually possessed a ledger that incontrovertibly tied the Kingpin to numerous crimes. Correctly doubting the Natchios brothers' ability to handle the problem, Fisk hired the assassin Benjamin Poindexter to eliminate Cullen. Poindexter succeeded in spite of the presence of Elektra Natchios, who had been sent to Cullen's safe house by her cousins to recover the ledger; however, William Savage, Cullen's lawyer, tried to blackmail the Kingpin with a copy of the ledger.

Kingpin again sent in Poindexter, who managed to kill Savage but failed to recover the second ledger thanks to the interference of Elektra and a young law student, Matt Murdock. Elektra, whose father had been wrongly accused of the Cullen slaying, delivered the book to Fisk in return for the Kingpin giving up Poindexter to the police and clearing her father's name; this proved to be the start of a lengthy working relationship between Fisk and Elektra. A few years later, the Kingpin was somehow involved in betraying burglar Jack Hardy to the police; Hardy was arrested, and in spite of a spirited defense from lawyer "Foggy" Nelson (ironically the partner of the now graduated Matt Murdock), he was sent to prison, where he later died. Hardy's daughter Felicia blamed Fisk, and would seek revenge years later.

Over time, Fisk's position began to seem unassailable; to the public he was a wealthy entrepreneur who supported worthy causes. The press dared not even suggest a link between him and the "Kingpin," though some dedicated reporters such as the Daily Bugle's Ben Urich continued to hunt for evidence which might bring him down. Even costumed vigilantes such as Hell's Kitchen's Daredevil proved only minor inconveniences. Other than his power and reputation, the only thing Fisk cared about was his wife, Vanessa. Fisk took few risks, rarely getting his own hands dirty with any direct involvement in criminality, employing others such as the Enforcers to act on his behalf.

When superpowered crimefighters began to spring up, Fisk evened the balance by trading construction contracts with industrialist Justin Hammer in return for the services of Electro; this turned out to be money well spent when Spider-Man broke into Fisk's offices. Electro overpowered the hero, whom the Kingpin then unmasked and interrogated; not recognizing him, the Kingpin had the youth thrown out a window, and then sent for Mr. Big, an underboss who had encountered Spider-Man days earlier. Fisk confronted Mr. Big, correctly accusing him of betrayal, then placed Spider-Man's mask over Mr. Big's head and crushed Big's skull with his bare hands. This personal touch proved to be a mistake when Spider-Man returned a few days later and stole the Kingpin's own surveillance footage of the murder. After his operatives failed to subdue the intruder, Fisk personally confronted Spider-Man as he attempted to leave with the footage; however, his immense strength could not counter Spider-Man's agility. He failed to land a single blow and ended up

REAL NAME: Wilson Fisk
KNOWN ALIASES: None
IDENTITY: Known to authorities
OCCUPATION: Kingpin of crime
CITIZENSHIP: U.S.A., accused of murder, charges dropped
PLACE OF BIRTH: Unknown
KNOWN RELATIVES: Vanessa Fisk (wife)
GROUP AFFILIATION: None
EDUCATION: Unknown
FIRST APPEARANCE: (mentioned) Ultimate Spider-Man #7 (2001); (seen) Ultimate Spider-Man #9 (2001)

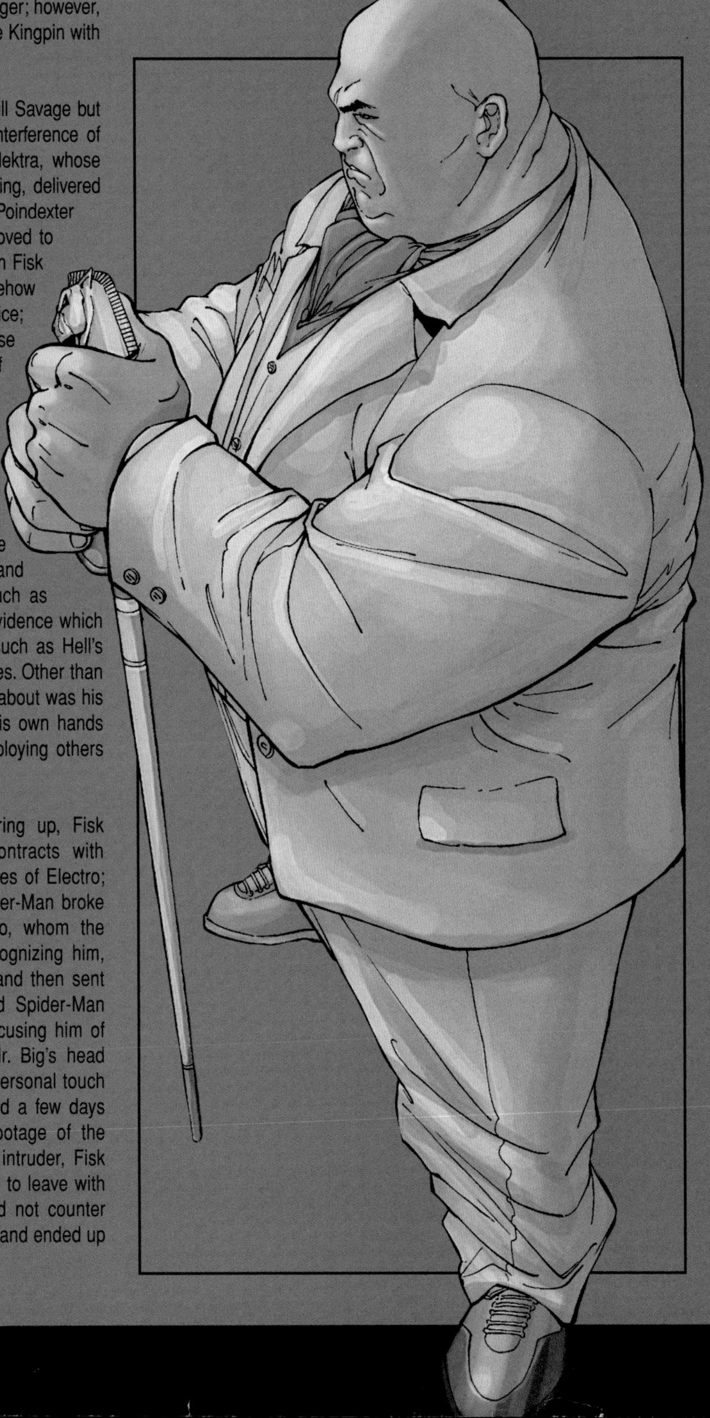

Art by Salvador Larroca

with his fists webbed to the wall. Spider-Man sent the surveillance discs to Ben Urich; Fisk was indicted and forced to flee the city, going into hiding in Brazil.

Eventually, Fisk's lawyer Walter Dini managed to get the tapes of the murder ruled inadmissible, and the case was dropped. Fisk returned to New York, determined to avenge himself on Spider-Man. He secretly backed Dini's partner, Sam Bullit, in a campaign to be elected D.A. on an anti-Spider-Man platform. At first the Daily Bugle backed Bullit, as its editor J. Jonah Jameson had his own dislike of the wall-crawler; but when Ben Urich provided Jameson with proof of Bullit's links to the crimelord, the endorsement was swiftly and publicly withdrawn. Fisk sent the Enforcers to threaten Jameson and scare him into reinstating his support, but thanks to the intervention of Spider-Man, this backfired. The defiant Jameson's next headline read "Kingpin Cronies Blow Lid," publicly declaiming Fisk's criminality. Fisk's lunch that day was interrupted by Spider-Man; both men swapped threats and each made it clear he intended to destroy the other.

Fisk's attentions were diverted from Spider-Man by his wife Vanessa's illness. After she fell into a coma, the Kingpin was prepared to clutch at any straw that might cure her. Mr. Moore, seeking a place in the Kingpin's organization, offered him a stone tablet that allegedly described a cure; but before Fisk could obtain it, the tablet was stolen by the Black Cat. Through a subordinate, the Kingpin hired Elektra to retrieve it and deal with the Cat. Though Elektra failed, in part due to the interference of Spider-Man, information she provided allowed the Kingpin to identify the Black Cat as Felicia Hardy, now seeking revenge for the death of her father. Accompanied by Elektra, the Kingpin went to Felicia's apartment to deal with her personally; he had her gripped in his enormous hands and pinned to the wall when Spider-Man arrived. This distraction allowed the Black Cat to break free, snatch the tablet and race to the roof where she threw the tablet into the sea. After Elektra seemingly slew Felicia for this, the Kingpin departed and spent the night by his wife's bedside, apologizing to her for his failure and pleading for her to awaken.

Recently, the Kingpin's dominance of the New York underworld has been challenged by rival crime lord Hammerhead. Federal agents arrested several of Fisk's men, including his lawyer Dini and underboss Sammy Silke; under close scrutiny from the Feds, the Kingpin found his hands tied as Hammerhead murdered his predecessor Silvermane, took over the remains of his organization, and began to target Kingpin's assets. Since the Enforcers had switched sides to work for Hammerhead, Kingpin again hired Elektra, then provided information to Spider-Man to encourage the vigilante to stop Hammerhead. This conflict's outcome remains to be seen.

HEIGHT: 6' 7"
WEIGHT: 500 lbs.
EYES: Brown
HAIR: Bald, was black

DISTINGUISHING FEATURES: Immense girth and height

ABILITIES: Though he rarely likes to get physical himself, the Kingpin is strong enough to crush a man's skull with his bare hands. He uses his bulk as a weapon when fighting.

POWER GRID	1	2	3	4	5	6	7
INTELLIGENCE							
STRENGTH							
SPEED							
DURABILITY							
ENERGY PROJECTION							
FIGHTING SKILLS							

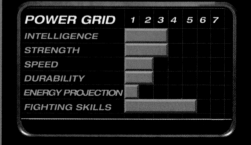

Art by Mark Bagley

KRAVEN

REAL NAME: Sergei Kravinoff
KNOWN ALIASES: None
IDENTITY: Publicly known
OCCUPATION: TV personality
CITIZENSHIP: Australia
PLACE OF BIRTH: Unknown
KNOWN RELATIVES: None
GROUP AFFILIATIONS: Norman Osborn's "Six"
EDUCATION: Unknown
FIRST APPEARANCE: Ultimate Spider-Man #16 (2002)

HISTORY: Reality TV star Kraven the Hunter had seen it all in the Australian outback. Battling crocodiles, boxing with kangaroos, and hunting wild game with his bare hands had gained him a cult following; but, as his agents put it, defeating the masked Spider-Man would put him on the map. Traveling to New York with his girlfriend, Tabidi, and production crew, Kraven promised a horde of reporters that he wouldn't just catch Spider-Man, he would kill him. Visiting P.S. 163 in Queens, Kraven examined the site of a recent battle between Spider-Man and a goblin monster, trying to pick up Spider-Man's scent. Unknown to Kraven, Spider-Man was right under his nose the whole time, in his secret identity as student Peter Parker. Later, Kraven learned that Spider-Man was spotted riding atop a limo on the New Jersey turnpike. Kraven and his production crew followed Spider-Man to a Hammer Industries laboratory where Spider-Man was battling Doctor Octopus. After Spider-Man defeated Doc Ock, Kraven challenged the exhausted Spider-Man, who wanted nothing to do with him. Kraven lunged at Spider-Man, throwing everything he had at him, but Spider-Man just dodged it all and eventually knocked Kraven out with a single punch. The police then arrested the humiliated Kraven and his production crew for public endangerment.

Because of his arrest, Kraven was deported and his show was cancelled. Even Tabidi left him. Obsessed with revenge, Kraven took illegal genetic enhancements and began a media tour, renewing his challenge to Spider-Man. When the Ultimates sought to arrest him for genetic tampering, Kraven tried to flee but Hawkeye shot him in the calf with an arrow. Placed in S.H.I.E.L.D. custody, Kraven was housed in the same cell block as fellow Spider-Man enemies Norman Osborn, Doctor Octopus, Electro, and the Sandman, escaping alongside them and hiding out in Wilson Fisk's summer house in the Hamptons.

While the Ultimates raided Kraven's production company, the escapees took advantage of this distraction to kidnap Spider-Man, whom Kraven saw unmasked. Enraged that a mere teen had humiliated him, Kraven attacked the bound Spider-Man, but his partners restrained him. Osborn tricked Spider-Man into joining them in an attack on the White House, but the Ultimates intervened and Spider-Man turned on Osborn. Knocked clear into the Oval Office, Spider-Man was stalked by a vengeful Kraven, whom Thor downed with a lightning bolt. Captured again, a desperate Kraven tried to claim that Doc Ock or Osborn had been using mind control on him.

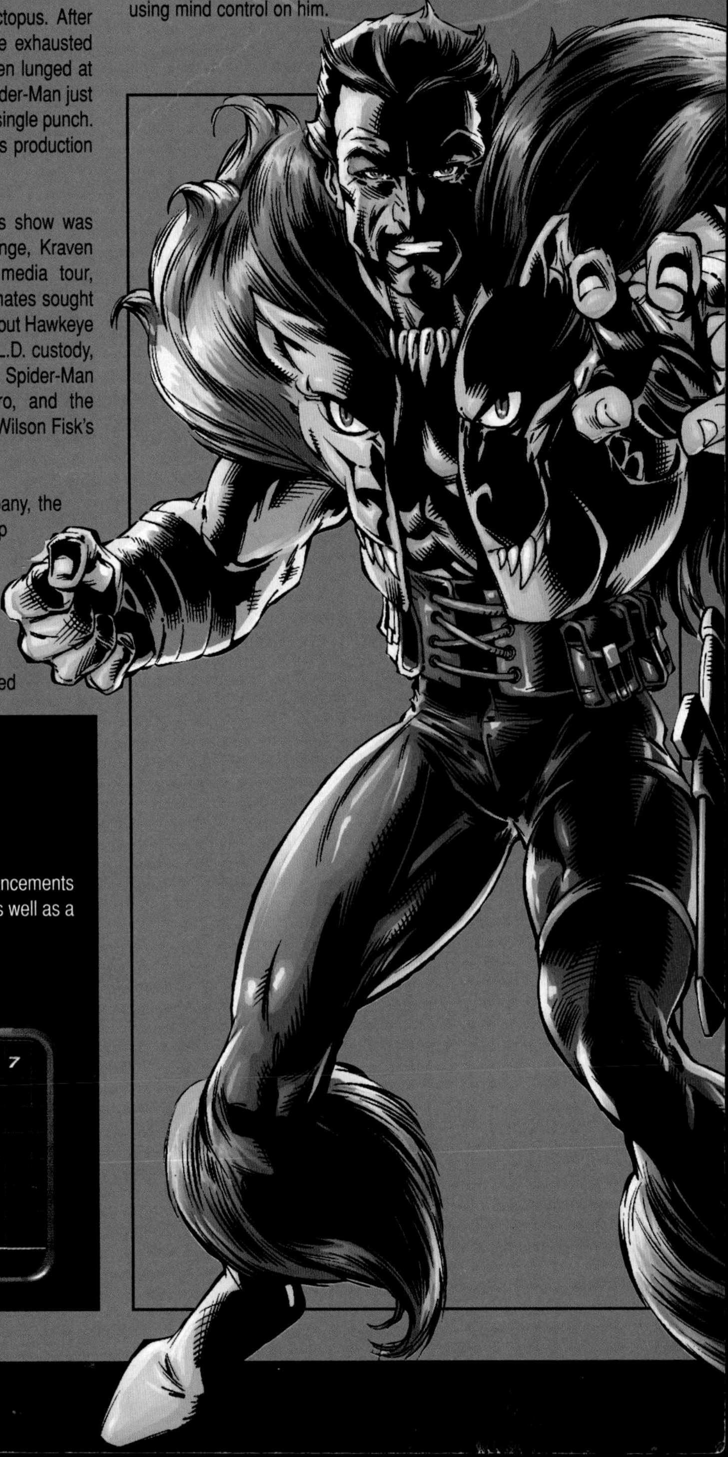

HEIGHT: 6'2"
WEIGHT: 240 lbs.
EYES: Blue
HAIR: Black

SUPERHUMAN POWERS: Kraven's genetic enhancements give him heightened strength, agility and senses, as well as a more animalistic appearance.

ABILITIES: Kraven is a skilled hunter and tracker.

POWER GRID	1	2	3	4	5	6	7
INTELLIGENCE	■	■					
STRENGTH	■	■	■	■			
SPEED	■	■					
DURABILITY	■	■					
ENERGY PROJECTION	■						
FIGHTING SKILLS	■	■	■	■			

Art by Mark Bagley

MAN-THING

REAL NAME: Ted Sallis
KNOWN ALIASES: None
IDENTITY: Secret
OCCUPATION: None, formerly scientist
CITIZENSHIP: Unrevealed
PLACE OF BIRTH: Unrevealed
KNOWN RELATIVES: None
GROUP AFFILIATION: None
EDUCATION: Unrevealed; as a scientist, Sallis may or may not hold a doctorate
FIRST APPEARANCE: Ultimate Marvel Team-Up #10 (2002)

HISTORY: Nothing is known of Ted Sallis save that he was a scientist entrusted with guarding an experimental serum; it is not known what the serum's original purpose was, nor if Sallis developed it independently or, indeed, had any direct role in its creation at all. Operatives in the employ of unidentified parties attempted to steal the serum, and Sallis was forced to inject it into himself — although, again, whether he did this in a foolhardy effort to keep the serum out of his enemies' hands or, on the contrary, was forced to do so by his enemies to test it remains a mystery.

In any event, the serum transformed Sallis into a monstrous form composed of swamp life and sewer waste; rendered virtually mindless, Sallis began a seemingly aimless life of wandering the sewers and waterways of the United States, occasionally compelled by an inexplicable empathic power that drew him to human fear. The extent of his adventures are unrevealed, but the confused accounts of those who survived their encounters with him gave him a whispered name: the Man-Thing.

In recent months, the Man-Thing's travels brought him to the New York sewer system. By coincidence, scientist Curt Conners, having been transformed into reptilian form, also made his way into the sewers, and tales of the Man-Thing's attacks upon fearful citizens became confused with reports of Conners' activities. Days later, the teenage adventurer Spider-Man ventured beneath the city in hopes of recovering Conners; unable to reach the scientist's human identity, Spider-Man found himself fighting the reptilian Conners until the Man-Thing intervened, his burning touch somehow reverting Conners back to human form. The stunned Spider-Man could only watch as the Man-Thing sank back into the sewage as mysteriously as he had appeared.

Since then, the Man-Thing's consciousness was somehow touched by the mind of young genius Reed Richards, recently empowered with three others as the Fantastic Four. Nothing has been heard of the Man-Thing since then, and it is not known whether or not he remains in the New York sewers or has wandered elsewhere.

HEIGHT: Unrevealed, currently 7'9"
WEIGHT: Unrevealed (in either form)
EYES: Unrevealed, currently red
HAIR: Unrevealed, currently none

SUPERHUMAN POWERS: The Man-Thing is superhumanly strong and moves more rapidly than his bulky appearance would suggest. His empathic senses can detect human emotion, most notably fear, and his touch can burn anyone who is sufficiently fearful. With the consciousness of Ted Sallis either submerged or destroyed, the Man-Thing is apparently motivated solely by instinct and reaction to his empathic senses.

POWER GRID	1	2	3	4	5	6	7
INTELLIGENCE							
STRENGTH							
SPEED							
DURABILITY							
ENERGY PROJECTION							
FIGHTING SKILLS							

Art by John Totleben and Bret Belvins

MISTER FANTASTIC

HISTORY: Growing up in Queens, the oldest child of three, Reed Richards was brighter than those around him. Reed's friend Ben Grimm protected him from bullying by lesser classmates, but Reed's father couldn't deal with his son's genius and treated his children harshly, leaving Reed and his sisters unhappy. While still a child, Reed discovered another dimension and built an oscillator which allowed him to view it. Six months later, in fifth grade, at the Midtown Middle School science fair, Reed demonstrated his ability to send items to that dimension. This caught the eye of Lieutenant Lumpkin, a "scout" for the Director of Mainland Technology Development who scoured the world for exceptional children.

Reed was placed under the supervision of internationally renowned scientist Dr. Franklin Storm at the Baxter Building, a midtown Manhattan government facility for gifted children. Reed's father was relieved to be rid of him, so Reed rarely saw his family thereafter. His only close contacts were fellow students and his dog Einstein. Missing his family, Reed covertly constructed a "Fantasti-Car," a fuel-free vehicle with the capacity to fly at MACH-7, but never used it. For five and a half years, Reed studied the N-Zone, never completely cracking its problems until fellow genius Victor Van Damme adjusted Reed's calculations; over the next five years Van Damme helped Reed with his N-Zone math while Reed aided Victor's work in miniaturized robotics. When the government built a life-sized N-Zone teleporter, Van Damme surreptitiously made some last minute alterations in the superposition calculations, and the activation of the gate created a phase-state fugue which altered Reed and his friends forever, granting them superhuman abilities.

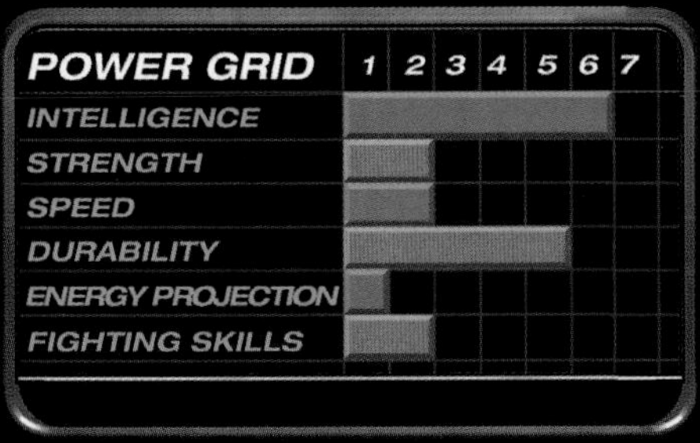

REAL NAME: Reed Richards
KNOWN ALIASES: None
IDENTITY: Secret
OCCUPATION: Scientist
CITIZENSHIP: U.S.A.
PLACE OF BIRTH: Unrevealed
KNOWN RELATIVES: Gary Richards (father), Mrs. Richards (mother), Enid Richards (sister), unnamed sister
GROUP AFFILIATION: Fantastic Four
EDUCATION: Multiple doctoral degrees
FIRST APPEARANCE: Ultimate Fantastic Four #1 (2004)

Unable to convince Van Damme to help him reverse the changes, Reed returned his focus to science, perfecting his N-Zone transporter and adapting it to both time travel and accessing parallel dimensions. After the team went public battling the alien Nihil in Las Vegas, Reed began craving the public approval of being a super hero, perhaps compensating for his father's disapproval. He now balances his obsessive love of science against his romantic relationship with Susan Storm and his new celebrity hero status.

HEIGHT: 6'1"
WEIGHT: 170 lbs.
EYES: Blue
HAIR: Brown

SUPERHUMAN POWERS: Reed's cells have been replaced with "pliable bacterial stacks," single cells which duplicate most of the larger functions of the human body. This allows Reed to stretch his body in myriad ways without disrupting the necessary functions of internal organs such as the kidneys, lungs, or even brain. Reed can stretch any or all of his body parts long distances, even assuming non-human shapes such as a sphere or parachute.

ABILITIES: Reed holds multiple doctoral level degrees in theoretical and applied physics fields.

PARAPHERNALIA: As a lead scientist at the Baxter Building, Reed has access to enormous governmental resources. He has developed technology such as the N-Zone transporter; the Fantasti-Cars, flying vehicles powered by zero-point generators; a NASA Space Shuttle uniquely modified for interdimensional travel; and a chrono-tunnel enabling travel through time. Reed's uniform stretches as he does without tearing.

POWER GRID	1	2	3	4	5	6	7
INTELLIGENCE							
STRENGTH							
SPEED							
DURABILITY							
ENERGY PROJECTION							
FIGHTING SKILLS							

Art by Stuart Immonen

ARTHUR MOLEKEVIC

REAL NAME: Arthur Molekevic
KNOWN ALIASES: "Moley Moley Mole Man"
IDENTITY: Publicly known
OCCUPATION: Scientist; explorer
CITIZENSHIP: U.S.A.
PLACE OF BIRTH: Unrevealed
KNOWN RELATIVES: None
GROUP AFFILIATION: None
EDUCATION: College graduate; multiple advanced degrees
FIRST APPEARANCE: Ultimate Fantastic Four #2 (2004)

HISTORY: Dr. Arthur Molekevic was employed at the Baxter Building in Manhattan as both a research scientist and a passionate teacher to the geniuses who studied there; however, his unpleasant personal appearance alienated the students (some of whom referred to him as the "Moley Moley Mole Man" behind his back), and his continual refusal to follow the facility's research guidelines alienated his superiors. When the government found his work on creating humanoid mold creatures, they sent General Ross to the Baxter Building to fire Molekevic, with the approval of Molekevic's supervisor, Dr. Franklin Storm (father of Susan and Johnny Storm).

In the subsequent five years, Molekevic went through various professional and personal changes, studying philosophy, religion, and ancient cultures as well as continuing his own work in bio-

technologies. He located the underground remains of a culture which he believed to be the lost continent of Atlantis. In one of these chambers, 1.4 miles beneath Manhattan, he monitored the Baxter Building's research while creating his own servile race of mold men, dubbed "ani-men." Using DNA scraped from weaponry found in the ruins, he also created a giant-sized serpentoid monster which served him.

When Reed Richards' N-Zone teleporter was tested in the Nevada desert, Molekevic covertly observed the test and the subsequent accident. He sent his ani-men after the five people who were teleported/transformed by the experiment; but he was unable to locate Van Damme, and of the other four only succeeded in reaching Susan Storm before the military could. Fascinated by the experiment's results and wanting to free the transformed others from government control, Molekevic sent his "monster" into New York to retrieve Reed, Ben, and Johnny from the Baxter Building. The threesome defeated the beast, and followed it to Molekevic's headquarters. When the trio arrived, Molekevic returned Sue to them and began discussing how they could aid each other in pursuing further scientific research.

Traumatized by their recent changes, the foursome refused to listen to Molekevic, who realized he once again faced minds closed to their own potential. Disgusted with their blindness, he ordered his ani-men to do as they wished with the four; however, the strength of the transformed Grimm was much greater than anyone realized, and in the subsequent fight, much of the ancient chamber was destroyed. Molekevic was last seen plummeting into a deep chasm, his dreams again destroyed by the world's inability to share his vision.

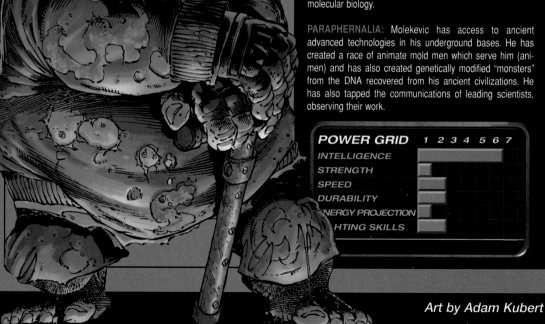

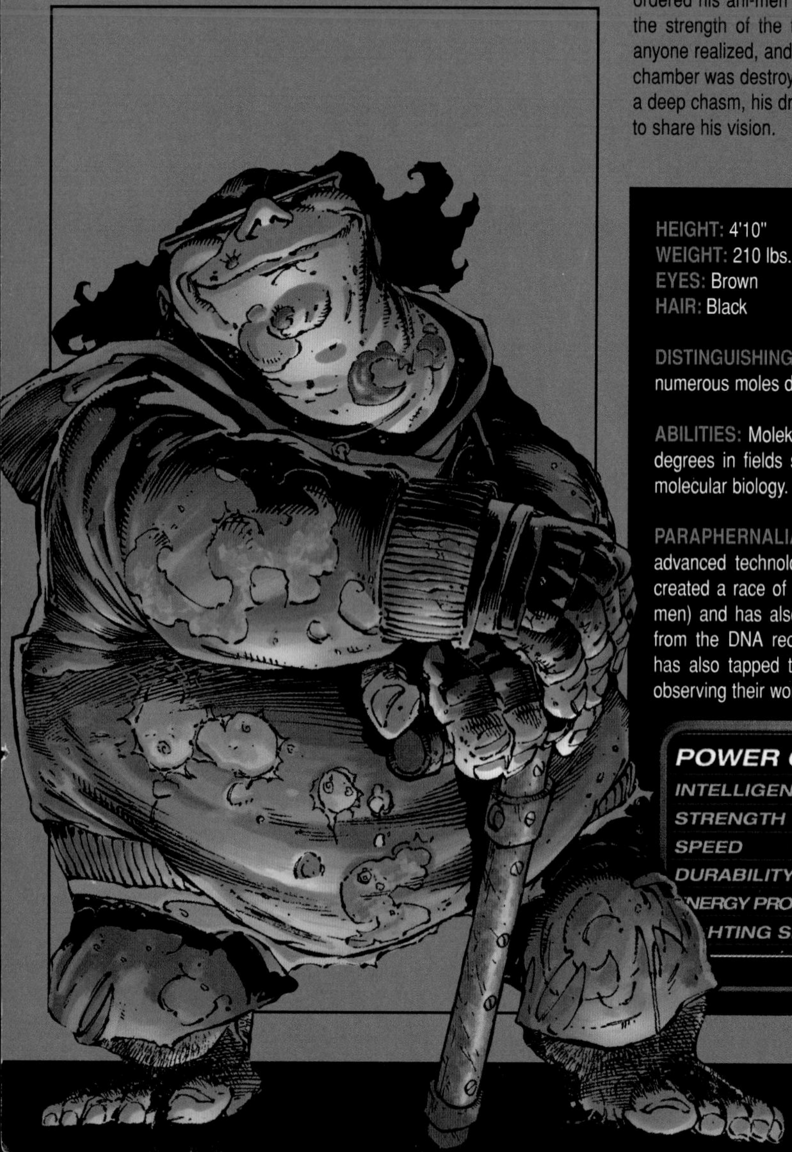

HEIGHT: 4'10"
WEIGHT: 210 lbs.
EYES: Brown
HAIR: Black

DISTINGUISHING FEATURES: Molekevic is covered with numerous moles due to a skin condition.

ABILITIES: Molekevic is a scientific genius, with advanced degrees in fields such as genetics, computer science, and molecular biology.

PARAPHERNALIA: Molekevic has access to ancient advanced technologies in his underground bases. He has created a race of animate mold men which serve him (ani-men) and has also created genetically modified "monsters" from the DNA recovered from his ancient civilizations. He has also tapped the communications of leading scientists, observing their work.

POWER GRID	1	2	3	4	5	6	7
INTELLIGENCE							
STRENGTH							
SPEED							
DURABILITY							
ENERGY PROJECTION							
FIGHTING SKILLS							

Art by Adam Kubert

HISTORY: Nihil's N-Zone universe is old, in the throes of final death with less than a million years before final collapse. The members of his space-borne race are exceedingly long lived, and Nihil could probably live until his N-Zone universe died. As Nihil's solar system has aged, he has slowly gathered the vessels of whatever life forms he found, melding their ships into one large conglomerated station, also apparently claiming whatever he needed from those he saved. In this manner, he built himself a large kingdom, a space station in which he took what he wanted while returning the necessities of life to his vassals. The name "Nihil" is actually a traditional caste title for leaders and punishers, dating back to feudal times of Nihil's race.

When Reed Richards and his team visited the N-Zone, Nihil detected them and sent out a hailing beacon to attract their attention. After the foursome's translation techniques proved ineffective, translating Nihil's name as "Annihil Us," Nihil provided the four with his own translation devices (which, unbeknownst to the four, contained explosive devices). Collecting information on their home system, Nihil determined they were from a parallel dimension which was younger and had a much longer prospective lifespan. The discussion was curtailed when Johnny Storm took ill and the quartet decided to leave. When Reed and Ben Grimm informed Nihil of this, Nihil decided to kill them both and take their ship for himself. Despite destroying their suits' integrities by detonating the translating devices he had attached to their helmets, Nihil was

REAL NAME: Nihil
KNOWN ALIASES: Annihil Us
IDENTITY: No dual identity
OCCUPATION: Ruler of an N-Zone star system
CITIZENSHIP: Alien
PLACE OF BIRTH: Unrevealed
KNOWN RELATIVES: None
GROUP AFFILIATION: None
EDUCATION: Centuries of accumulated learning.
FIRST APPEARANCE: Ultimate Fantastic Four #15 (2005)

still defeated in hand-to-hand combat by Grimm, who managed to tear off one of Nihil's wings during the fight. While his vassals delayed Reed and Ben's escape, Nihil got to a ship and pursued the foursome to their home dimension. Both ships crashed on the Sunset Strip in Las Vegas, Nevada, and while the Fantastic Four defeated his servants, Nihil himself was apparently killed by one of his own weapons while battling Reed Richards.

HEIGHT: 6'5"
WEIGHT: 250 lbs.
EYES: Iridescent and insectile
HAIR: None

DISTINGUISHING FEATURES: Nihil has an insectoid face and leathery bat wings (one of which was recently torn off), and though four-limbed like a human, both upper limbs divide at the equivalent of his elbows into two lower arms and hands, each hand possessing two talons and an opposing claw. Nihil is an extra-dimensional alien, with completely non-human internal organ structures.

SUPERHUMAN POWERS: Nihil can fly and possesses very sharp talons. He can survive in various atmospheres toxic to humans, as well as in Earth's atmosphere. He is immensely old, with a life expectancy of more than one million years ahead of him.

ABILITIES: Though not a scientific genius, Nihil has accumulated untold years of scientific knowledge.

PARAPHERNALIA: Nihil has access to technologies from hundreds of alien races, including translation devices, weaponry, and space ships. As feudal ruler of his ship and surrounding areas, Nihil controls and demands the service of those on his ship, willing or not.

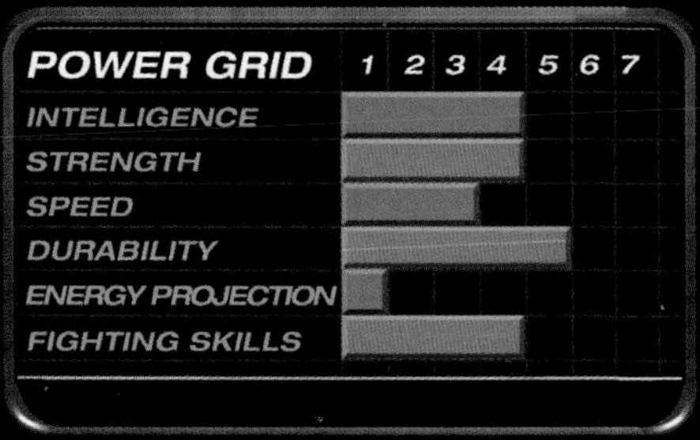

POWER GRID	1	2	3	4	5	6	7
INTELLIGENCE							
STRENGTH							
SPEED							
DURABILITY							
ENERGY PROJECTION							
FIGHTING SKILLS							

Art by Adam Kubert

HARRY OSBORN

REAL NAME: Harold "Harry" Osborn
KNOWN ALIASES: Hobgoblin
IDENTITY: Secret
OCCUPATION: Student
CITIZENSHIP: U.S.A.
PLACE OF BIRTH: Unrevealed, probably New York City
KNOWN RELATIVES: Norman Osborn (a.k.a. the Green Goblin, father); unnamed mother (deceased); Amberson (grandfather); unnamed uncle, Cher Osborn (aunt)
GROUP AFFILIATION: None
EDUCATION: High school (not yet graduated)
FIRST APPEARANCE: Ultimate Spider-Man #1 (2000)

HISTORY: The only son of industrialist Norman Osborn, Harry was secretly subjected to hypnotherapy from age 11 so that his father could better control him; aside from this, Norman mostly ignored Harry, as did Harry's alcoholic mother. He instead found emotional support at school, where he was friends with Peter Parker and dated Mary Jane Watson. When Norman grew more secretive after the incident that, unknown to Harry, mutated Peter Parker, Harry investigated and discovered his father undergoing an experimental mutation process. Caught in a lab explosion, Harry, like his father, was mutated, though in his case the transformation

was initially suppressed. Later, Norman, driven insane following his mutation into a monstrous goblin, murdered his wife before Harry's eyes, then set out to attack Peter, now the costumed Spider-Man. In the wake of the goblin's assault, the distraught Harry revealed the goblin's identity. Sent to his uncle in Colorado, Norman's employee Dr. Warren stepped up his hypnotherapy, erasing Harry's memories of his father's transformation and murder of his mother. Harry was then reunited with his father, unaware of the madman's continued designs on his friend Peter. Returning to Midtown High, Harry recanted his earlier claims, unaware that Norman had threatened Peter's family unless the youth agreed to enter his service. Later, Spider-Man confronted the goblin, who responded by abducting Mary Jane right in front of Harry's appalled eyes. Minutes later, when the fight between Spider-Man and the Goblin brought them back to the Osborn home, Harry walked in on the battle; recognizing Spider-Man's unmasked face, the desperate Harry ended the fight by impaling his father, who was taken into S.H.I.E.L.D. custody; S.H.I.E.L.D. director Nick Fury also took the by now near-catatonic Harry into custody, hoping to deprogram Osborn's hypnotherapy.

Months later, when Norman led superhuman criminals to attack the White House, Harry, informed of the situation, volunteered to confront his father in the hope of talking sense to him. However, as a result of Harry's distraction, Osborn was defeated by the Ultimates and Spider-Man, and Harry believed him dead; deeply distraught, Harry vowed vengeance on all involved. Nevertheless, Fury eventually deemed Harry's treatment successful and released him from custody. But Harry was far from recovered. He began hallucinating that his father's old henchman Shaw had returned; "Shaw" proceeded to poison Harry's mind against Spider-Man, whom he claimed had murdered Osborn. Unnerving Peter with a second reappearance at school, Harry soon confronted him at the Osborn penthouse where he transformed into his own mutated form and attacked. A prolonged battle erupted until Harry, despondent at what his father had done to him, begged Spider-Man to end his suffering. The hero could not kill his friend, but Fury intervened, bringing Harry down using extreme force and nearly killing him. After the enraged hero departed, Fury had Harry taken into custody.

HEIGHT: (Harry) 5'7" (Hobgoblin) 7'
WEIGHT: (Harry) 151 lbs.; (Hobgoblin) 900 lbs.
EYES: Blue
HAIR: Brown

SUPERHUMAN POWERS: Harry can transform into a large, muscular, orange-skinned form with superhuman strength and endurance. His body produces flames which he can hurl as weapons. Harry is apparently wracked with pain while transformed, and his mental state is highly precarious; he is susceptible to certain trigger words implanted by hypnotherapy.

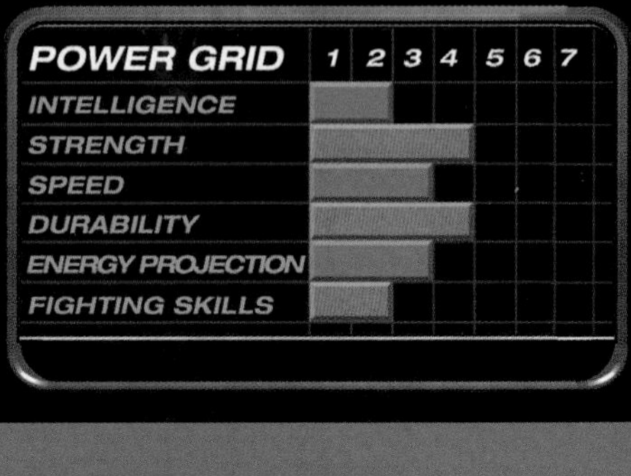

POWER GRID	1	2	3	4	5	6	7
INTELLIGENCE							
STRENGTH							
SPEED							
DURABILITY							
ENERGY PROJECTION							
FIGHTING SKILLS							

Art by Mark Bagley

HISTORY: Ex-hippy Ben Parker lived in a commune for a short time before he met his wife, May. A kind and good-natured man, Ben found married life agreeable and his family welcomed his wife as one of their own. Ben was close to his younger brother Richard and his family, often spending time with them and the family of Richard's partner, Eddie Brock; when Richard and his wife died in a plane crash, Ben and May took in their nephew Peter. Uncle Ben took over as Peter's father figure, and as Peter grew older, Ben recognized his nephew's intelligence and did his best to encourage him in academics. Perhaps because of his intelligence, Peter was often bullied, and Ben did his best to prevent it, even going so far as to join Peter during a certain lunch hall and convincing Peter's old friend Mary Jane Watson to sit with them. During a field trip to Oscorp the next day, Peter was bit by the experimental "00" spider, causing him to faint and giving him amazing powers — powers Ben never suspected. Norman Osborn, fearful the Parkers would sue, picked up the hospital bill, but Ben never considered a lawsuit, worrying it would break up Peter's friendship with Harry Osborn.

Several days later, Flash Thompson's parents called Ben and threatened to sue the Parkers because Peter had accidentally broken Flash's hand defending himself in a fight. Ben agreed to pay the hospital bill, even though he believed the altercation to be Flash's fault, as there was no way they could afford a lawyer. Their financial worry abated when they began receiving letters filled with cash allegedly donated by Peter's teachers; in truth the money was from their nephew, who was secretly earning it by wrestling.

As Peter took advantage of his newfound powers by joining the basketball team, his grades plummeted, causing a loud argument with Ben. Peter ran away from home, staying at classmate Kong Harlan's house. In his parents' absence, Kong threw a large party; arriving there, Ben pulled Peter outside for a heart-to-heart talk. Ben told Peter his father's philosophy on life: "If there are things you do better than anyone else, things that you could do to help people, it is your responsibility to do them." Overcome with emotion, Peter ran away again.

Dejected, Ben went home where he discovered a burglar, ironically a man Peter had refused to stop during another robbery just hours before. The burglar demanded money, but Ben joked with him, saying, "You probably have more money than we do." Angered, the burglar shot Ben, killing him.

REAL NAME: Benjamin "Ben" Parker
KNOWN ALIASES: None
IDENTITY: No dual identity
OCCUPATION: Unknown
CITIZENSHIP: U.S.A.
PLACE OF BIRTH: Unrevealed
KNOWN RELATIVES: May (wife), Richard (brother, deceased), Mary (sister-in-law, deceased), Peter (nephew), unnamed sister-in-law (deceased), unnamed mother-in-law
GROUP AFFILIATIONS: None
EDUCATION: Printing plant employee
FIRST APPEARANCE: Ultimate Spider-Man #1 (2000)

HEIGHT: 6'
WEIGHT: 190 lbs.
EYES: Blue
HAIR: Gray

POWER GRID	1	2	3	4	5	6	7
INTELLIGENCE							
STRENGTH							
SPEED							
DURABILITY							
ENERGY PROJECTION							
FIGHTING SKILLS							

MAY PARKER

REAL NAME: May Parker
KNOWN ALIASES: None
IDENTITY: No dual identity
OCCUPATION: Office worker
CITIZENSHIP: U.S.A.
PLACE OF BIRTH: Unknown
KNOWN RELATIVES: Unnamed mother, Ben (husband, deceased), Richard Parker (brother-in-law, deceased), Mary Parker (sister-in-law, deceased), Peter Parker (Spider-Man, nephew), unnamed sister (deceased)
GROUP AFFILIATION: None
EDUCATION: Unknown
FIRST APPEARANCE: Ultimate Spider-Man #1 (2000)

HISTORY: As a girl, May was a wild child; she once shouted a proposal to Jimi Hendrix at a concert, and at fifteen she ran away from home, sleeping in a San Francisco basement for a while. Her

family problems were presumably resolved over time, as she now has a good relationship with her mother, who retired to Florida. After marrying Ben Parker, May befriended his brother Richard, Richard's wife Mary and their son Peter. When Richard and Mary died in a plane crash around the same time May lost her own sister, whom she considered her best friend, May and Ben took Peter in and raised him as their own. May became a responsible adult, working in an office cubicle and attending PTA meetings.

May's life took a tragic turn when Ben was shot dead by a burglar before her eyes. She became sole guardian to Peter, who started acting up and keeping odd hours. She comforted him when he had nightmares, but was unsure if Peter even liked her since he never seemed to be around anymore; in truth, Peter had secretly become the super hero Spider-Man. Terrified she might lose Peter, too, May angrily overreacted whenever she couldn't account for his whereabouts, subconsciously pushing him away because she feared losing another loved one. One night, May caught Peter coming home extremely late and grounded him, but soon relented; however, reports of Peter's erratic attendance and attitude at school continued to cause her concern.

After Peter befriended new classmate Gwen Stacy, May became friendly with and romantically interested in Gwen's father, John — ironically, the police officer who had investigated Ben's death. When John was killed by a Spider-Man imposter and Gwen's absentee mother refused to take responsibility for her daughter, May took Gwen in. John Stacy's death prompted May to see a therapist to whom she confessed her fear of loss, her guilt over being attracted to John so soon after Ben's death, and her concern that she was only using Gwen as a way of keeping herself too busy to think about the ghosts surrounding her. She also admitted she was terrified of the chaos Spider-Man and his ilk represented, as he seemed to keep appearing during times of crisis in her life. May's therapist helped her see she needed to let herself love people without always fearing she would lose them.

Realizing this seemed to give May new strength. When Peter's employer J. Jonah Jameson unjustly fired Peter, May called Jameson and gave him a piece of her mind; and when Mary Jane's father accosted Peter for endangering his daughter, May again defended her nephew. She even held her ground against agents of S.H.I.E.L.D. when they took her into protective custody after several of Spider-Man's enemies escaped. However, tragedy struck again when Gwen was murdered in the Parkers' backyard. With too many bad memories now filling their home, May and Peter have recently made plans to move.

HEIGHT: 5'7"
WEIGHT: 120 lbs.
EYES: Blue
HAIR: Gray

POWER GRID	1	2	3	4	5	6	7
INTELLIGENCE							
STRENGTH							
SPEED							
DURABILITY							
ENERGY PROJECTION							
FIGHTING SKILLS							

HISTORY: One of the NYPD's finest, Frank Castle refused to stand by while his partner and other officers took bribes from the mysterious underworld figure known as the Owl. Turning them in to Internal Affairs, Frank made himself a target — the officers he exposed sought revenge, gunning Frank and his family down while they were on a picnic in the park. The sole survivor, Frank became the twisted, murderous vigilante known as The Punisher. Gaining a cult following for his extreme brand of justice, the Punisher eventually went too far when he killed one of the cops who had slaughtered his family. Imprisoned on Ryker's Island, the Punisher continued his work, killing nine unrepentant criminals, including Jim Washington, a convicted rapist who had been apprehended by Daredevil; but Frank had unfinished business, and took the first opportunity to escape. Free again, the Punisher killed two more of the crooked cops behind his family's murder, including his former partner, Bruce Greenwood, who was visiting his attorney, Matt Murdock, at the time. Chased by Daredevil, the Punisher managed to escape, nearly killing Daredevil in the process.

Tracking Artie Jillette, the final living member of the group who had killed his family and the go-between between the Owl and the other corrupt cops, to his apartment, the Punisher held him at gunpoint, but was unable to kill the man in front of his children. Forcing Artie up to the roof, the Punisher was once more confonted by Daredevil, who appealed to his sense of justice, claiming he would make sure Jillette was sentenced for his crimes. Before the Punisher could consider Daredevil's claims, Spider-Man blindsided him, knocking him out and letting Artie escape. Daredevil ordered Spider-Man to take the Punisher to the police while he captured Artie; later, as attorney Matt Murdock, he defended the Punisher in court. Jillette was reunited with the Punisher in jail, where Frank's friends on the inside made sure they were cellmates, ensuring the Punisher's revenge.

While in jail, the Punisher became a cultural phenomenon whose case was much-discussed and featured on several popular evening news programs. Unsatisfied with merely avenging his family's death, the Punisher broke out again, continuing his cold-blooded campaign against crime. He encountered Spider-Man while trying to gun down an unidentified bank robber employing a boomerang motif. Spider-Man easily defeated the Punisher again, and left both Castle and his target for the cops to pick up.

REAL NAME: Frank Castle
KNOWN ALIASES: None
IDENTITY: Publicly known
OCCUPATION: Vigilante; former police officer
CITIZENSHIP: U.S.A.
PLACE OF BIRTH: New York
KNOWN RELATIVES: Unnamed wife (deceased), unnamed daughter (deceased), unnamed son (deceased)
GROUP AFFILIATIONS: Formerly NYPD
EDUCATION: College graduate
FIRST APPEARANCE: Ultimate Team-Up #6 (2001)

HEIGHT: 6'5"
WEIGHT: 240 lbs.
EYES: Blue
HAIR: Black

ABILITIES: Frank is an excellent marksman who is skilled in the usage of a large variety of conventional weapons.

POWER GRID	1	2	3	4	5	6	7
INTELLIGENCE							
STRENGTH							
SPEED							
DURABILITY							
ENERGY PROJECTION							
FIGHTING SKILLS							

GENERAL ROSS

REAL NAME: Ross (full name unrevealed)
KNOWN ALIASES: None
IDENTITY: No dual identity
OCCUPATION: U.S. Army general, former Head of S.H.I.E.L.D.
CITIZENSHIP: U.S.A.
PLACE OF BIRTH: Unknown
KNOWN RELATIVES: Betty Ross (daughter)
GROUP AFFILIATION: S.H.I.E.L.D.
EDUCATION: Unknown
FIRST APPEARANCE: Ultimate Marvel Team-Up #3 (2001)

HISTORY: As head of the S.H.I.E.L.D. Global Security organization, General Ross commanded men such as Colonel Nick Fury, who policed violations of the Superhuman Test-Ban Treaty. He oversaw numerous U.S. defense projects: the Super-Soldier Research Facility in Pittsburgh, where Ross' prospective son-in-law, Bruce Banner, headed the research team trying to rediscover the serum which had created WW II's Captain America; Weapon X, S.H.I.E.L.D.'s premier counter-terrorism division run by Colonel John Wraith, which kidnapped young mutants from around the world to turn them into covert agents; and Dr. Storm's Baxter Building, where child geniuses worked on scientific breakthroughs. When the Baxter Building's Doctor Molekevic defied orders by developing forbidden bio-technology, Ross confronted him and fired him.

Banner continually suggested downsizing the conventional military to free resources for a small superhuman unit, but Ross mostly ignored him. As pressure mounted on Banner to produce results, he tested a super-soldier serum on himself, transforming into a monstrous Hulk, which the military chased all the way from Nevada to New York. When Banner reverted to human form at the Chelsea Piers waterfront, Spider-Man tried to calm the situation; but Banner panicked, transformed again, and bounded away with Ross and his men in pursuit.

Following the Hulk's capture, S.H.I.E.L.D. lost Fury on a mission in Delhi. Ross reluctantly assigned Wraith's Weapon X to recover Fury and complete his mission: to retrieve the scientist behind an Indian genome project. Ross was horrified to discover Wraith had recently kidnapped the X-Men, mutants on first-name terms with the U.S. President, and even angrier to discover the one X-Man they hadn't retrieved was Wolverine. The decision was made to phase out Weapon X and replace it with a new super soldier initiative. Wraith retaliated by trying to kill Ross in an explosion, but Ross survived, perhaps because Xavier was resisting the device controlling him; however, while recovering, Ross was replaced by Fury as head of S.H.I.E.L.D.

Ross returned to working with Dr. Storm at the Baxter Building, and observed teenage scientist Reed Richards' first major test of his N-Zone teleporter, an experiment which inadvertently mutated Richards and several of his friends. Ross later authorized Reed's use of an outdated Space Shuttle to explore the otherdimensional N-Zone, interested in N-Zone teleportation's potential for instantaneous troop movements. When Reed's group very publicly crashed into Las Vegas upon returning from the N-Zone, Ross was initially outraged at them for blowing the secrecy of their group, but was mollified when Reed provided him with a "death-ray" they had acquired.

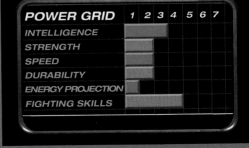

HEIGHT: 6'
WEIGHT: 180 lbs.
EYES: Brown
HAIR: Gray

ABILITIES: General Ross is a highly experienced soldier.

POWER GRID	1	2	3	4	5	6	7
INTELLIGENCE							
STRENGTH							
SPEED							
DURABILITY							
ENERGY PROJECTION							
FIGHTING SKILLS							

SANDMAN

HISTORY: After a failed armored car heist, Flint Marko returned home and beat his girlfriend so badly their neighbors called the cops. When the police arrived, Marko assaulted an officer to the point that he eventually died of his injuries. Sentenced to 50 years in Ryker's Island maximum security prison, Flint Marko eventually found his way to the scientists at Hammer Industries, who were seeking test subjects for their illegal genetic research projects. Flint became the guinea pig for their Sandman Project. Granted the ability to transform into a mass of sentient sand, Marko was temporarily driven insane, unable to control his newfound powers. When the owner of Hammer Industries, Justin Hammer, who was being stalked by Dr. Octopus, called his lab in New Jersey, he was horrified to see how the Sandman Project had turned out. Despite Marko's condition, lab chief Dr. Skrtic remained hopeful about his future use. Only a few days later, Doctor Octopus assaulted the lab, killed Skrtic, and then lured Hammer there, intending to murder him in front of the assembled media.

After Spider-Man apprehended Octopus, S.H.I.E.L.D. agents Woo and Carter arrived at the lab and found some surviving technicians hiding within. Carter carelessly freed Marko, who went on a rampage before Spider-Man intervened. Attacking both Spider-Man and the S.H.I.E.L.D. agents, Marko was slowed down when Spider-Man used a fire hose to mix water with his granular form, then was knocked out by one of the lab techs using an experimental gun designed to stun him; Marko was taken into S.H.I.E.L.D. custody. Housed in the same top secret cell block as Norman Osborn, Doctor Octopus, Electro, and Kraven, Marko escaped alongside them. When the Ultimates raided Kraven's production company, the escapees took advantage of the situation and kidnapped Spider-Man from S.H.I.E.L.D.'s protective custody, with Electro and Sandman causing most of the damage. Osborn then tricked an unmasked Spider-Man into joining their attack on the White House by threatening his Aunt May, but when they reached their target, they were intercepted by the Ultimates. Marko attacked Iron Man, but was hit by a laser which caused him to explode. The clumps of Marko's sand form were later housed in separate jars in S.H.I.E.L.D. custody.

REAL NAME: Flint Marko
KNOWN ALIASES: None
IDENTITY: Known to authorities
OCCUPATION: None
CITIZENSHIP: U.S.A.
PLACE OF BIRTH: Unknown
KNOWN RELATIVES: None
GROUP AFFILIATIONS: Norman Osborn's "Six"
EDUCATION: Unknown
FIRST APPEARANCE: Ultimate Spider-Man #17 (2002)

HEIGHT: 6'2" (variable in sand form)
WEIGHT: 230 lbs. (variable in sand form)
EYES: Brown
HAIR: Brown

SUPERHUMAN POWERS: Flint Marko can shift his DNA into an organic sand-like state, allowing him to alter his shape and size and become a living mass of sand. He can seep through small gaps, move like a sandstorm at high speed ripping through anyone in his path, or harden to a stonelike density.

ABILITIES: He is not particularly confident in his control over his abilities.

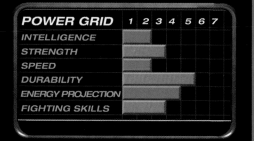

POWER GRID	1	2	3	4	5	6	7
INTELLIGENCE							
STRENGTH							
SPEED							
DURABILITY							
ENERGY PROJECTION							
FIGHTING SKILLS							

SHANG-CHI

REAL NAME: Shang-Chi
KNOWN ALIASES: Master of Kung Fu
IDENTITY: No dual identity
OCCUPATION: Floor sweeper at Wu's Fish Market
CITIZENSHIP: China (presumably)
PLACE OF BIRTH: Unknown, presumably China
KNOWN RELATIVES: Fu Manchu (father)
GROUP AFFILIATION: None
EDUCATION: Trained from birth in martial arts, other education unknown
FIRST APPEARANCE: Ultimate Marvel Team-Up#15 (2002)

HISTORY: Shang-Chi is the son of the international criminal known as Fu Manchu. Trained from birth to be the ultimate living weapon, he became the world's greatest martial artist. A noble spirit, he eventually renounced his father's evil criminal empire and dedicated himself instead to protecting the innocent. Seeking to live beyond his father's reach, he eventually came to New York. At some point during his wanderings, he befriended fellow martial artist Danny Rand, the Iron Fist; they shared a mutual respect for a Master Kee and his school, which may well be where they met.

In New York's Chinatown, Shang-Chi found employment sweeping floors at Wu's Fish Market; disgusted to learn three separate gangs were menacing the locals, he vowed to stop the predators. He became the only person in the area willing to stand up to the gangs. One day, he stopped three gang members from mugging a newcomer to the area, Leiko, unaware that she was an agent of his father's sent to retrieve him. Shortly after this, more gang members attacked him in an alley; though outnumbered seven to one, he swiftly overcame them before Peter Parker, who had witnessed the altercation begin, had time to change into Spider-Man and lend a hand. Realizing Shang-Chi didn't need help, Spidey departed. The police soon arrived and questioned Shang-Chi, but let him go without charging him.

Leiko promised the local Chinese gangs exclusive rights to the local drug trade if they broke, but did not kill, Shang-Chi. Wu Kwan overheard and warned his friend of the plot, suggesting he leave for his own safety. Before Shang-Chi could do so, he was confronted by a heavily armed gang, outnumbered at least forty to one. Shang-Chi began to cut a swath through them, but was nearly overwhelmed by sheer numbers until Spider-Man arrived; impressed by Shang-Chi's martial arts skills, he had come to ask to be taught some moves. The newcomer swiftly ended the fight by webbing up the entire gang, then carried Shang-Chi out of the area. In gratitude, Shang-Chi taught his rescuer the white ape maneuver, then departed the city.

Shang-Chi secretly returned, feeling the people of New York's Chinatown needed someone to protect them. He was recently drawn into the gang war between the Kingpin and Hammerhead after the latter targeted him to win the Chinatown gangs to his cause. His friends Spider-Man and Danny Rand have also joined this conflict.

HEIGHT: 5'7 1/2"
WEIGHT: 128 lbs.
EYES: Black
HAIR: Black

ABILITIES: Shang-Chi has mastered every fighting style invented by man, and understands ancient techniques forgotten for centuries. He is capable of catching a bullet in mid-air, even when it is fired at point-blank range.

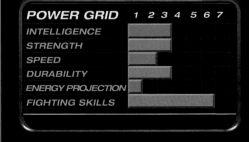

POWER GRID	1	2	3	4	5	6	7
INTELLIGENCE							
STRENGTH							
SPEED							
DURABILITY							
ENERGY PROJECTION							
FIGHTING SKILLS							

HISTORY: Herman Schultz designed and built his vibro-shock units in a rehabilitation program while serving time in Ryker's Island Maximum Security Prison. Upon release he tried to establish a new career as the Shocker; but while committing a daylight robbery of a Krinks Security Van at the First Union Bank, he was interrupted by Spider-Man, who taunted him and broke his nose. When Shocker tried to use his weapon, Spider-Man webbed his hand, causing a backfire that shocked Herman into unconsciousness. He was returned to Ryker's, but was swiftly released when his lawyer managed to get his conviction overturned, claiming Spider-Man had infringed his client's rights.

Shocker improved his costume and equipment and returned to robbing. Yet another daylight bank raid found him in a standoff with the police, whom he easily dispatched, until Spider-Man showed up in a new, strength-enhancing costume. The panicked Shocker blasted Spider-Man at close range, only to see the upgraded hero literally shrug off the attack. As Shocker stared in disbelief, Spider-Man kicked him, sending him flying into the side of a police car. Unconsciousness, he was again captured.

Several months later, improved and once more on the loose, the Shocker committed another robbery but his luck remained true; as he attempted to flee with his loot, he encountered both Wolverine and Spider-Man (who had temporarily swapped bodies, though Herman was unaware of this). Shocker stood frozen in terror as the two argued, virtually ignoring him, until Spider-Man webbed him in the chest, then yanked him through the air straight into Wolverine's upraised fist. Shocker's mask shattered and he slammed to the ground unconscious.

Ever persistent, Shocker soon tried again, robbing another armored car outside a bank in the middle of the day; as ever, his luck was poor and he was cornered by arriving police units. Before anyone could open fire, the costumed Kitty Pryde confronted Shocker, but when the terrified crook tried to blast her, he found his attack had no effect on the immaterial girl. She phased through his shock units, causing them to short out; when he realized Spider-Man was also present, he fled in abject terror, straight into a wall of webs. For the moment, he is back in custody.

REAL NAME: Herman Schultz
KNOWN ALIASES: None
IDENTITY: Public
OCCUPATION: Criminal
CITIZENSHIP: U.S.A. with criminal record
PLACE OF BIRTH: Unknown
KNOWN RELATIVES: None
GROUP AFFILIATION: None
EDUCATION: Unknown
FIRST APPEARANCE: Ultimate Spider-Man #8 (2001)

HEIGHT: 5'11"
WEIGHT: 155 lbs.
EYES: Blue
HAIR: Silver

ABILITIES: Shocker is a skilled mechanical engineer who managed to build high-tech weapons using only the equipment available to him while in prison.

PARAPHERNALIA: The Shocker wears vibro-shock units (vibratory weapons resembling over-large knuckle-dusters) and a metallic protective mask covering his upper face.

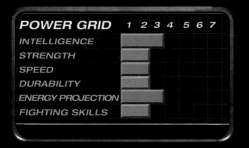

POWER GRID	1	2	3	4	5	6	7
INTELLIGENCE							
STRENGTH							
SPEED							
DURABILITY							
ENERGY PROJECTION							
FIGHTING SKILLS							

SPIDER-MAN

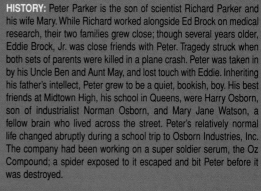

REAL NAME: Peter Parker
KNOWN ALIASES: Arthur Simek
IDENTITY: Known to S.H.I.E.L.D.; otherwise secret
OCCUPATION: Student; Daily Bugle intern and website maintainer; former wrestler
CITIZENSHIP: U.S.A.
PLACE OF BIRTH: Unknown
KNOWN RELATIVES: Richard Parker (father, deceased), Mary Parker (mother, deceased), Ben Parker (uncle, deceased), May Parker (aunt)
GROUP AFFILIATION: Formerly Osborn's "Six", member of UCW (Unlimited Class Wrestling)
EDUCATION: High school (not yet graduated)
FIRST APPEARANCE: (as Parker) Ultimate Spider-Man #1 (2000); (as Spider-Man) Ultimate Spider-Man #3 (2001)

HISTORY: Peter Parker is the son of scientist Richard Parker and his wife Mary. While Richard worked alongside Ed Brock on medical research, their two families grew close; though several years older, Eddie Brock, Jr. was close friends with Peter. Tragedy struck when both sets of parents were killed in a plane crash. Peter was taken in by his Uncle Ben and Aunt May, and lost touch with Eddie. Inheriting his father's intellect, Peter grew to be a quiet, bookish, boy. His best friends at Midtown High, his school in Queens, were Harry Osborn, son of industrialist Norman Osborn, and Mary Jane Watson, a fellow brain who lived across the street. Peter's relatively normal life changed abruptly during a school trip to Osborn Industries, Inc. The company had been working on a super soldier serum, the Oz Compound; a spider exposed to it escaped and bit Peter before it was destroyed.

Peter soon discovered that he had been mutated, gaining superhuman strength and agility and various spider-like powers. After Peter accidentally broke jock Flash Thompson's hand in a fight, the Parkers were hit with expensive medical bills; to help pay them, Peter secretly took up a wrestling challenge, wearing a mask to hide his youth and identity. The fight promoter gave him a more colorful costume and dubbed him Spider-Man, but his new career was cut short when he was accused of stealing money. Peter allowed a robber he encountered on the way home to escape because of his bad mood, an action that would later haunt him. He subsequently argued with his uncle over his slipping grades and recent poor attitude, and ran off to cool down; but when he returned home, he learned that a burglar had slain Uncle Ben in his absence. Overhearing some cops mention a cornered criminal who might be the burglar, Peter donned his costume and raced to capture him, only to find it was the same criminal he had allowed to escape earlier. Guilt-ridden, Peter finally accepted the great responsibility which came with his powers, becoming a crime fighter as Spider-Man.

Norman Osborn transformed into a monstrous, green goblin-like menace after mainlining the Oz Compound and attacked Peter's school, battling Spider-Man until he was shot down by police marksmen and presumed dead; Harry vanished into police custody for protection and questioning. Spider-Man encountered the criminal Shocker, the mutant Wolverine (on the run from Weapon X) and the rampaging Hulk. To help his aunt pay the bills, Peter tried to sell photos of Spider-Man to the Daily Bugle, and ended up hired to maintain the newspaper's website. Learning that Uncle Ben's killer worked for Wilson Fisk, the Kingpin of Crime, Peter set out to bring him down. After trying to get information from the Enforcers, he learned the Kingpin's whereabouts from ambitious underboss Mr. Big. Breaking into the Kingpin's office while Fisk hosted a party elsewhere in Fisk Tower, Spider-Man was spotted on the security cameras, defeated by Fisk's superpowered henchman Electro, unmasked, and thrown out a window. Kingpin, having figured out who had provided his intruder's information, personally murdered Mr. Big before having his body dumped in the river wearing Spider-Man's mask. Peter returned to Fisk's building, and after defeating Electro, the Enforcers and Fisk, sent the Daily Bugle security footage he had stolen showing the murder of Mr. Big; Fisk swiftly went into hiding.

Peter soon revealed his dual identity to Mary Jane, and they began dating. He fought alongside Iron Man at the U.N.; ran into Daredevil in Hell's Kitchen and helped apprehend the Punisher, a killer vigilante; encountered a lizard creature and a monster composed of swamp vegetation (both transformed scientists) in the sewers; and was mesmerized by Xandu into attacking the sorcerer Dr.

Strange. He encountered the former Russian spy, the Black Widow, who stole his webshooters; met the martial artist Shang-Chi; ran into a vampire and unidentified vampire slayer; and prevented a murder by the assassin Elektra. A new girl, Gwen Stacy, whose policeman father had investigated Uncle Ben's killing, joined Peter's school; soon after, Peter went to the mall with his friends where they bumped into the off-duty X-Men after Wolverine recognized Peter. Parker next faced the twin threats of Otto Octavius, alias Doctor Octopus, an Osborn scientist who had gained powers at the same time as Osborn himself; and Kraven, a reality TV show hunter who announced his intention to hunt and kill Spider-Man. After losing his first fight with Octopus, Spider-Man soundly defeated both him and Kraven outside an illegal genetic research lab in front of a horde of assembled press. The televised fight and a quick interview afterwards helped turn around negative public opinion about Spider-Man; minutes later, he fought one of the lab's rogue creations, the Sandman.

The next day at school, Harry returned — but Peter's joy evaporated when Norman resurfaced, too. The senior Osborn offered Peter a stark choice: work for him or see his loved ones killed by the Goblin. The following day, Peter learned from General Nick Fury that S.H.I.E.L.D. was monitoring him and was aware of the Osborn situation, but could not intervene unless the Goblin made a public move. Spider-Man confronted Osborn to say he would not be intimidated, unaware that Harry had invited Mary Jane over; the Goblin seized her and carried her to the Queensboro Bridge, then dropped her off it; Spider-Man only narrowly managed to catch her. Facing both Spidey and S.H.I.E.L.D. attack helicopters, Osborn fled back home and overdosed on the serum, mutating further. Peter pursued but was nearly killed before Harry walked in on the fight and saved him by driving a spike into the Goblin's back. The pursuing helicopters shot the Goblin, who turned back to Osborn and was taken into custody. In the aftermath, Nick Fury told Peter that when he turned 18 and was an adult, he would be forced to work for S.H.I.E.L.D.

Peter's friendship with Gwen Stacy grew as she began to confide in him regarding family troubles, though this meant he arrived minutes too late to help Iron Man capture the rampaging Rhino. When an imposter dressed as Spider-Man committed a string of robberies, the real Spider-Man was shot in the shoulder by police trying to apprehend him, and Fury sent the Wasp over to Peter's school to patch him up. While this was happening, the fake Spider-Man killed Captain John Stacy, Gwen's father. Enraged, Spider-Man foiled the imposter's latest bank robbery, beat him to a pulp and left him for the police, clearing his name. As her mother had run off with another man, Gwen moved in with the Parkers; Mary Jane, meanwhile, broke up with Peter, fearful he would one day be killed.

Finding boxes full of mementos of his parents in the basement prompted Peter to track down Eddie Brock. Now a university student, Eddie was trying to complete their parents' Venom Project, a protoplasmic medical dip nicknamed "the Suit" which could enhance its wearer's abilities while healing illness and injury — even curing cancer; however, some of Eddie's comments led Peter to wonder if their parents had been murdered by their corporate employers. As Spider-Man, he broke into Eddie's lab to examine the dip, but it enveloped his body, creating a new black costume. He briefly enjoyed this new look, easily stopping a kidnapping and beating an upgraded Shocker; but after the Suit took control of Peter and nearly killed a mugger, Peter had to electrocute himself to remove it. Seeing the danger of the dip, Peter went back

to the lab to destroy the rest of it, confiding in Eddie that he was Spider-Man and apparently convincing Eddie to let him destroy the dip, unaware Eddie had more hidden away. Exposing himself to the Suit, Eddie became an insane, monstrous menace and attacked Peter. In the end, an accidental electrocution seemingly killed Eddie, though the subsequent disappearance of his belongings suggested Brock may have survived. After confronting Nick Fury to ask if his parents had been murdered, Peter returned to the lab where he found the rest of the dip gone and encountered Eddie's professor, Curt Conners, the former lizard-man, who deduced Peter was Spider-Man.

Shortly thereafter, Spider-Man got back together with Mary-Jane as Peter; offered guidance to unstable Latverian mutant teen Geldoff alongside the X-Men; and stopped martial artist Danny Rand from using his "Iron Fist" on an aggressive man during a street fight.

Wounded X-Man Wolverine later sought refuge in Peter's home while fleeing remnants of Weapon X. The Enforcers returned, as did their boss, the Kingpin, who had gone free after the murder evidence against him was ruled inadmissible. Sam Bullit ran for D.A. on an anti-Spider-Man platform, supported by Jameson and the Bugle, and when Peter spoke out against the Bugle's anti-Spidey stance, he was fired; however, reporter Ben Urich learned that Bullit was tied to the Kingpin and the Bugle withdrew its support. The Enforcers tried to intimidate Jameson into reversing this, but Spider-Man intervened. Soon after, Jameson admitted his mistake to Peter and reinstated him. Spider-Man next encountered the burglar known as the Black Cat, who became attracted to him. She had stolen a stone tablet sought by the Kingpin, and Elektra was hired to retrieve it. After a fruitless three-way skirmish between Black Cat, Elektra and Spider-Man, Peter and the Kingpin both figured out the Black Cat was secretly Felica Hardy, who was soon trapped by Kingpin and Elektra. Spider-Man's arrival allowed her to free herself, and she threw the tablet into the river, only to be seemingly slain by Elektra.

Several of Spider-Man's foes, led by Norman Osborn, escaped S.H.I.E.L.D. captivity. Fearing for Peter, Fury brought him to the Triskelion base used by the Ultimates and placed his loved ones under observation. The escapees attacked the Triskelion and captured Peter, blackmailing him into joining Osborn's "Six." This group attacked the White House but was opposed by the Ultimates, who informed Peter that Aunt May was safely in protective custody, prompting Spider-Man to turn on Osborn and help the Ultimates recapture the criminals. While Aunt May visited Florida, Peter heard a Spider-Man movie was being filmed and angrily confronted its film crew, but learned he had no legal recourse to stop the film. Equally put out by the news, Doctor Octopus attacked the movie set; when Spider-Man stepped in, Octopus defeated him and abducted him to Brazil, where Spider-Man bested Octopus in a rematch and hitched a ride back to the States in the cargo hold of a passenger jet. He narrowly beat his aunt home, only to be confronted by an angry Gwen, who had figured out his double identity and blamed him for her father's death. Peter managed to convince her otherwise, and she forgave him, joining his trusted circle of confidants. A short while later, the movie opened to great success.

Spider-Man stopped the maniac Gladiator, who had taken hostages in a museum, and met Captain Jeanne De Wolfe of the NYPD. Injured by Gladiator's blades, he sought medical assistance from Dr. Conners, who later experimented with Peter's blood in search of cures for disease, having obtained Peter's reluctant permission to do so. A few months later, a creature Conners had created by mixing Peter's DNA with his own reptile-infected DNA escaped, killing a number of people, including Gwen Stacy, as it followed echoes of Peter's memories back to his home. Peter accused Conners of being behind Gwen's death, and Conners revealed what he had done, just as the creature came out of hiding. Peter attacked it, eventually tricking it into leaping into a fiery factory smokestack. Later, an angry Peter convinced Conners to turn himself in. Deciding that Spider-Man had caused enough death, Peter told Mary Jane he was dropping his dual identity, but he could not avoid his sense of responsibility, stopping a mugging while wearing a makeshift mask; he soon realized he could not quit.

When the X-Men's Jean Grey used her telepathy to punish Wolverine for an indiscretion, she unwittingly swapped the minds of Spider-Man and Wolverine, trapping each in the other's body. After a series of misadventures, the duo foiled another robbery attempt by the Shocker before Grey restored them to their rightful bodies. Later, Peter enjoyed a trip to the beach with Mary Jane,

Kong, Liz and a new kid in school that Liz liked, Johnny Storm. After the secretly superhuman Storm was unexpectedly ignited by their campfire and flew off, he came back the next day to apologize to Liz; as Spider-Man, Peter offered Storm advice and they formed what might prove to be an enduring friendship. Together, they rescued people from a tenement fire.

After helping the Ultimates capture a rogue cyborg, Peter accompanied Ben Urich to interview the now-celebrity sorcerer Dr. Strange. Turned away by the Doctor's manservant Wong, Peter sensed something was wrong and returned as Spider-Man to investigate. Witnessing what he thought was Wong attacking the unconscious Doctor, he broke in through the window, unwittingly shattering the mansion's mystic defenses. The nightmare being who had been attacking Strange pulled Peter into a horrifying dream world until Strange managed to wake him, and Peter fled in terror. When Harry Osborn returned, Peter learned that he had dated Mary Jane prior to Peter, and that he too had been mutated in the same explosion that empowered Doctor Octopus and his father. Now mentally unstable and hallucinating, Harry transformed into a monstrous hobgoblin. He went on a rampage, trying to get Peter to kill him, but Peter refused; when Fury and S.H.I.E.L.D. arrived, they took Harry down hard, and an enraged Peter struck the government man. Afterwards, Peter broke up with Mary Jane, fearful for her safety and feeling he could no longer trust her.

Recently, Spider-Man has gotten caught up in a gang war between Kingpin and his rival Hammerhead, and has encountered the mysterious vigilante Moonknight, as well as fighting Hammerhead and the Enforcers alongside Shang-Chi, Iron Fist and Black Cat. He has also started dating Kitty Pryde of the X-Men.

HEIGHT: 5'5"
WEIGHT: 140 lbs.
EYES: Brown
HAIR: Brown

SUPERHUMAN POWERS: Spider-Man possesses superhuman strength, reflexes and equilibrium, the ability to cling to most surfaces, and a sixth sense that warns him of impending danger.

ABILITIES: Peter is an accomplished scientist for his age.

PARAPHERNALIA: Spider-Man's wrist-mounted web-shooters discharge thin strands of web-fluid at high pressure. On contact with air, the long-chain polymer knits and forms an extremely tough, flexible fiber with extraordinary adhesive qualities.

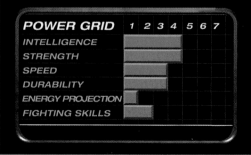

POWER GRID	1	2	3	4	5	6	7
INTELLIGENCE							
STRENGTH							
SPEED							
DURABILITY							
ENERGY PROJECTION							
FIGHTING SKILLS							

LIZ ALLEN

REAL NAME: Liz Allen
KNOWN ALIASES: None
IDENTITY: No dual identity
OCCUPATION: Student
CITIZENSHIP: U.S.A.
PLACE OF BIRTH: Unknown
KNOWN RELATIVES: Unnamed uncle (deceased), Becky (cousin), unnamed mother, unnamed father
GROUP AFFILIATION: None
EDUCATION: High school (not yet graduated)
FIRST APPEARANCE: Ultimate Spider-Man #1 (2000)

HISTORY: Liz Allen is Mary Jane Watson's best friend at Midtown High. She is uncomfortable, almost to the level of phobia, with mutants and superhumans, and even the discussion of them distresses her; Liz claims this is because she had a mutant uncle in Washington who disappeared, perhaps killed by either the Sentinels or during Magneto's attack on the capital. Unfortunately for Liz, unwittingly going to school with one of New York's premier super heroes has meant she has encountered more than her fair share of superpowered weirdness. She has been present during various Goblin attacks and witnessed Spider-Man fighting them; she and her friends ran into the X-Men at the mall, causing Liz to flee in terror; and she was present when reality-TV star Kraven visited her school hunting for Spider-Man. When Mary Jane temporarily broke up with Peter Parker, Liz tried to help her get over him by getting her cousin Becky to invite them to a party, unaware that both Peter and the explosive mutant Geldoff would be attending. Liz later became instantly smitten by a new boy in school, Johnny Storm; she got Mary Jane to arrange a meeting with him after school, and successfully asked him out on a date. With her friends, they spent a pleasant day at Rockaway Beach until their campfire set Storm ablaze, unintentionally revealing he had superhuman powers. Unsurprisingly, Liz fled. Storm secretly returned to Midtown High a few days later, hoping to explain himself to Liz, but she wanted nothing to do with him.

HEIGHT: 5'5"
WEIGHT: 125 lbs.
EYES: Blue
HAIR: Blonde

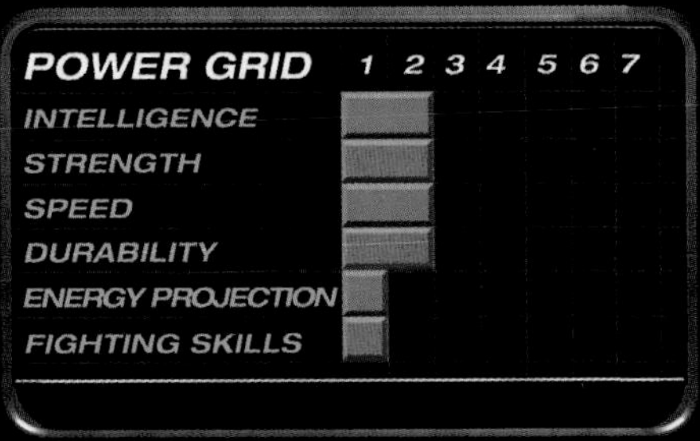

POWER GRID	1	2	3	4	5	6	7
INTELLIGENCE							
STRENGTH							
SPEED							
DURABILITY							
ENERGY PROJECTION							
FIGHTING SKILLS							

JEANNE DEWOLFE

REAL NAME: Jeanne De Wolfe
KNOWN ALIASES: None
IDENTITY: No dual identity
OCCUPATION: Police captain
CITIZENSHIP: U.S.A.
PLACE OF BIRTH: Unrevealed
KNOWN RELATIVES: None
GROUP AFFILIATIONS: The NYPD
EDUCATION: College graduate
FIRST APPEARANCE: Ultimate Spider-Man #32 (2003)

HISTORY: An eleven-year veteran of the New York Police Department, Jeanne De Wolfe succeeded the late John Stacy as Captain. Jeanne first encountered the costumed vigilante Spider-Man when the Spider-Man imposter who had killed Captain Stacy was robbing a bank. Jeanne and several officers surrounded the building, but the real Spider-Man snuck in and defeated the imposter. Demanding that anyone in a Spider-Man costume come out with their masks off and their hands in the air, Jeanne was unable to apprehend the true Spider-Man as the bank's customers flooded out, allowing his escape, but she found the imposter webbed up with a note, "From the REAL Spider-Man," pinned to him. When police held an injured Spider-Man at gunpoint after he defeated Gladiator, Jeanne ordered them to stand down and let him go. Jeanne later headed the investigation of a rash of murders where the victims appeared to be drained of all life, and was one of the first to arrive at the Parker house where Gwen Stacy was found dead. Dr. Curt Conners later admitted his part in the murders to Jeanne, who placed him in custody. After beating a criminal so badly he had to be hospitalized, Spider-Man came to Jeanne to turn himself in; but Jeanne appreciated all of his help and offered him her card, which he promptly lost. Following a lunch with the Kingpin, Spider-Man gave Jeanne information on the crime boss Hammerhead. Hindered by police procedure, Jeanne suggested Spider-Man handle it himself.

HEIGHT: 5'8"
WEIGHT: 125 lbs.
EYES: Blue
HAIR: Brown

POWER GRID	1	2	3	4	5	6	7
INTELLIGENCE							
STRENGTH							
SPEED							
DURABILITY							
ENERGY PROJECTION							
FIGHTING SKILLS							

KONG HARLAN

REAL NAME: Clifford Kenneth Harlan
KNOWN ALIASES: King Kong, Kong
IDENTITY: No dual identity
OCCUPATION: Student
CITIZENSHIP: U.S.A.
PLACE OF BIRTH: Unknown
KNOWN RELATIVES: Unnamed parents, unnamed uncle
GROUP AFFILIATION: Midtown High Tigers basketball team and football team
EDUCATION: High school (not yet graduated)
FIRST APPEARANCE: Ultimate Spider-Man #1 (2000)

HISTORY: Clifford Harlan prefers to go by his middle name, Kenny — or, even better, Kong, the nickname he earned playing basketball and football. Though not a malicious boy, he follows the lead of his fellow jock and best friend, Flash Thompson, and often makes fun of non-jock students such as Peter Parker. He was present on the school trip where Parker was bitten by a mutated spider, and killed the creature himself afterwards, stamping on it. Costumed crimefighters fascinate him; he was present when Spider-Man first beat Crusher Hogan in the wrestling ring, and again when the webbed wonder took on a Green Goblin at Midtown High; he was thrilled when he and his friends ran into the X-Men at the mall, questioning them about their powers; and he idolized the killer vigilante dubbed the Punisher. Kong followed news reports about Spider-Man, and quickly figured out his classmate Peter Parker was the hero; Peter fooled him into thinking he had made a mistake by letting Kong get in a sneak kick against him in the school corridors. Another classmate, Gwen Stacy, pulled a knife on Kong for this act of bullying, and things remained tense between them for some time.

Kong's greatest moment was probably when he successfully auditioned to be an extra in the Spider-Man movie; though he had only a single line, he was inordinately proud of his big screen debut.

HEIGHT: 6'2"
WEIGHT: 190 lbs.
EYES: Brown
HAIR: Black

POWER GRID	1	2	3	4	5	6	7
INTELLIGENCE							
STRENGTH							
SPEED							
DURABILITY							
ENERGY PROJECTION							
FIGHTING SKILLS							

JOE ROBERTSON

REAL NAME: Joe Robertson
KNOWN ALIASES: Robbie
IDENTITY: No dual identity
OCCUPATION: Newspaper editor
CITIZENSHIP: U.S.A.
PLACE OF BIRTH: Unknown
KNOWN RELATIVES: None
GROUP AFFILIATION: Daily Bugle staff
EDUCATION: Unrevealed
FIRST APPEARANCE: Ultimate Spider-Man #7 (2001)

HISTORY: Joe Robertson has known J. Jonah Jameson for twenty years; the calming yin to Jameson's raging yang, he has helped his friend cope with drinking problems and personal bereavement. He often serves to balance Jameson's temper and act as his conscience: telling him off for going overboard on the mutant scare; wanting to run reporter Ben Urich's sewer monster piece when Jameson knocked it back; expressing sadness in contrast to Jonah's jubilation when Spider-Man was accused of being a bank robber; and admitting to a new employee that the reason the Daily Bugle didn't pursue Wilson Fisk's criminal activities more vigorously was because the crimelord owns stock in the company. In fact, Robertson is often the only person whom Jameson will listen to when he has dug his heels in. Joe was unhappy when Jameson endorsed prospective D.A. Sam Bullit's election campaign without clearing it with him first, and berated Jameson for firing Peter Parker simply for questioning the paper's reporting of the Kingpin escaping murder charges. Robertson has also acted as a mentor to younger staff members; Ben Urich claims Joe taught him to always have a backup, and Peter Parker has often found his wisdom extremely useful.

HEIGHT: 6'
WEIGHT: 160 lbs.
EYES: Brown
HAIR: Graying black

ABILITIES: Joe is an excellent reporter whose calm rationality often balances Jameson's raging temper.

POWER GRID	1	2	3	4	5	6	7
INTELLIGENCE							
STRENGTH							
SPEED							
DURABILITY							
ENERGY PROJECTION							
FIGHTING SKILLS							

FLASH THOMPSON

REAL NAME: Thompson (first name unrevealed)
KNOWN ALIASES: Flash
IDENTITY: No dual identity
OCCUPATION: High school student, athlete
CITIZENSHIP: U.S.A.
PLACE OF BIRTH: Unknown
KNOWN RELATIVES: Unnamed parents
GROUP AFFILIATION: Midtown High Tigers basketball team and football team
EDUCATION: High school (not yet graduated)
FIRST APPEARANCE: Ultimate Spider-Man #1 (2000)

HISTORY: Flash Thompson has been Peter Parker's classmate since both were 7, but they have never been friends. The sporty Flash was worlds away from the bookish Peter, and took delight in tormenting him. For Flash, the most important things in the world are basketball and football, interests shared by his best friend "Kong" Harlan and his idol Mark Raxton. Flash fancies himself a ladies man, though his track record suggests otherwise. When he hit on Mary Jane Watson soon after the Peter Parker secretly gained superhuman abilities, the jealous Peter knocked him Flash down with a basketball to the face. After school, Flash tried to fight Peter, who eventually blocked a punch and broke Flash's hand; to add insult to injury, Peter temporarily replaced the incapacitated Flash on the basketball team. Flash's parents threatened to sue Parker's guardians if they did not pay for Flash's medical bills.

For all the students of Midtown High, the last few months have been interesting, but for Flash, the most important person to enter his life was Gwen Stacy. A new girl in class, Flash wanted to ask her out, but couldn't figure out how to; when she moved in with the Parker's following the death of her father's death, Flash repeatedly tried to ask Peter for help on this front, only to be rebuffed each time before he could reveal what he wanted. It wasn't until after her Gwen's untimely death that Mary Jane Watson deduced Flash had feelings for Gwen.

HEIGHT: 5'10"
WEIGHT: 155 lbs.
EYES: Blue
HAIR: Blond

POWER GRID

	1	2	3	4	5	6	7
INTELLIGENCE							
STRENGTH							
SPEED							
DURABILITY							
ENERGY PROJECTION							
FIGHTING SKILLS							

GLADIATOR

REAL NAME: Unrevealed
KNOWN ALIASES: None
IDENTITY: Known to authorities
OCCUPATION: Unknown
CITIZENSHIP: Unknown
PLACE OF BIRTH: Unknown
KNOWN RELATIVES: None
GROUP AFFILIATIONS: None
EDUCATION: Unknown
FIRST APPEARANCE: Ultimate Spider-Man #60 (2004)

HISTORY: For reasons only understood by his own demented mind, the madman who called himself the Gladiator took an entire museum hostage, ranting about the unjust imprisonment of Nurhachi, presumably referring to the 16th century founder of the Manchu Dynasty (a.k.a. Geren Gurun Be Ujire Genggiyen or "Brilliant Emperor Who Benefits All Nations"). By the time Spider-Man arrived, the Gladiator had already killed at least one security officer. Declaring "the Emperor" had given the attack signal, Gladiator shot blades from his gauntlet at Spider-Man, destroying several priceless artifacts when the hero dodged. He avoided Gladiator's next blow just as easily, and the madman's gauntleted fist shattered a concrete pillar instead. Spider-Man landed on Gladiator's shoulders and pounded away at him, but was dislodged when blades sprang from Gladiator's pauldrons. As the hero leapt away, Gladiator grabbed his leg and threw his opponent through some display cases. Tangled in some ropes, Spider-Man was unable to dodge the next set of blades Gladiator fired. As Gladiator moved in for the killing blow, the injured Spider-Man webbed his eyes and repeatedly bashed a metal stand over his head, knocking Gladiator out.

HEIGHT: 6'8"
WEIGHT: 280 lbs.
EYES: Brown
HAIR: Unknown

ABILITIES: Gladiator is a skilled fighter.

PARAPHERNALIA: The Gladiator's armored suit gives him heightened durability and is fitted with retractable blades on the shoulders. His gauntlets also feature retractable blades, which he can eject and fire at a target.

POWER GRID

	1	2	3	4	5	6	7
INTELLIGENCE							
STRENGTH							
SPEED							
DURABILITY							
ENERGY PROJECTION							
FIGHTING SKILLS							

IRON FIST

REAL NAME: Danny Rand
KNOWN ALIASES: The Iron Fist
IDENTITY: No dual identity
OCCUPATION: Adventurer
CITIZENSHIP: U.S.A.
PLACE OF BIRTH: Unknown
KNOWN RELATIVES: None
GROUP AFFILIATION: None
EDUCATION: Unknown
FIRST APPEARANCE: Ultimate Spider-Man #1/2 (2002)

HISTORY: Danny Rand trained in martial arts for many years, eventually learning a rare discipline which allowed him to focus his life energy, or chi, in his hand, rendering it hard as iron. At some point he befriended Shang-Chi, possibly in the school of Master Kee. Inspired by the example of individuals like Spider-Man, Danny considered dedicating himself to crimefighting, or community service as he called it; thus, when he saw a street altercation involving a large man grabbing a smaller man by the head and threatening violence, he intervened. When the larger man refused to let his victim go, Danny knocked him down with a kick to the head; when his opponent rose to attack, Danny began to focus his "iron fist", only to be sent flying by an unexpected blow from Spider-Man, who happened by and assumed Danny was the villain of the piece. This poor start did not deter Danny's community spirit, but a later incident where he used his "iron fist" on a man saw him sentenced to six months on Ryker's Island. Released on parole after four, he sought out his old friend Shang-Chi; however, when Shang-Chi was attacked by the arrival of the Dragons, a local gang; the ambitious crimelord Hammerhead; and his Enforcers, Danny was drawn into the gang war between Hammerhead and the Kingpin, and encountered Spider-Man again, this time as an ally.

HEIGHT: 6'1"
WEIGHT: 150 lbs.
EYES: Blue
HAIR: Blond

SUPERHUMAN POWERS: Rand can focus his spiritual energy into an impervious fist of iron.

ABILITIES: Rand is an expert martial artist.

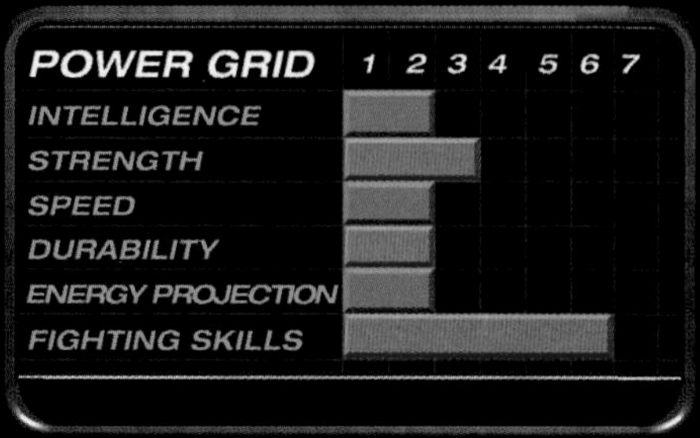

POWER GRID	1	2	3	4	5	6	7
INTELLIGENCE							
STRENGTH							
SPEED							
DURABILITY							
ENERGY PROJECTION							
FIGHTING SKILLS							

RHINO

REAL NAME: Unrevealed
KNOWN ALIASES: None
IDENTITY: Known to authorities
OCCUPATION: None
CITIZENSHIP: Unknown
PLACE OF BIRTH: Unknown
KNOWN RELATIVES: None
GROUP AFFILIATIONS: None
EDUCATION: Unknown
FIRST APPEARANCE: Ultimate Spider-Man #28 (2002)

HISTORY: Under unknown and classified circumstances, the man who became the Rhino stole an experimental suit of armor from the U.S. military. Using the suit's incredible strength, the Rhino robbed a Manhattan bank, charging the vault head-first and destroying it. He then rampaged through a busy street attempting to make his escape, destroying anything in his path, including police cars, with ease. While Spider-Man raced to the scene, Iron Man arrived, stopped the Rhino's assault and captured him. Sometime later, the Rhino rampaged through the Brooklyn Naval Yard, battling the police and Spider-Man, who seemed to be more of an annoyance than a threat, constantly evading the Rhino's clumsy blows. After knocking Spider-Man clear across the street into an office building, the Rhino was confronted by the U.S. army, who were hoping to retrieve his experimental armor. Spider-Man used the distraction to sneak up on the Rhino and rip his armor open, sabotaging its internal circuitry and knocking him out. The Rhino was taken into military custody.

HEIGHT: Unknown (8' in armor)
WEIGHT: Unknown (1250 lbs. in armor)
EYES: Unknown (red in armor)
HAIR: Unknown

SUPERHUMAN POWERS: The Rhino's experimental suit of armor gives him superhuman strength and durability, allowing him to crush bank vaults and motor vehicles with little effort, but makes him extremely slow and limits his range of motion.

POWER GRID	1	2	3	4	5	6	7
INTELLIGENCE							
STRENGTH							
SPEED							
DURABILITY							
ENERGY PROJECTION							
FIGHTING SKILLS							

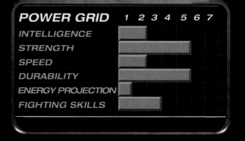

CAPTAIN STACY

HISTORY: NYPD veteran Captain John Stacy's dedication to his job was eroding his family life; his wife Ginger was having an affair while his daughter Gwen grew up a rebellious teen, barely seeing her father due to his police schedule. John was the detective assigned to the Ben Parker murder where he first encountered May and Peter Parker, the victim's wife and nephew. Later, Stacy was called to a factory where Ben Parker's killer was holed up, and glimpsed Spider-Man (secretly Peter Parker) as he delivered the bound criminal to the police.

Gwen began attending Midtown High after being expelled from her last school. While investigating a horrific crime scene where Dr. Octopus had killed a woman, Captain Stacy received a call from the Midtown High principal informing him Gwen had been caught with a knife in school. Meeting reporter Ben Urich outside of the crime scene, Stacy let off some steam; he "thanked" him for cracking the Kingpin case, sending every wannabe gangster in the tri-state area into a power-grabbing frenzy, and asked him why he wasn't chasing sewer monsters. Back at his station, John argued with Gwen, reminding her that if she didn't have a police captain for a father, she would probably be jailed for bringing a weapon into school. Gwen explained that she was sticking up for Peter Parker, who was being bullied at the time, but John was interrupted by a call from Ben Urich before they could finish the conversation. Urich provided John with information about Otto Octavius and his link to the brutal murder, but Gwen ran off during their conversation. John barely managed to get his daughter back into Midtown High, promising the principal there would be no more such incidents.

Ginger finally ran off with another man, abandoning her husband and daughter; with her father at work and nowhere else to go, Gwen turned up at Peter's house in the middle of the night. Peter's Aunt May called John, who came over to collect her, and the two adults bonded. A few days later, with a large detectives' conference in Atlantic City coming up, John asked May if she could watch Gwen for the weekend; May agreed. While there, John witnessed Spider-Man (actually an imposter) robbing an armored car. The false Spider-Man attempted to escape while several officers opened fire on him and a bullet hit his backpack. The imposter tossed the smoking backpack as far as he could, nearly hitting a child. Stacy ran towards the child, pushing him out of the way of the backpack, which he caught. The backpack exploded, killing him. The true Spider-Man later caught the imposter during a bank robbery. With Ginger Stacy unwilling to take responsibility for her child, May Parker offered Gwen a place to stay.

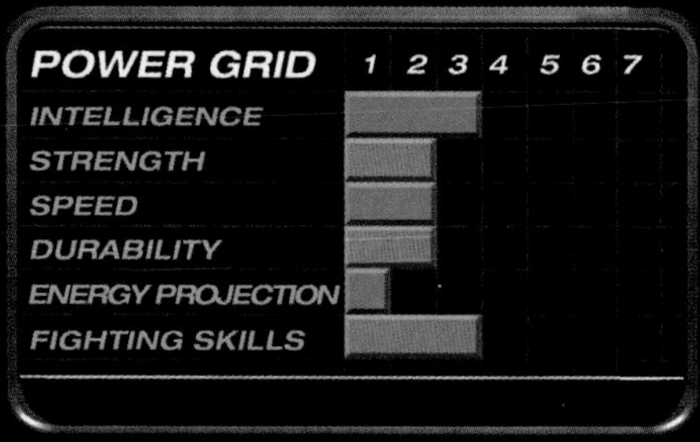

REAL NAME: John Stacy
KNOWN ALIASES: None
IDENTITY: No dual identity
OCCUPATION: Police Captain
CITIZENSHIP: U.S.A.
PLACE OF BIRTH: Unknown
KNOWN RELATIVES: Gwen Stacy (daughter, deceased); Ginger Stacy (wife, separated), unnamed mother
GROUP AFFILIATIONS: NYPD
EDUCATION: College graduate
FIRST APPEARANCE: Ultimate Spider-Man #5 (2001)

HEIGHT: 6'
WEIGHT: 180 lbs.
EYES: Brown
HAIR: Reddish-brown

ABILITIES: John Stacy was a competent and dedicated detective.

POWER GRID	1	2	3	4	5	6	7
INTELLIGENCE							
STRENGTH							
SPEED							
DURABILITY							
ENERGY PROJECTION							
FIGHTING SKILLS							

Art by Mark Bagley

GWEN STACY

REAL NAME: Gwen Stacy
KNOWN ALIASES: None
IDENTITY: No dual identity
OCCUPATION: Student
CITIZENSHIP: U.S.A.
PLACE OF BIRTH: Unrevealed
KNOWN RELATIVES: John (father, deceased); Ginger (mother); unnamed paternal grandmother, unnamed aunt
GROUP AFFILIATION: None
EDUCATION: High school (unfinished)
FIRST APPEARANCE: Ultimate Spider-Man #14 (2001)

HISTORY: The daughter of police captain John Stacy, Gwen was a rebellious girl who dressed for attention and used her intellect and wit to keep it. Transferring to Midtown High, she was among the handful of teens who chanced to meet the X-Men at a local mall, unaware that she was far closer to another costumed adventurer, her fellow student Peter Parker who was secretly Spider-Man. Soon after, she made a more negative impression on the student body when she pulled a knife on Kong Harlan after he assaulted Peter. Having thus earned a dangerous reputation, she soon befriended Peter and his girlfriend Mary Jane and was grudgingly accepted by most of her fellow students. When Gwen's irresponsible mother ran off with another man, the near-suicidal girl sought reassurance from Peter, whose Aunt May took Gwen under her wing and helped her deal with her family problems. Days later, when it became clear that Mrs. Stacy was not returning, May offered to let Gwen stay at the Parker home when necessary so that Captain Stacy, plagued by a police officer's unpredictable routine, would know that she was safe in his absence. Gwen's presence inadvertently drove a wedge between Peter and Mary Jane, who was unnerved by the beautiful blonde's proximity to Peter.

Unfortunately, Captain Stacy was killed by a criminal impersonating Spider-Man, and Gwen, formerly a supporter of costumed heroes, nurtured a hatred for the hero which not even the imposter's exposure could wholly diminish. When her mother refused to take custody of her, Gwen remained with the Parkers, whom she came to regard as a surrogate family. When she accidentally discovered Peter's secret identity, Gwen, still unsure of just which Spider-Man had murdered her father, confronted him at gunpoint, tearfully demanding justice, but Peter calmed her and convinced her of his innocence. Gwen's knowledge of his secret drew her closer than before to Peter and Mary Jane, who was assured by Gwen that she was no competition for Peter's heart. Gwen even confessed to Mary Jane that she considered Peter to be like her little super-hero brother.

Tragically, Gwen Stacy was slain by the creature called Carnage, who had been drawn to the Parker home; her death was a stunning blow to Spider-Man, and its long-term emotional impact has left an even larger wedge between him and Mary Jane.

HEIGHT: 5'6"
WEIGHT: 101 lbs.
EYES: Hazel
HAIR: Blonde

ABILITIES: Gwen Stacy was an intelligent if erratic student with a unique perspective on many topics; she claimed to possess a near-superhuman "sixth sense" which enabled her to evaluate whether or not someone was a good person. She wielded a knife on occasion and possessed at least average self-defense skills.

POWER GRID	1	2	3	4	5	6	7
INTELLIGENCE							
STRENGTH							
SPEED							
DURABILITY							
ENERGY PROJECTION							
FIGHTING SKILLS							

Art by Mark Bagley

HISTORY: Athletically and intellectually gifted, young Ben Grimm, regarded as a future football star as early as fourth grade, was nicknamed "Grimm Reaper" for his linebacking skills. At the age of seven, Grimm had befriended fellow student Reed Richards, protecting Reed from bullying students. In turn, Reed helped Ben with his studies, tutoring him in math and science; he also shared his research with Ben, showing him his devices built for accessing other dimensions. In fifth grade, Reed was moved uptown to a government research facility. Ben seldom saw his friend thereafter.

Ben finished high school and soon began college in the New York area. He remained in occasional contact with Reed over the years, and when the time came for Reed to demonstrate his teleportation device, Ben was invited to observe. As the test was during Ben's spring break, he rode cross-country to the Nevada test site, where he watched the test beside Reed, Susan and Johnny Storm, and Victor Van Damme. The device malfunctioned and Ben woke up in Mexico City, transformed into a rocky, brutish Thing. He was taken to the Baxter Building by the U.S. government. When the Baxter Building was attacked by Arthur Molekevic's monster, Ben leapt from the skyscraper and battled the beast. Ben, Reed and Johnny pursued the monster into Molekevic's hidden headquarters beneath Manhattan, where they retrieved Susan Storm, though Ben's massive strength inadvertently collapsed Molekevic's chambers.

As the U.S. government wanted to keep the foursome a secret, Ben was confined to the Baxter Building for months after his change and limited to weekly phone calls to his family. He accompanied his teammates to Denmark to confront Victor Van Damme, and again into the N-Zone on a voyage of exploration. While Reed and Sue had each other, and Johnny was allowed out in public, Ben was the most isolated of the four, unable to pursue his interests or see his friends, his pro football dreams dead. His first real joy since being changed came when the quartet entered the N-Zone and Ben space-walked for the first time; he found similar moments venturing into the Jurassic Era. After the team went public as the Fantastic Four while battling the alien Nihil in Las Vegas, Ben slowly began to accept what he'd become, even adopting an old football coach's slogan as his battle cry: "It's Clobberin' Time!"

REAL NAME: Ben Grimm
KNOWN ALIASES: Grimm Reaper
IDENTITY: Secret
OCCUPATION: Adventurer
CITIZENSHIP: U.S.A.
PLACE OF BIRTH: Unrevealed
KNOWN RELATIVES: Mrs. Grimm (mother)
GROUP AFFILIATION: Fantastic Four
EDUCATION: Unfinished college education
FIRST APPEARANCE: Ultimate Fantastic Four #1 (2004)

HEIGHT: 7'5"
WEIGHT: 1650 lbs.
EYES: Blue
HAIR: None

DISTINGUISHING FEATURES: Ben has orange rock-like skin, three fingers and a thumb on each hand, and four toes on each foot.

SUPERHUMAN POWERS: Ben's strength limit is still unknown. His arm strength was measured at over seven tons per square inch, sufficient to tear through a twelve-inch-thick steel door. The resistance of Ben's hide is also not fully measured; however, he is bulletproof, and has taken a bazooka in the chest at close range, which was sufficient to knock him off his feet but not to damage him. Ben is capable of surviving in alien atmospheres such as Nihil's toxically acidic environment.

PARAPHERNALIA: Ben's impact suit can withstand immense damage without shredding.

POWER GRID	1	2	3	4	5	6	7
INTELLIGENCE							
STRENGTH							
SPEED							
DURABILITY							
ENERGY PROJECTION							
FIGHTING SKILLS							

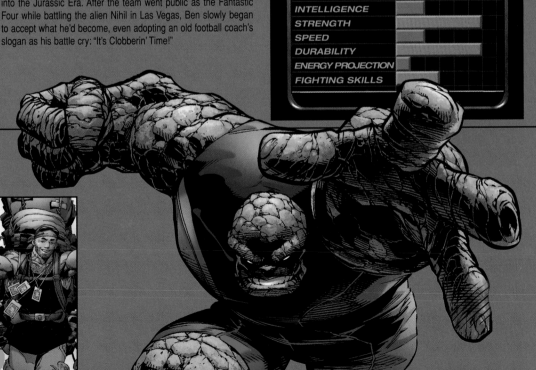

BEN URICH

REAL NAME: Ben Urich
KNOWN ALIASES: None
IDENTITY: No dual identity
OCCUPATION: Reporter, novelist
CITIZENSHIP: U.S.A.
PLACE OF BIRTH: Unknown
KNOWN RELATIVES: None
GROUP AFFILIATION: Daily Bugle staff
EDUCATION: Unknown
FIRST APPEARANCE: Ultimate Spider-Man #7 (2001)

HISTORY: Ben Urich is the veteran star reporter for the Daily Bugle, armed with an incisive mind and an uncanny knack for being where the story is. His many confidential sources include a General who tipped him off about the Hulk's first New York rampage before it happened. Willing to consider stories others write off as outlandish, such as monsters in the sewer system, Urich's main challenges include getting Bugle editor J. Jonah Jameson to print his weirder findings and enduring frequent disrespect from city officials. A longtime foe of organized crime, Urich learned

the identity of the city's Kingpin, Wilson Fisk, researching stories such as the "Murdock Case" to seek proof tying Fisk to his crimes. When Spider-Man first appeared, Jameson ordered Urich to set aside his "family tree of organized crime" and investigate this newcomer instead; ironically, Spider-Man soon provided Urich with the evidence he had sought when the crimefighter anonymously delivered surveillance recordings showing Fisk murdering Frederick Foswell, the criminal underboss known as Mr. Big, with his bare hands. Urich's subsequent story forced Fisk to flee the city and garnered Ben a book deal, which he later lost when the evidence was deemed inadmissible and Fisk returned to the city.

Ben's greatest strength lies in being able to connect the pieces of the puzzle; investigating a particularly brutal murder, Urich soon deduced that the supposedly deceased scientist Otto Octavius was the killer and that Octavius had somehow become a dangerous superhuman. Shortly thereafter, Urich was present at the press launch for Justin Hammer's Big Apple Energy Dome when Octavius, now calling himself Doctor Octopus, attacked it, proving Urich's theories. Later, when Octopus fought Spider-Man outside an illegal Hammer genetics lab, Urich first saw the wall-crawler in person.

A keen observer, Urich saw through the disguise of a Spider-Man-costumed bank robber, noting the imposter's different body language; but Jameson ordered him to cover the story without including this speculation. Later, after Spider-Man had been cleared, Urich got his first, brief interview with the hero, getting his side of things after Spider-Man assaulted would-be do-gooder Danny Rand.

After the Kingpin returned, the evidence against him dropped, Urich interviewed prospective D.A. Sam Bullit. Jameson wanted a fluff piece since the Bugle endorsed Bullit's anti-Spider-Man campaign, but Urich swiftly noted a connection between Bullit and the Kingpin, and tricked Bullit into admitting his mob connections. Enraged, Bullit destroyed Urich's tape recorder and threatened him, unaware the canny reporter had a second such device hidden on his person; with this evidence, Urich convinced Jameson to revoke the Bugle's support of Bullit and wrote a scathing piece that effectively ended Bullit's political career. Soon after this, Jameson assigned Urich to mentor young Peter Parker (ironically Spider-Man's secret identity), taking Parker along on certain stories; the first such instance was when Jameson sent them to interview celebrity sorcerer Doctor Stephen Strange. Urich has recently started to cover the first shots in the growing gang war between the Kingpin and Hammerhead.

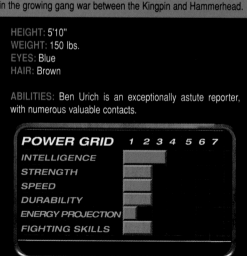

HEIGHT: 5'10"
WEIGHT: 150 lbs.
EYES: Blue
HAIR: Brown

ABILITIES: Ben Urich is an exceptionally astute reporter, with numerous valuable contacts.

POWER GRID   1 2 3 4 5 6 7

INTELLIGENCE	
STRENGTH	
SPEED	
DURABILITY	
ENERGY PROJECTION	
FIGHTING SKILLS	

VICTOR VAN DAMME

HISTORY: On Victor's tenth birthday, his father taught him his lineage: Van Damme was descended from Vlad Tepes Dracula, whose descendents were scattered across Europe. Those who settled in Belgium married into the Van Damme family. Around age twelve, Victor was brought to America and began studying at the Baxter Building, an American think-tank for genius children. Taught by his father that most others were beneath him, Victor rarely even spoke to his fellow students for four years until, needing help from Reed Richards with his robotics designs, he broke into Reed's room and showed him how to correct his physics calculations. Over the next five years, the two formed a loose partnership. As the final construction of Reed's full-sized N-Zone transporter neared, Victor came to believe Richards' super-position calculations were faulty and changed the settings just before the test. The machine transported Van Damme, Richards, and three others across the world, physically changing them. Victor found himself transformed into a mechanical form, reminiscent of the armors of his Wallachian heritage.

Victor returned to his native Europe where he founded a Permanent Autonomous Zone (PAZ), also known as the Keep or the Freezone, in Copenhagen. Using his technology, Van Damme provided those who came to the PAZ with free food, water, shelter, and power in exchange for their loyalty, marking them with a dragon tattoo that included microfibers through which he could control them against their will. Seeking to destroy Richards and his fellows so as to eliminate rival knowledge of the N-Zone transporter and its capabilities, Van Damme used junk electronics to construct a swarm of fist-sized mechanical mosquitoes capable of committing murder and sent them to attack the Baxter Building. As Victor was

REAL NAME: Victor Van Damme
KNOWN ALIASES: None
IDENTITY: Public
OCCUPATION: Scientist
CITIZENSHIP: Belgian
PLACE OF BIRTH: Unrevealed
KNOWN RELATIVES: Mr. Van Damme (father), Vlad Tepes Dracula & Cneajna; Mihnea & Voica; Mircea (distant ancestors)
GROUP AFFILIATION: None
EDUCATION: Multiple doctoral degrees
FIRST APPEARANCE: Ultimate Fantastic Four #2 (2004)

unprepared for the Fantastic Four's new powers, the mosquitoes were quickly destroyed, and the Four confronted Van Damme in Denmark. The fight ended in a standstill when the American and Danish armies intervened; Van Damme was left free by international law, though Richards destroyed Victor's control over his followers.

HEIGHT: 6'1"
WEIGHT: 450 lbs.
EYES: Blue, occasionally glowing red
HAIR: None

DISTINGUISHING FEATURES: Van Damme's skin is completely mechanical in appearance. His legs are shaped like those of a satyr, complete with cloven hooves. His normally blue eyes glow red when he is angry or using his natural powers.

SUPERHUMAN POWERS: Van Damme's skin has been replaced by a regenerative mechanical surface; his internal organics are also of a techno-organic nature. He is highly resistant to physical damage, can throw his armor's spines at a distance, and can project a poisonous gas through his mouth.

ABILITIES: Van Damme holds multiple doctoral level degrees.

PARAPHERNALIA: Van Damme's creations include a swarm of mechanical mosquitoes capable of breaking through shatterproof glass.

POWER GRID	1	2	3	4	5	6	7
INTELLIGENCE							
STRENGTH							
SPEED							
DURABILITY							
ENERGY PROJECTION							
FIGHTING SKILLS							

Art by Stuart Immonen with Adam Kubert (inset)

VENOM

REAL NAME: Edward "Eddie" Brock Jr.
KNOWN ALIASES: "The Suit"
IDENTITY: Secret
OCCUPATION: Student
CITIZENSHIP: U.S.A.
PLACE OF BIRTH: New York City
KNOWN RELATIVES: Edward Brock (father, deceased), unnamed mother (deceased), unnamed grandparents
GROUP AFFILIATION: None
EDUCATION: College student, extensive Bioengineering studies
FIRST APPEARANCE: Ultimate Spider-Man #33 (2003)

HISTORY: Eddie Brock was the son of a brilliant scientist who teamed with Richard Parker to create a protoplasmic dip nicknamed "The Suit," designed as a cure for cancer; but the Suit's potential as a weapon tempted financiers Trask Industries, who seized control of the project. Mostly unaware of his father's troubles, Eddie befriended Parker's son, the slightly younger Peter. When both sets of parents were killed in a tragic plane crash, Eddie went to live with his grandparents and lost contact with Peter for years. Eddie's grandfather eventually gave him a frozen sample of the Suit, hidden away by Ed Brock Sr. Eddie threw himself into a study of his father's work, seeing it as a way to connect with his lost parent. This pursuit eventually led him to Empire State University and a close relationship with Doctor Curt Conners, who helped Eddie study the Suit, dubbed the Venom Project.

While Eddie's academic career seemed to take off, his personal life was in shambles. Plagued by a quick temper and an inability to connect with women on any level, Eddie became isolated. When his old friend Peter Parker contacted him, he felt a rush of enthusiasm: here, at last, was someone with whom he could truly bond. Eddie shared the secret of the Suit with Peter, but was shocked when he saw a black-suited Spider-Man on the news shortly thereafter. Already frustrated by his failed attempt to seduce Gwen Stacy, an angry Eddie raced back to the lab where he caught Peter taking the rest of the dip, intent on destroying it. Expressing a deep sense of betrayal, Eddie felt that Peter was stealing the only thing his father had left him. Parker tried to warn Eddie of the Suit's dangers, including its powerful hunger for violence, but Eddie was unconvinced. After Parker left to destroy the Suit, Eddie pulled a second sample out of storage and allowed the black liquid to flow over him. The intense pain may have mentally damaged Eddie, who immediately killed a female custodian and two campus security guards. In his new form, Brock began stalking Peter and finally lured him into battle. Eddie felt that the Suit craved Peter and he wanted to force Peter to take it from him. Caught in a crossfire of police bullets and accidentally electrocuted by a downed power line, Brock was seemingly killed; but his belongings later disappeared from his dorm room, leading Peter to believe that his old friend is still alive.

HEIGHT: 5'11"
WEIGHT: 175 lbs.
EYES: Blue
HAIR: Blond

SUPERHUMAN POWERS: Venom's powers all stem from the suit that has bonded to Brock. The suit was designed to restore and rebuild damaged body tissues, granting Venom tremendous regenerative abilities and augmenting his physical abilities. It can also project organic "webbing," and is capable of limited shapeshifting.

ABILITIES: Eddie has a natural aptitude for bioengineering.

POWER GRID	1	2	3	4	5	6	7
INTELLIGENCE							
STRENGTH							
SPEED							
DURABILITY							
ENERGY PROJECTION							
FIGHTING SKILLS							

Art by Mark Bagley

ACADEMY OF TOMORROW

HISTORY: Able to assume an unbreakable crystalline form, Emma Frost was a former student and lover of fellow mutant Charles Xavier. She broke up with him after disagreeing over Homo Superior's role in society. Charles felt mutants could avoid racial conflict with humanity by policing themselves, while Emma felt mutants must become role models and educators. Emma moved to Chicago, becoming a schoolteacher and running mutant education seminars. After the public debut of Xavier's X-Men, Emma approached the government with a proposal to create a group of popular, attractive mutant spokespeople from various backgrounds and ethnicities to win over public opinion and launch her education campaign. Though a number of her candidates were rejected, the President approved her plan. She recruited Alex Summers, elder brother to the X-Men's Cyclops, an energy generator who had turned down Xavier's school; Alison Blaire, lead singer of the punk band Dazzler, who could absorb sound and generate light; and Hank McCoy, a.k.a. Beast, a disenchanted Xavier dropout. At the President's behest, Emma also added S.H.I.E.L.D. Black Ops agent Xi'an Coy Mahn, codename Karma, who could possess people. However, at the group's press launch on the Capitol steps, rogue government elements that feared mutants influencing the President unleashed Sentinels. Beast was killed saving others from the Sentinel attack. The X-Men intervened to destroy the Sentinels, and Karma revealed Nick Fury had placed her in the group to uncover the anti-mutant conspiracy within the President's inner circle. In the aftermath, Frost and her remaining charges moved into Xavier's estate to re-evaluate their mission.

After a brief stay, Frost and Alex departed for Chicago, still feeling the X-Men were taking the wrong path. Frost established the Academy of Tomorrow, which accepted all outstanding individuals, mutant or not. Among her new students were computer genius Doug Ramsey; mutant speedster Jean-Paul Beaubier, a.k.a. Northstar, son of the Canadian ambassador; Alex's magnetic-powered girlfriend Lorna Dane (Polaris); Sam Guthrie (Cannonball), able to generate a protective forcefield and fly; and Roberto DaCosta, known as Sunspot because he could generate solar blasts. While trying to rescue people from a fire, Polaris seemingly lost control of her powers, causing the deaths of three people. To prevent all her students being arrested, Emma handed Polaris over to S.H.I.E.L.D., who incarcerated her in the Triskelion. Her loss of control was actually due to a device planted by Brotherhood of Mutant's Forge, who knew that due to the similar nature of their powers, she would be imprisoned in same cell as Magneto. While Doug tried to figure out the real reason Polaris had lost control, the rest of her classmates decided to break her out. Learning of these plans, the X-Men moved to intercept the Academy students before they turned themselves into fugitives, but instead both groups ended up clashing with one another and the Ultimates, unwittingly providing a distraction which enabled the Brotherhood to free Magneto. In the aftermath of the Academy's incursion into the Triskelion Polaris was freed thanks to evidence found by Doug; Nick Fury would have imprisoned Havok for leading the break-in, but the X-Man Wolverine blackmailed Fury into dropping the charges. Angel joined the Academy, apparently expelled from Xavier's but in truth acting as an undercover operative for Professor X, who believed Emma could not be trusted to keep an eye on her students. And the openly gay Northstar asked Colossus to the Homecoming Dance, finally giving the metallic X-Man the courage to come out to his team-mates.

CURRENT MEMBERS: Angel (Warren Worthington III), Cannonball (Sam Guthrie), Emma Frost, Havok (Alex Summers), Northstar (Jean Paul Beaubier), Polaris (Lorna Dane), Doug Ramsey, Sunspot (Roberto DaCosta)
FORMER MEMBERS: Beast (Henry McCoy), Dazzler (Alison Blaire), Karma (Xi'an Coy Mahn)
BASE OF OPERATIONS: Chicago
FIRST APPEARANCE: (as Emma Frost's "new mutants") Ultimate X-Men #44 (2004); (as Academy of Tomorrow) Ultimate X-Men #62 (2005)

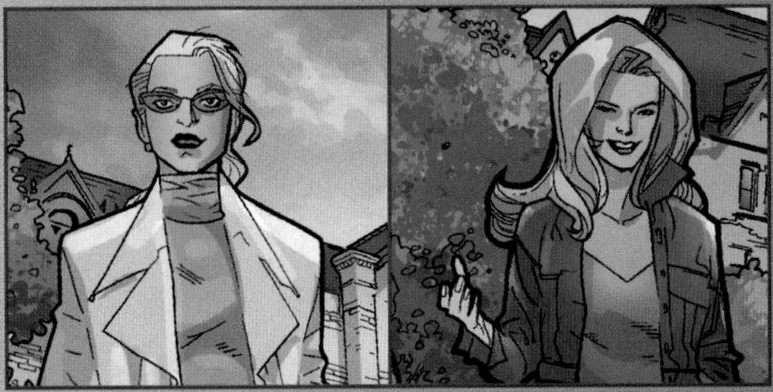

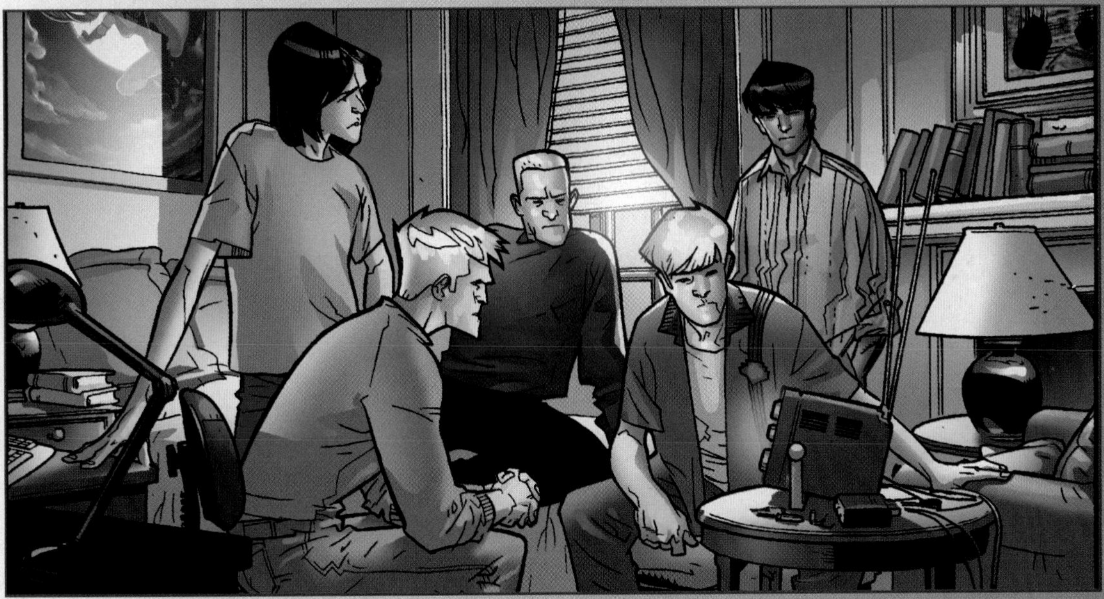

Art by Stuart Immonen

ANGEL

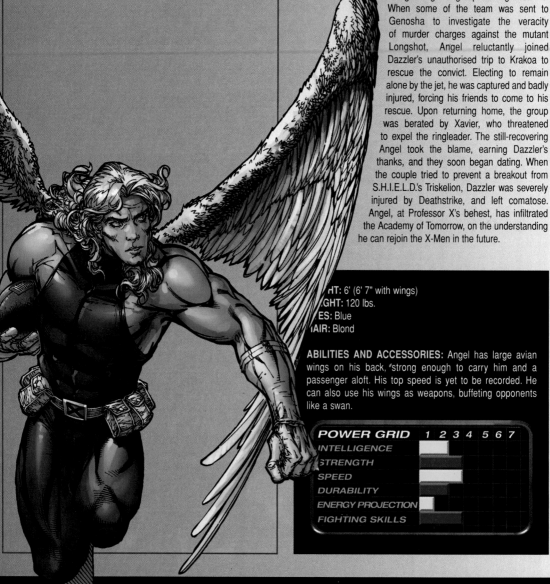

REAL NAME: Warren Worthington III
KNOWN ALIASES: Captain Eagle, War
IDENTITY: Publicly known
OCCUPATION: Student
CITIZENSHIP: U.S.A.
PLACE OF BIRTH: Unrevealed
KNOWN RELATIVES: Charles Xavier (legal guardian), parents (names unrevealed)
GROUP AFFILIATION: Academy of Tomorrow; formerly X-Men
EDUCATION: Currently undertaking college level classes
FIRST APPEARANCE: Ultimate X-Men #40 (2004)

HISTORY: Though Warren Worthington III's bigoted parents claimed to love their son, they could not cope with his visible mutation (a huge pair of wings) and had him raised by servants on a secluded private estate. They considered risky surgery, but when Warren's father heard of the Xavier Institute, he hastily unloaded his problem son, paying Charles Xavier to become Warren's legal guardian. Warren's arrival at the Institute caused a stir. Teammate Rogue felt that an "angel" in their midst might be a sign. This feeling was shared by religious pro- and anti-mutant groups who demonstrated outside within days of his arrival, having read about him from Beast's website. Feeling like an outsider, and mistaking his female teammates' stares for disgust rather than admiring glances, Warren flew away. Storm convinced him to return, and he informed the demonstrators that he was not a religious figure, merely a mutant, ending their interest.

Now codenamed Angel, Warren asked Wolverine to teach him combat skills. The first time they sparred, Angel panicked, unprepared for combat. Though he felt ill suited for battle, he soon went through a baptism of fire, overcoming his fears to help his teammates fight a Sentinel robot. When serial killer Sinister invaded Xavier's school, Angel proved his mettle, confronting him solo and successfully disarming him before Sinister regained the upper hand with his hypnotic power. Rogue finally subdued the villain, and Sinister's assault failed.

Angel soon formed strong friendships with his fellow X-Men, covertly playing Captain Eagle to Nightcrawler's Dread Pirate Bluetail in secret Danger Room adventures, and taking charge in group training sessions. When some of the team was sent to Genosha to investigate the veracity of murder charges against the mutant Longshot, Angel reluctantly joined Dazzler's unauthorised trip to Krakoa to rescue the convict. Electing to remain alone by the jet, he was captured and badly injured, forcing his friends to come to his rescue. Upon returning home, the group was berated by Xavier, who threatened to expel the ringleader. The still-recovering Angel took the blame, earning Dazzler's thanks, and they soon began dating. When the couple tried to prevent a breakout from S.H.I.E.L.D.'s Triskelion, Dazzler was severely injured by Deathstrike, and left comatose. Angel, at Professor X's behest, has infiltrated the Academy of Tomorrow, on the understanding he can rejoin the X-Men in the future.

HT: 6' (6' 7" with wings)
WGHT: 120 lbs.
ES: Blue
AIR: Blond

ABILITIES AND ACCESSORIES: Angel has large avian wings on his back, strong enough to carry him and a passenger aloft. His top speed is yet to be recorded. He can also use his wings as weapons, buffeting opponents like a swan.

POWER GRID	1	2	3	4	5	6	7
INTELLIGENCE							
STRENGTH							
SPEED							
DURABILITY							
ENERGY PROJECTION							
FIGHTING SKILLS							

Art by Brandon Peterson

HISTORY: Henry McCoy grew up taunted as "Monkey Boy" and "Joe Bananas" because of his apelike appearance; when he was identified as a mutant, his parents rejected him as well. In his late teens he was recruited by Jean Grey (Marvel Girl) and dubbed Beast, becoming a founding member of Charles Xavier's X-Men. He helped rescue Bobby Drake (Iceman) from Sentinels in Times Square and fell in love with his teammate Storm, though low self esteem prevented him from openly expressing it. When the X-Men battled the Brotherhood of Mutants in Croatia to rescue the U.S. President's kidnapped daughter, Beast was critically injured. A revolutionary transplant technique saved his life, but a side effect turned his hair blue. In spite of this close call, he soon returned to action when Magneto led a Sentinel attack on Washington, an attack that ended in Magneto's apparent death. Beast and Storm became an item, though he couldn't understand why such a beautiful girl would be interested in a "fat guy."

When the X-Men were abducted by rogue government agency Weapon X, Doctor Cornelius enhanced Beast's animalistic qualities, leaving him with blue fur, claws and fangs. Even more insecure about his looks, Beast began an online correspondence with "Naomi," actually the Brotherhood's Blob playing a prank. After rogue telepath David Xavier claimed his father Charles had made Storm fall for Hank in order to keep Hank in the school, Beast shut Storm out, fearing it was true; he increasingly confided in Naomi, eventually revealing Magneto's survival. The Brotherhood ambushed Beast, beating him until he disclosed Magneto's location. With Magneto's return, the X-Men became fugitives, hunted by the authorities, battling S.H.I.E.L.D. and the Ultimates; they finally redeemed themselves by recapturing Magneto and preventing him from destroying Florida. With the X-Men recognized as heroes, Hank was shocked to find his parents now accepted him, though he realized they merely wished to cash in on his newfound fame. Renewing his relationship with Storm, Beast continued to be active on the Internet , carelessly discussing the X-Men's angelic new recruit Warren Worthington on his fan website. When religious demonstrations ensued, Hank's teammates berated him for his foolishness. Feeling insecure again, and aware of the handsome Warren's attraction to Storm, Beast quit the X-Men after he was approached for Emma Frost's new mutant spokesperson

REAL NAME: Henry "Hank" McCoy
KNOWN ALIASES: Beast666, X11
IDENTITY: Publicly known
OCCUPATION: Student, adventurer
CITIZENSHIP: U.S.A.
PLACE OF BIRTH: Unrevealed
KNOWN RELATIVES: Norton McCoy (father), mother (name unrevealed)
GROUP AFFILIATION: Emma Frost's "new mutants;" X-Men
EDUCATION: College graduate, taking post-graduate courses at time of death
FIRST APPEARANCE: Ultimate X-Men #1 (2001)

program. At the group's public unveiling, a rogue government faction released a Sentinel; while trying to get others to safety, Beast was struck by debris and killed. He was buried in the Xavier Mansion grounds in a private ceremony; his parents did not bother to attend.

HEIGHT: 5'7"
WEIGHT: 180 lbs.
EYES: Blue; (originally) Brown
HAIR: Blue; (originally) Black

DISTINGUISHING FEATURES: Covered in blue fur

ABILITIES AND ACCESSORIES: Beast was exceptionally agile, a skilled acrobat and superhumanly strong. His clawed hands and prehensile feet made him an excellent climber. Weapon X's experiments heightened his sense of smell.

POWER GRID	1	2	3	4	5	6	7
INTELLIGENCE							
STRENGTH							
SPEED							
DURABILITY							
ENERGY PROJECTION							
FIGHTING SKILLS							

BLACK WIDOW

REAL NAME: Natalia Romanova
KNOWN ALIASES: Natasha Romanov (anglicised name), Nanci Roman, countless other aliases
IDENTITY: Known to various authorities
OCCUPATION: U.S. government super-operative; former freelance spy, K.G.B. agent
CITIZENSHIP: Russia (plus fabricated U.S. status)
PLACE OF BIRTH: St. Petersburg, Russia
KNOWN RELATIVES: Alexi Shostakov (husband, deceased), other ex-husbands (deceased), Tony Stark (fiancé)
GROUP AFFILIATION: Ultimates, S.H.I.E.L.D., former K.G.B. agent
EDUCATION: Graduate of the Red Room (Moscow's spy academy)
FIRST APPEARANCE: Ultimate Marvel Team-Up #14 (2002)

HISTORY: A descendant of Russian royalty, Natasha Romanov was abandoned as a child and found by soldier Ivan Petrovich. A ballerina in her youth, she joined Russia's K.G.B. and became an elite intelligence operative, a combination of consummate skill and classified government enhancements of her natural abilities. She also became infamous as an often-wed, often-widowed heartbreaker whose husbands (beginning with test pilot turned intelligence agent Alexi Shostakov) tended to suffer "unfortunate accidents," a quirk which may have influenced her choice of long-term code name: the Black Widow. She eventually embarked on a lucrative freelance spy career, which culminated in her infiltration of New York City's Latverian Embassy. Manipulating the naïve young superhero Spider-Man into helping her escape Latverian security, Natasha used the information she gathered to audition successfully for the American-based international spy agency S.H.I.E.L.D. She became a mainstay of S.H.I.E.L.D.'s black ops division, often partnered with Hawkeye (Clint Barton).

After Hawkeye and the Widow exterminated over five hundred Chitauri extraterrestrial subversives, the duo was promoted to the ranks of the Ultimates, S.H.I.E.L.D.'s celebrity super-agents, helping save Earth from a Chitauri plot. Widow and teammate Iron Man (wealthy genius Tony Stark) became lovers, though Natasha feuded with Stark's butler, Edwin Jarvis. Giving Natasha the female equivalent of his Iron Man battle armor, Stark asked her to marry him and she said yes. More recently, a traitor within the Ultimates has leaked secrets, framed Captain America for slaughtering Hawkeye's family, and helped a foreign super-army conquer both the Ultimates and America. At the same time, Natasha has suddenly, violently turned against Tony for reasons unknown.

HEIGHT: 5'7"
WEIGHT: 125 lbs.
EYES: Green
HAIR: Red-auburn

SUPERHUMAN POWERS: Black Widow's physical and mental abilities — notably her speed, agility, reflexes, stamina, recall and concentration — have been enhanced slightly beyond human limits through unspecified secret technologies. Nanites recently bonded to her body enable her to link with and control her Stark-designed battle armor. The Black Widow is a master martial artist, an expert markswoman, a natural actress, an infamous seductress, and a gifted veteran spy. She carries assorted firearms and various miniaturized tools and weapons, such as communications equipment, tear gas pellets, various drugs, an electrostatic discharge weapon, spring-loaded cables and surveillance devices; her costuming has also included microscopic suction cups enabling her to cling to walls and ceilings. Her Stark-designed armor gives her tremendous superhuman strength and durability, the capacity for supersonic flight, and assorted built-in weapons such as repulsor rays, wrist-mounted machine guns and mind-impairing "thought-scramblers."

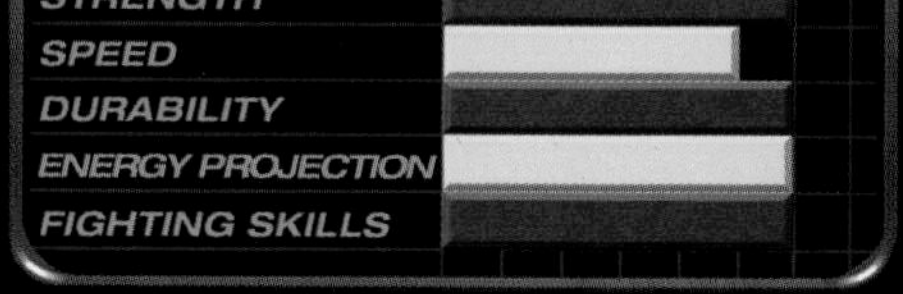

POWER GRID	1	2	3	4	5	6	7
INTELLIGENCE							
STRENGTH							
SPEED							
DURABILITY							
ENERGY PROJECTION							
FIGHTING SKILLS							

BETSY BRADDOCK

HISTORY: While her brother Brian became a scientist like their father, Sir James Braddock, Betsy Braddock chose another path. A mutant telepath, she used her family name to avoid Sentinel attack and joined the Psi Division of S.T.R.I.K.E., the British division of the international espionage agency S.H.I.E.L.D. She swiftly rose to the rank of Colonel.

When the telepathic, reality-warping mutant David Xavier escaped the medical facility on Scotland's remote Muir Island, killing several people in the process, Betsy and Agent Dai Thomas were assigned to recapture him. They placed Moira MacTaggert, David's mother and facility head, under house arrest until Charles Xavier, her estranged husband and David's father, arrived on the island with his students, the X-Men. The elder Xavier's psi powers swiftly located his son, and the group cornered David inside a Burger King in Aberdeen. David took possession of Wolverine's form and cut a swath through the X-Men, until Storm hit him with a lightning bolt and Betsy stunned him with a psychic grenade. David fled, jumping out of Wolverine and into the driver of an oncoming truck; right after the vehicle crashed, he jumped into Betsy's mind.

Hidden within Betsy, David lured his parents and the X-Men to Germany, claiming that her psychic powers had tracked him there; however, Charles confronted him after realizing "Betsy's" mannerisms were those of a teenage boy, not an adult woman. David dropped the charade, took his parents hostage and transformed Betsy's body to resemble his own. He defeated the X-Men, but as he tried to kill Charles, Betsy's personality kicked in, jamming his powers. She told Charles he had to kill her before David could regain control, or flee; Charles refused, but the X-Man Colossus crushed Betsy with a car, killing her body and apparently slaying both the minds within.

Betsy, however, escaped the reaper; her mind made contact with Kwannon, a young Asian woman. Kwannon was relieved to have a chance to finally move on after ten years in a coma, and let Betsy claim her body. Awakening, she called her father, who had only just buried her and was overjoyed to find his daughter alive, whatever her form. Returning to active S.T.R.I.K.E. duty, Betsy was redeployed to help assemble the European Defence Initiative. She later met Colossus at a Xavier Institute reception, and told him she did not blame him for killing her, and in fact had found dying a fascinating experience.

REAL NAME: Colonel Betsy Braddock
KNOWN ALIASES: None
IDENTITY: No dual identity
OCCUPATION: S.T.R.I.K.E. agent
CITIZENSHIP: U.K.
PLACE OF BIRTH: U.K.
KNOWN RELATIVES: Sir James Braddock (father), mother (name unrevealed), Brian Braddock (Captain Britain, brother)
GROUP AFFILIATION: S.T.R.I.K.E. Psi Division
EDUCATION: Unknown
FIRST APPEARANCE: Ultimate X-Men #16 (2002)

HEIGHT: (Betsy) 5'8"; (Kwannon) 5'7"
WEIGHT: (Betsy) 130 lbs.; (Kwannon) 125 lbs.
EYES: (both bodies) Brown
HAIR: (both bodies) Black

ABILITIES AND ACCESSORIES: Betsy is telepathic and can set off "psychic grenades" in people's heads, leaving them weak and nauseous and incapacitating them for lengthy periods.

POWER GRID	1	2	3	4	5	6	7
INTELLIGENCE							
STRENGTH							
SPEED							
DURABILITY							
ENERGY PROJECTION							
FIGHTING SKILLS							

BROTHERHOOD OF MUTANTS

FORMER MEMBERS: Blob, Cyclops (Scott Summers), Detonator (Ricky Gibson), Forge, Hard-Drive, HHVX, Juggernaut (Cain), Kathleen, Magneto (Erik Lensherr), Mastermind, Multiple Man, Mystique, Orb-Weaver, Prosimian, Quicksilver (Pietro Lensherr Maximoff), Rogue (Marian), Sabretooth, Saluki, Scarlet Witch (Wanda Lensherr Maximoff), Sumatran, Toad, Unus, Vanisher, Wolverine (James Howlett), Professor Charles Xavier; many unidentified others
BASE OF OPERATIONS: Unknown; formerly the Citadel, Arctic Circle; Savage Land; San Francisco mansion
FIRST APPEARANCE: Ultimate X-Men #1 (2001)

HISTORY: Nearly a decade ago, Charles Xavier and Erik Lensherr founded a sanctuary for persecuted mutants: the Brotherhood of Mutants. They viewed it as a school, but others considered it a cult. Feeling unsafe in their San Francisco mansion, they relocated to the Savage Land, a remote Pacific island, to build a new community. However, Lensherr, now calling himself Magneto, came to believe that mutantkind should eliminate mankind for the good of the planet. Fearing Magneto would provoke a genocidal war, Xavier fled back to the States, though Magneto crippled him before he left. While Xavier was recovering, the Brotherhood launched its first terrorist attack when Detonator blew up part of the Pentagon.

After several years of similar attacks, Magneto openly declared his plans to supplant humanity, generating anti-mutant hysteria and provoking the U.S. government to unleash giant Sentinel robots, which indiscriminately killed any mutant they found. The Brotherhood responded by kidnapping the President's daughter, threatening to kill her if another mutant was slain. She was rescued by Xavier's new students, the X-Men, and the grateful President halted the Sentinel hunts.

The disillusioned X-Man Cyclops defected to the Brotherhood, feeling that Xavier was currying favor with an enemy regime. In response to plans for British Sentinels, he helped the Brotherhood bomb the British Houses of Parliament and MI6 building in London, though he tried to limit human casualties. The U.S.A. found the Savage Land and launched a massive Sentinel attack, but Magneto reprogrammed them and attacked Washington. The X-Men and his own son, Quicksilver, halted Magneto's genocidal plan. With Magneto believed dead, Quicksilver led a less murderous Brotherhood. When the X-Men were captured by Weapon X, the Brotherhood freed them; many of Weapon X's liberated mutant captives joined the Brotherhood. They freed sentient mutant animals and attacked financial institutions. Quicksilver called a cease fire, and held talks with the U.N.

Splinter groups such as the Acolytes broke from the Brotherhood and resumed terrorism. Asserting his authority, Quicksilver led the Brotherhood in disarming the nuclear arsenals of Pakistan and India. Certain followers such as militant animal evolutionary Prosimian remained dissatisfied, and, learning his death had been faked, they tracked down an amnesiac Magneto and restored his memories. Magneto promptly "purified" the Brotherhood by slaying the evolved animals who had rescued him. He re-launched the bombing campaign, and gave humanity six months to surrender. Fearing their father's retaliation, Quicksilver and Scarlet Witch defected to the Ultimates. Based in the Citadel in the Arctic Circle, Magneto plotted to destroy the established world by reversing Earth's magnetic fields. Forge built a power boosting device, and other Brotherhood members stole art treasures and recruited more mutants. The X-Men thwarted this plan, Magneto was apprehended, and much of the Brotherhood dispersed. Some of the Brotherhood, Forge and Mystique, subsequently helped arrange Magneto's jailbreak. Magneto has informed his newest follower, Longshot, that he has no intentions of reforming the Brotherhood.

CAPTAIN AMERICA

HISTORY: Steve Rogers grew up in Brooklyn, a scrawny kid protected from neighborhood bullies by his best friend "Bucky" Barnes. Enlisting around the time the United States entered World War II, Steve voluntarily underwent six months of steroids, surgery, and other experimental treatments supervised by Dr. Erskine, becoming the world's first genetically-enhanced super-soldier. The authorities seemed unable to replicate the process thereafter. Clad in stars-and-strips military fatigues, he became "Captain America," his image used to bolster Allied recruiting.

Over the next three years Captain America undertook numerous covert operations, often accompanied by Bucky, now a war photographer, and sometimes alongside Canadian "Lucky" Jim Howlett (later the X-Men's Wolverine). In Poland in 1944 he battled Kleiser, one of the Nazi's secret extraterrestrial Chitauri masters, blowing up a train delivering parts for a super weapon. A year later, he led an assault on an Icelandic base where the Nazis were launching a prototype nuclear bomb at the White House. As the rocket launched, he climbed aboard and wrecked its guidance system, causing it to explode seconds later. Though believed dead, Steve was thrown clear into the icy Arctic waters. Rather than dying, he seemingly fell into suspended animation and was found decades later by a team of marine biologists.

Steve awoke in a S.H.I.E.L.D facility, and was soon appointed leader of the Ultimates, America's new superhuman strike force. Struggling to adjust to 21st century life, he helped subdue the rampaging Hulk and attempted to recruit Hawk-Owl, coming to blows with the Chicago vigilante. After teammate Giant Man abused and nearly killed his wife, the Wasp, Steve tracked him down and hospitalized him. When the Chitauri resurfaced, Steve led a successful counterattack during which he duped the Hulk into slaying Kleiser. Soon after this mission, he and the Wasp became a couple.

Captain America has led the Ultimates against the Brotherhood of Mutants, the X-Men, and Norman Osborn's "Six" (super-criminals mostly empowered by failed attempts to reproduce the super-soldier process). On a Tunguska expedition he learned of a Soviet super-soldier project and fought a man who claimed to be his Russian counterpart. When his former teammate Thor seemingly betrayed

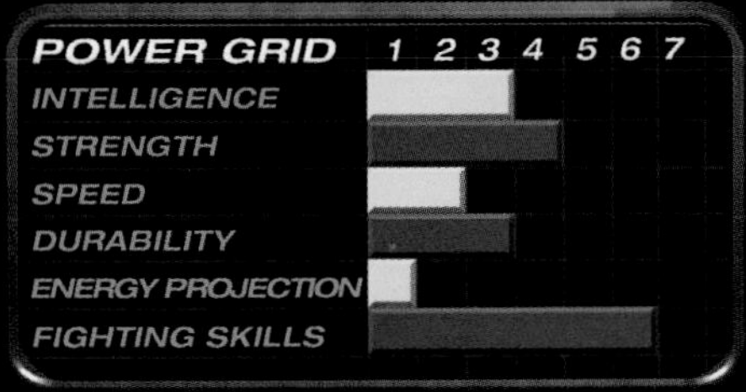

REAL NAME: Steve Rogers
KNOWN ALIASES: None
IDENTITY: Publicly known
OCCUPATION: Soldier, U.S. government super-operative
CITIZENSHIP: U.S.A.
PLACE OF BIRTH: Brooklyn, New York
KNOWN RELATIVES: Joseph Harvey Rogers (father, deceased), Sarah Alicia Rogers (mother, deceased), Douglas Lincoln Rogers (brother, deceased), unidentified nephew (deceased), unidentified niece, unidentified nephew-in-law
GROUP AFFILIATION: Ultimates; formerly U.S. Armed Forces
EDUCATION: Unrevealed
FIRST APPEARANCE: Ultimates #1 (2002)

the Ultimates, Steve angrily confronted Thor, and later led the team in capturing him. Ironically, Steve himself was soon after accused of betraying the team, murdering Hawkeye, and not truly being the W.W. II hero; he has been taken into S.H.I.E.L.D. custody.

HEIGHT: 6'3"
WEIGHT: 250 lbs.
EYES: Blue
HAIR: Blond

ABILITIES AND ACCESSORIES: Captain America has enhanced strength, speed, endurance, agility and regenerative capacity; even severe injuries heal in days. A tactical and strategic genius, he has mastered numerous fighting forms and weapons, and can operate most standard military vehicles. His costume is bulletproof Kevlar, and he carries a metallic, round, bulletproof shield.

POWER GRID	1	2	3	4	5	6	7
INTELLIGENCE							
STRENGTH							
SPEED							
DURABILITY							
ENERGY PROJECTION							
FIGHTING SKILLS							

CAPTAIN BRITAIN

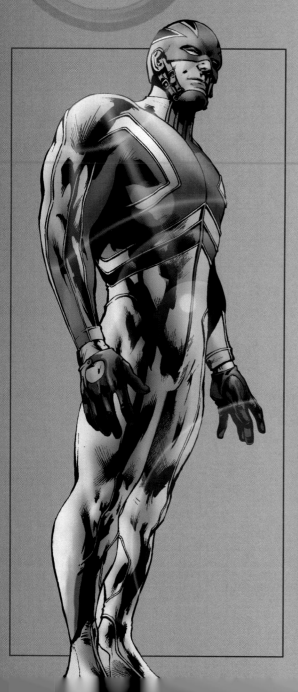

REAL NAME: Brian Braddock
KNOWN ALIASES: None
IDENTITY: Secret
OCCUPATION: Scientist, government agent
CITIZENSHIP: U.K.
PLACE OF BIRTH: U.K.
KNOWN RELATIVES: Sir James Braddock (father), mother (name unrevealed), Betsy Braddock (sister)
GROUP AFFILIATION: European Defense Initiative, presumably the Corps
EDUCATION: PhD
FIRST APPEARANCE: (as Braddock) Ultimate X-Men #19 (2002); (as Captain Britain) Ultimates 2 #2 (2005)

HISTORY: As a teenager, Brian Braddock was fascinated by the World War II super-soldier Captain America, even hanging a poster of the hero in his room at Fettes College, his Edinburgh boarding school. Inheriting the scientific aptitude of his bio-engineer father, Sir James Braddock, Brian eventually joined him at the Dome in Brussels, working for the European Defence Initiative's super-soldier program. Each member country provided a team that worked on its own designs, with the elder Braddock overseeing the project as a whole. Brian worked on designing an exo-suit which could enhance the wearer's abilities. Allegedly Thorlief Golman stole the Norwegian team's successful prototypes to become Thor. Despite this setback, the project continued working to create a European Union equivalent of the Ultimates taskforce forming in the United States.

Personal tragedy hit the Braddocks when Brian's sister Betsy, a Psi agent of S.T.R.I.K.E. (the British branch of S.H.I.E.L.D.), was possessed by the rogue mutant David Xavier and slain by the X-Men, though the family soon learned she had survived by taking over the body of a long-term coma victim. Soon after this, Brian perfected his armor and took the codename Captain Britain. With twelve other candidates from the E.U. member states in various states of readiness, the E.D.I. prepared to go public. One of Brian's earliest missions prior to this unveiling was to raise a downed submarine, assisted by two fellow E.D.I. agents and the Ultimates' Iron Man.

Weeks later, S.H.I.E.L.D. decided Thor had become a dangerous liability who needed to be apprehended. The four combat-ready E.D.I. super-soldiers — Captain Britain, Captain Spain (Carlos Fraile), Captain France (Hugo Etherlinck) and Captain Italy (Umberto Landi) — accompanied the Ultimates to Norway to confront Thor. After a protracted melee, the European super-soldiers helped their allies strip Thor of his belt, the source of his powers, and placed Thor in custody. Soon after, the entire E.D.I. team helped the Ultimates invade and disarm a rogue Middle Eastern state.

HEIGHT: 6'3"
WEIGHT: 250 lbs.
EYES: Blue
HAIR: Blond

ABILITIES AND ACCESSORIES: Captain Britain's exo-suit allows him to fly at supersonic speeds and enhances his physical attributes, giving him superhuman strength, endurance and durability.

POWER GRID	1	2	3	4	5	6	7
INTELLIGENCE							
STRENGTH							
SPEED							
DURABILITY							
ENERGY PROJECTION							
FIGHTING SKILLS							

CAPTAIN MAHR VEHL

HISTORY: For millennia an ancient extraterrestrial race called the Kree have tracked and studied a mysterious planet-eating creature they called Gah Lak Tus. The Supreme Intelligence restricted this knowledge to specially trained high-level Kree, fearing that if the true nature of Gah Lak Tus became common knowledge, it would drive their race insane. Several years before Gah Lak Tus was due to arrive in the Sol system, the Kree staged a covert observation mission on Earth and Pluskommander Mahr Vehl underwent massive nanosurgery to appear human, going undercover as physicist Dr. Philip Lawson to investigate the human race. Growing fond of humans, Vehl joined S.H.I.E.L.D.'s Asis program to speed up humanity's progress to the stars, helping develop a zero point energy source for manned space flight.

On the day the Asis 01 test article was to be launched, the base was attacked by a Kree killform with orders for Vehl to aid humanity no further. Refusing, Vehl slew the killform, but the effort left him powerless and he was captured by S.H.I.E.L.D. After questioning by General Nick Fury and Captain Carol Danvers, Vehl briefed them, the Fantastic Four, Iron Man and Thor regarding the existence of a Gah Lak Tus database aboard his ship. Vehl led a strikeforce consisting of Mr. Fantastic, Invisible Girl, Hawkeye and Iron Man to steal the database while Fury, Danvers, Thor, Human Torch, Thing, Black Widow and S.H.I.E.L.D. forces engaged the Kree soldiers on Earth. Vehl transferred the database into Iron Man's computers and the team escaped the spacecraft moments before a self-destruct sequence initiated by the insane Shipthane Yahn Rgg destroyed the ship. Under the watchful eyes of his bodyguard Danvers, Vehl aided the Falcon in deciphering the database to learn the true nature of the threat they were facing.

REAL NAME: Geheneris HalaSon Mahr Vehl
KNOWN ALIASES: Captain Marvel, Doctor Philip Lawson
IDENTITY: Publicly known (Kree territories); known to authorities (Earth)
OCCUPATION: Pluskommander in the Kree Void Navy; (as Lawson) physicist
CITIZENSHIP: Kree citizen
PLACE OF BIRTH: Unrevealed, presumably the Kree territories
KNOWN RELATIVES: Geheneris Kohl HalaSon (3father/trial-father)
GROUP AFFILIATION: S.H.I.E.L.D.; formerly the ship Night's Inquiry
EDUCATION: Unknown
FIRST APPEARANCE: Ultimate Secret #1 (2005)

HEIGHT: (Kree) 7'; (human) 5'9"
WEIGHT: (Kree) 350 lbs.; (human) 200 lbs.
EYES: (Kree) Glowing white; (human) green
HAIR: (Kree) None; (human) black

DISTINGUISHING FEATURES: Vehl's original form has translucent dark aquamarine skin, four-fingered hands the length of his forearm with a thumb on either side of his palm, webbing beneath his arms, four-toed anisodactyl feet, 'cobra-like' neck, a head fin, and a mouth full of sharp teeth.

ABILITIES AND ACCESSORIES: Vehl's cybersurgery allows him to change between his original and human forms. He can be changed against his will in to his original form until he gets a chance to reboot his cybersytems. Vehl has unspecified combat training, and sufficient physics knowledge to pass as a top human scientist. Vehl has an implanted device that looks like a wristwatch when in human guise. It allows him to access Kree technology, such as contact lenses used to see through invisibility shields and his uniform which has flight capabilities, energy shields, invisibility shields, and an onboard totalkannon.

POWER GRID	1	2	3	4	5	6	7
INTELLIGENCE							
STRENGTH							
SPEED							
DURABILITY							
ENERGY PROJECTION							
FIGHTING SKILLS							

CHITAURI

KNOWN MEMBERS: Kleiser, Gunther, Siegfried, Suverkrubb, Wigbert, countless others (Earth contingent apparently largely deceased)
BASE OF OPERATIONS: Active throughout the universe
FIRST APPEARANCE: Ultimates #8 (2002)

HISTORY: The Chitauri are an ancient, technologically advanced race of extraterrestrial fanatics dedicated to controlling all other life in the universe, eradicating that which they cannot control. Determined to bring harmony to the universe since the dawn of time, they regard themselves as the universe's immune system, purging diseases such as chaos, disorder and independent thought. Dubbed the Chitauri by Africans who encountered them on Earth, these aliens have been known as the Annakui or Skrulls on other worlds. Within their own society, they have little use for individual names or personalities, functioning as a collective with shared goals and values; however, they do assume identities while infiltrating the races of other worlds. They can replicate the appearance of other life forms, but must consume their victims first in order to assume their shapes. In their natural state, the Chitauri are eight feet tall and reptilian in appearance. At least some of them possess enhanced strength, durability, senses, and regenerative powers. Their ruling class apparently possesses these traits in greater abundance than the rank and file. They reportedly spend at least part of their lives in realms beyond three-dimensional space, but use their shape-shifting powers to assume forms better suited to three dimensions when operating within our reality.

One of at least eleven different extraterrestrial species known to be active on Earth, the Chitauri came to this planet in 1777 and have been responsible for multiple genocidal disasters. In World War II, they secretly supported Germany's Nazi party and its leader, Adolf Hitler. The leader of Earth's Chitauri contingent, in human form as the Nazi officer Kleiser, repeatedly battled the Allied super-soldier Captain America, who opposed Chitauri efforts to create nuclear weapons for the Nazis. After blowing up a Nazi/Chitauri supply train full of weapons components in 1944, Captain America thwarted the 1945 launch of a Nazi/Chitauri nuclear missile aimed at Washington, throwing it off course and detonating it in the sky above the North Atlantic, seemingly sacrificing his life. Earth's Chitauri were apparently wiped out during the latter stages of the war, purged from Europe and Africa, their training camps bombed at Hiroshima and Nagasaki. A few Chitauri survived and went underground — slowly, subtly, secretly undermining human society from within, lacing drinking water supplies with thought-dampening chemicals, inserting mind-influencing devices into popular new technologies, and placing their operatives in key positions of influence.

In recent years, the intelligence agency S.H.I.E.L.D. and its Ultimates superhuman strike force (including a revived Captain America) became aware of continued Chitauri activity on Earth. After agents Hawkeye and Black Widow wiped out a nest of 528 Chitauri sleeper agents in New York, S.H.I.E.L.D. recovered intelligence leading to an explosively booby-trapped Chitauri base in Micronesia. Twenty thousand S.H.I.E.L.D. troops died, but the core Ultimates team survived. Meanwhile, Kleiser's Chitauri force took over the Ultimates' Triskelion headquarters, planning to accelerate their subversive activities by taki over S.H.I.E.L.D. from within. Plans changed when a massive Chita invasion fleet arrived. They informed their Earth-based brethren that th were fighting a losing war with other enemies throughout the univers and that they didn't have time to convert Earth. They swiftly assemble bomb that would have wiped out the entire solar system, but the Ultima neutralized the bomb and wiped out the Chitauri invaders. This was mos due to the assistance of the monstrous Hulk, whom they tricked i attacking the aliens; Hulk even killed and ate Kleiser himself.

COLOSSUS

HISTORY: Piotr Rasputin was smuggled into the U.S. from Russia at age nine, for his own personal safety as opposed to anything threatening his family, most of whom still live in Russia. After a childhood described as violent and miserable, Rasputin discovered his mutant powers and began earning money by performing feats of super-strength for tourists. He also realized that he was gay. Eventually returning to Russia, he faced death from a Siberian firing squad, but was rescued and recruited by the Red Mafiya (the Russian Mafia). Not a criminal by nature but unable to resist the attractive profits, Piotr became an arms dealer and sent almost all his earnings to his family. When an arms merchant employed by Magneto's Brotherhood of Mutants double-crossed him during a transaction, Piotr exposed himself as a mutant by assuming metallic form to repel his attacker's bullets. In the aftermath of the battle, Jean Grey, who was tracking down potential X-Men, came upon the scene and recruited Piotr. As Colossus, Piotr proved an exceptional combatant against X-Men foes such as the Sentinels and Magneto's Brotherhood of Mutants, and he developed a crush on fellow recruit Wolverine.

After a few months of action Colossus decided the X-Men only valued his strength, and grew jealous of the romances among his teammates. He returned to Russia, vowing never to use his powers again; however, after Cyclops and Marvel Girl followed him and urged him to return, he rescued an endangered submarine, winning worldwide recognition. Colossus rejoined the X-Men, frequently teaming with Wolverine. When the Brotherhood of Mutants resurfaced, again led by Magneto, Colossus almost confessed his feelings to Wolverine during battle. When Magneto used his control over Wolverine's metallic skeleton to torment him, Colossus beat the villain savagely.

Although Colossus remains protective of Wolverine, he realizes his affections are unrequited. Piotr was briefly interested in Longshot, a mutant whom he and his teammates rescued in Krakoa, but later learned Longshot was a murderer. More recently mutant speedster Northstar (Jean-Paul Beaubier) has asked Peter out to a Homecoming Dance. Peter has accepted, and come out to his X-Men team-mates.

REAL NAME: Piotr "Peter" Nikolaievitch Rasputin
KNOWN ALIASES: X8
IDENTITY: Publicly known
OCCUPATION: Student, adventurer, former factory worker, arms dealer, street performer
CITIZENSHIP: Russia
PLACE OF BIRTH: Siberia, Russia
KNOWN RELATIVES: Father, mother, sister and brother (names unrevealed); Illyana (sister)
GROUP AFFILIATION: X-Men; formerly Red Mafiya
EDUCATION: Little or no formal schooling prior to X-Men membership
FIRST APPEARANCE: Ultimate X-Men #1 (2001)

HEIGHT: 6'5"
WEIGHT: 283 lbs. (500 lbs. in metal form)
EYES: Blue
HAIR: Black

ABILITIES: Colossus can convert his body into a form of organic steel, almost doubling his weight and rendering him impervious to most conventional weaponry. In this form he possesses a staggering level of superhuman strength, sufficient to move a submarine weighing thousands of tons with extreme effort.

POWER GRID	1	2	3	4	5	6	7
INTELLIGENCE		2					
STRENGTH						6	
SPEED		2					
DURABILITY					5		
ENERGY PROJECTION	1						
FIGHTING SKILLS			3				

CYCLOPS

REAL NAME: Scott Summers
KNOWN ALIASES: Mutant number 118, X9
IDENTITY: Publicly known
OCCUPATION: Student, adventurer
CITIZENSHIP: U.S.A.
PLACE OF BIRTH: Unrevealed
KNOWN RELATIVES: Alex Summers (Havok, brother), father (name unrevealed)
GROUP AFFILIATION: X-Men; formerly Brotherhood of Mutants
EDUCATION: Currently taking college level courses
FIRST APPEARANCE: Ultimate X-Men #1 (2001)

HISTORY: When Scott Summers developed his mutant eye beams, he trained himself to operate blind, fearful of the damage he could cause with his powers. He dated Lorna Dane, a fellow mutant with magnetic powers, until she dumped him for his older brother, Alex. Later, Scott was rescued from a lynch mob by the telepath Charles Xavier, who recruited him to be the first X-Man, Cyclops; Alex turned down a similar invitation. Scott fell in love with Jean Grey (Marvel Girl), Xavier's next recruit, but hesitated to tell her. After the X-Men rescued the President's kidnapped daughter, Cyclops became disillusioned, allegedly because of Xavier's dealings with an anti-mutant U.S. administration, but also because Jean had become involved with new recruit Wolverine. Scott defected to the terrorist Brotherhood of Mutants. When their leader, Magneto, set out to annihilate Washington, Cyclops rejoined the X-Men, even convincing Magneto's son Quicksilver to help defeat him.

When teammate Colossus quit and returned to Russia, Cyclops and Marvel Girl followed and convinced him to rejoin; during this period they grew closer, and soon after, became an item. Though his relationship with Jean had already ended, a jealous Wolverine fought with Scott. Xavier tried to force them to learn to co-exist, sending them on a mission to the Savage Land to find missing U.S. marines. They faced a sentient computer and its army of cyborg zombies; while fleeing a collapsing underground complex, Wolverine deliberately let Cyclops fall into a chasm. Cyclops survived the fall, albeit severely injured, and clung to life by eating grubs and worms to survive. After twenty-six days he was found by Brotherhood members, who failed to recognize him as "the traitor Cyclops," and took him back to their new base, the Citadel, for medical treatment. When Magneto plotted to reverse Earth's magnetic fields, Cyclops summoned the X-Men in time to stop him. After the battle, Cyclops confronted a penitent Wolverine and violently removed him from the team. Months later, Cyclops reconsidered and invited Wolverine back, feeling it was his best chance to rehabilitate.

Scott was reunited with his estranged brother Alex, who joined Emma Frost's rival mutant educational program. They failed to resolve their differences. Later, when Lorna, now called Polaris, apparently lost control of her powers and killed several people, Cyclops tried to prevent Alex and other Frost students from breaking into the Triskelion to rescue her.

HEIGHT: 6'
WEIGHT: 170 lbs.
EYES: Unknown
HAIR: Brown

ABILITIES AND ACCESSORIES: Cyclops generates beams of force from his eyes, powerful enough to penetrate several inches of steel; he has no control over this power, and must wear special glasses or visors at all times to contain the blast. He is an excellent tactician and strategist, and has trained himself to operate blind.

POWER GRID	1	2	3	4	5	6	7
INTELLIGENCE							
STRENGTH							
SPEED							
DURABILITY							
ENERGY PROJECTION							
FIGHTING SKILLS							

HISTORY: Alison Blaire was lead singer in the heavy metal band "Dazzler," known for its obscene lyrics and spectacular visual effects (secretly supplied by her mutant powers). After two less-than-successful records, Ali considered outing herself as a mutant for extra publicity. Before she could, she was approached by teacher Emma Frost, who was forming a group of young mutant spokespeople to distance the current presidential administration from the X-Men. Uninterested in Frost's politics, Ali said she would join in exchange for a record deal, a requirement she reiterated when the X-Men tried to recruit her. Ali joined Emma Frost's mutant spokesperson group. However, an anti-mutant military faction programmed giant robot Sentinels to attack the group's introductory press conference; the X-Men, on hand for the event, counterattacked and defeated the Sentinels. The anti-mutant conspirators were exposed, and Professor X offered Ms. Frost's charges a place at his own school. Ali was the only one to accept, albeit claiming she was doing it for free room and board.

After overindulging at an Atlantic City rave, Ali (now called "Dazzler" by her fellow mutants) returned to the school in an intoxicated stupor; however, she recovered in time for Sinister's attack on the X-Men. Despite her claims of disinterest, Ali helped fight off the serial killer, who was defeated shortly thereafter by Rogue. Ali dissolved her band, unconvincingly claiming this was induced by Professor X's telepathy. Later, when Gambit attacked the X-Men at a carnival while trying to abduct Rogue on behalf of the Strucker twins, Dazzler helped rescue civilians trapped in a Ferris wheel. She then accompanied the team to rescue Rogue, who nevertheless left of her own free will.

Soon afterward, Professor X sent half of the team to investigate criminal charges against the Genoshan mutant Longshot. Her interest piqued, Dazzler persuaded Angel, Colossus and Nightcrawler to accompany her on an unauthorized mission to rescue Longshot. When Angel was abducted by Longshot's captors, Dazzler demonstrated leadership skill in rallying the team against their foes. Following Angel's rescue and Longshot's escape, Dazzler and the others learned Longshot was indeed guilty of murder. An infuriated Professor X resolved to punish the one responsible for the unauthorized mission, but Angel, realizing Dazzler was more likely to be expelled than he, claimed he had been the ringleader. Impressed by Angel's selflessness, Dazzler rewarded him with a kiss, and the two became romantically involved. However, when the pair tried to prevent the release of Magneto from the Triskelion,

REAL NAME: Alison "Ali" Blaire
KNOWN ALIASES: None
IDENTITY: Secret
OCCUPATION: Student, adventurer; former mutant spokesperson, musician
CITIZENSHIP: U.S.A.
PLACE OF BIRTH: Unrevealed
KNOWN RELATIVES: None
GROUP AFFILIATION: X-Men; formerly Emma Frost's "new mutants," Dazzler (her band)
EDUCATION: Unrevealed, possibly high school drop out prior to X-Men membership
FIRST APPEARANCE: Ultimate X-Men #42 (2004)

Dazzler was severely injured by Deathstrike, and she now lies in a coma.

HEIGHT: 5'5"
WEIGHT: 119 lbs.
EYES: Blue
HAIR: Black

ABILITIES: Dazzler can convert sound into light and energy, which she can utilize for various effects from scintillating light shows to laser-like blasts powerful enough to send people flying.

POWER GRID	1	2	3	4	5	6	7
INTELLIGENCE							
STRENGTH							
SPEED							
DURABILITY							
ENERGY PROJECTION							
FIGHTING SKILLS							

DEFENDERS

CURRENT MEMBERS: Black Knight (Alex), Hellcat (Patsy Walker), Nighthawk (unrevealed), Power Man (Luke Cage), Son of Satan (Damien), Valkyrie (Barbara), Whiz-Kid (unrevealed)
FORMER MEMBERS: Ant-Man/Giant-Man (Hank Pym)
BASE OF OPERATIONS: Nighthawk's apartment, Manhattan, NYC
FIRST APPEARANCE: Ultimates 2 #6 (2005)

HISTORY: As super-beings proliferate, the world is increasingly filled with stories of wonder, grandeur and high adventure; this is not one of those stories. The Defenders fancy themselves an up-and-coming super-team, but are little more than a handful of exhibitionist, athletic wannabes, superhero fans playing at being superheroes. The group's idealistic, somewhat self-deluded leader, Nighthawk, wears a striking, vaguely batlike costume stuffed with home-made gadgets. He is more dork than dark knight, a mediocre fighter with a flair for the dramatic and little skill to back it up. He is often preoccupied with seeking media attention and corporate sponsorship for the Defenders, though he seems to aspire to the heroic ideal more genuinely than some of his teammates. The Black Knight, for instance, seems to be little more than a fame-seeking medieval role player, and is often late for Defenders business since he has to commute across the Brooklyn Bridge from his day job. Valkyrie calls herself a female Thor equivalent, but is really just a scantily-clad novice martial artist with a super-hero fetish. The similarly underdressed and underpowered Hellcat and Power Man seem likewise preoccupied with celebrity. Though they do not realize it, the group's most capable member is probably the goth-clad Son of Satan, who is secretly a reservist with the elite government-sponsored Ultimates superteam, assigned to spy on the Defenders.

The team found its first new recruit in Hank Pym, formerly the Ultimates' Giant-Man, before he was fired in disgrace for abusing his wife and teammate the Wasp. Claiming the sorcerer Doctor Strange was a member of their group and that several X-Men were considering joining, the Defenders convinced Pym to join their team. He had to do so in his new self-shrinking guise as Ant-Man since the Giant-Man powers and identity were considered property of the government. Unable to reach the scene of a major fire before Iron Man went to the rescue instead, the Defenders decided to make a name for themselves by ambushing some young cigarette thieves later that same night, tipping off the media. However, Nighthawk was badly beaten by the thieves and nearly killed, saved only by the reluctant last-second intervention of a giant-sized Pym (who went into action nude since he no longer had his Giant-Man costume). The thieves escaped, the team was humiliated in the press, and Pym quit shortly after his new girlfriend Valkyrie tried to convince him to dress up like Captain America for her gratification. The group replaced Pym with a new super-powered recruit, the polio-afflicted, wheelchair-bound Whiz Kid, who can vary the temperature of certain inorganic objects. Whiz Kid was annoyed when he realized that the Defenders (who kept calling him "little guy" and "little wheel-fellow") had an ulterior motive, using his disabled status to seek new corporate sponsorship, including a four-thousand-dollar transportation grant with which the team bought a used Pontiac Firebird. Meanwhile, they are soliciting new media attention from outlets like *USA Today* and *Spin*. Wherever there is corporate money, media coverage or moderately hazardous adventure to be had, the Defenders will be there.

HISTORY: Following an army stint, Sam Wilson explored various fields of interest before he began working for S.H.I.E.L.D. Director Nick Fury. Sam agreed to give S.H.I.E.L.D. first refusal rights for any discovery or invention his research yielded. Wilson invented his remarkable "wing-pack," which enables him to fly. He also occasionally participated in secret S.H.I.E.L.D. operations. In recent months, he visited the Amazon River Basin to study various plant derivatives and their potential effects on human physiology.

Wilson was recalled to active duty by S.H.I.E.L.D. when overwhelming psionic messages of doom were transmitted worldwide from Tunguska, a region of Russia where an unidentified object had crashed in 1908. Wilson, Fury, and super-soldiers Captain America and Black Widow of the Ultimates located the transmission's source, an abandoned Soviet research base. Wilson deciphered the code to unlock the facility; once inside, they were attacked by an immensely powerful superhuman, powered by a horn-like device implanted in his skull. Wilson slew this cyborg "Unicorn," and after discovering several other cyborgs, the team realized the facility was creating super-soldiers via the surgical attachment of components from the mysterious Tunguska object.

As Wilson and the Ultimates moved deeper into the facility, they encountered Marvel Girl, Wolverine, and Colossus of the X-Men, who erroneously believed the worldwide distress message came from endangered mutants. When the agitated mutants attacked, Wilson disabled Colossus by attacking his metallic, but still vulnerable, eyes. In the battle's aftermath, Wilson discovered the signal was emanating from an alien android known as Vision, around whom the facility had been built. Unable to repair himself for nearly a century, Vision had been cannibalized by Soviet scientists, his alien technology used to create the cyborgs. Wilson convinced Vision to cease broadcasting the psionic signal, and Vision informed him and the others of his purpose: to warn the Earth of the coming of an alien menace known as "Gah Lak Tus." Fury assigned Wilson to accompany Vision back to a S.H.I.E.L.D. base and learn everything he could about the android, information which might prove vital if Earth was to have a chance of surviving the approaching Gah Lak Tus.

REAL NAME: Sam Wilson
KNOWN ALIASES: None
IDENTITY: Secret
OCCUPATION: Research scientist, government operative, adventurer; formerly soldier
CITIZENSHIP: U.S.A.
PLACE OF BIRTH: Unrevealed
KNOWN RELATIVES: None
GROUP AFFILIATION: S.H.I.E.L.D.; formerly U.S. Army
EDUCATION: Unrevealed, presumably one or more doctorates
FIRST APPEARANCE: Ultimate Nightmare #1 (2004)

HEIGHT: 5'11"
WEIGHT: 193 lbs.
EYES: Brown
HAIR: Black

ABILITIES AND ACCESSORIES: Wilson is a brilliant scientist with expertise in many fields, as well as an exceptional marksman and hand-to-hand combatant. Wilson wears a "wing-pack" capable of extending wings that allow him to fly. The wings are extremely sharp and can be used as weapons.

POWER GRID	1	2	3	4	5	6	7
INTELLIGENCE							
STRENGTH							
SPEED							
DURABILITY							
ENERGY PROJECTION							
FIGHTING SKILLS							

Art by Steve Epting

NICK FURY

REAL NAME: Nick Fury
KNOWN ALIASES: November Foxtrot (his Gulf War call sign)
presumably many undercover aliases
IDENTITY: No dual identity
OCCUPATION: U.S. Army General, National Chief of Security,
S.H.I.E.L.D. Director, leader of the Ultimates
CITIZENSHIP: U.S.A.
PLACE OF BIRTH: Unrevealed
KNOWN RELATIVES: Mother (name unrevealed); three ex-wives
(names unrevealed), Nicole Barton (goddaughter, deceased)
GROUP AFFILIATION: Ultimates, S.H.I.E.L.D.; liaison to the X-Men
EDUCATION: College degree
FIRST APPEARANCE: Ultimate Marvel Team-Up #5 (2001)

HISTORY: Details of Nick Fury's early life and career are sketchy and contradictory. He has claimed both that he was orphaned as a child, and that his mother is still alive; that he graduated college in India less than a decade ago and that he personally contributed to the end of the Cold War. Regardless, his status as a "war hero" is generally considered unquestionable. He has also said he has been prepared to die since the age of eighteen, but what happened then and how it affected his life remains a mystery.

Years ago, Fury worked closely with spy Clint Barton (a.k.a. Hawkeye) to develop S.H.I.E.L.D., a worldwide high-tech security organization; however, S.H.I.E.L.D.'s directorship itself went to Fury's commanding officer, General Ross. Fury participated in the Gulf War, during which he lost an eye and the mutant adventurer Wolverine saved his life. When the most recent revival of the U.S. super-soldier program failed to yield results for six years, Fury recommended private enterprises offer competitive bids to develop the required technology and procedures. Companies such as Norman Osborn's Oscorp and Hammer Industries vied for this government contract, experimenting upon and empowering both willing and unwilling subjects. Meanwhile, S.H.I.E.L.D. developed the technology that would empower some of the government operatives known as the Ultimates. As such, Fury is both directly and indirectly responsible for the recent, sudden upsurge of non-mutant super humans. Fury personally cut ties between S.H.I.E.L.D. and the ethically-compromised Oscorp, earning him the hatred of Osborn, who soon mutated himself into the Green Goblin.

Around the same time, Fury went to significant trouble to free Wolverine from the mutant-enslaving Weapon X, a barely controlled subdivision of S.H.I.E.L.D. Interestingly, this was the same timeframe as Magneto's break with his fellow mutant scholar, Charles Xavier. Whether or not Fury anticipated Wolverine's subsequent intervention in their conflict is unclear. Fury also participated in various activities of questionable legality in his quest for advanced technology, such as cooperating with a Latverian effort to steal Tony Stark's Iron Man technology.

Not long ago, Fury (now a colonel) was sent to Delhi, India, to investigate alleged violations of international superhuman test-ban treaties. He discovered a major project involving mass replication of mutant DNA, but was captured by enemy operatives. En route to Nepal, where the international secrets he held were to be auctioned off, Fury was rescued by the X-Men, at this time unwilling operatives of Weapon X. Shortly afterward, acting on a recorded message left by Wolverine, Fury led a S.H.I.E.L.D. invasion of the Weapon X facility, shutting down its inhumane operations and personally executing unit leader John Wraith. In the operation's aftermath, Fury established peaceful relations with the X-Men and recruited Quicksilver and Scarlet Witch, leaders of the Brotherhood of Mutants, as covert government operatives.

When General Ross stepped down from S.H.I.E.L.D. directorship, Fury, promoted to general, took his place. One of his first initiatives was the establishment of a black ops unit of mutant trainees, among them the mind-controlling Karma. Also serving in S.H.I.E.L.D.'s black ops division under Fury were his old friend Hawkeye and ex-K.G.B. espionage legend the Black Widow, whom Fury had personally recruited. Fury also gave the super-soldier program its first serious jumpstart in years, playing upon concern over mutant terrorists to win unprecedented funding used to form the Ultimates, a combination of mutants, mutated humans and wielders of advanced technology. This team included the recently recovered Captain America, and operated out of the high-tech base called the Triskelion. The Ultimates faced an array of personal

Art by David Finch

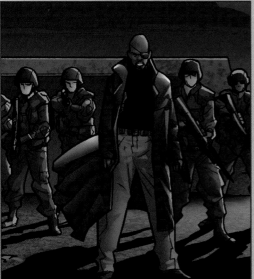

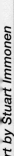
Art by Stuart Immonen

Fury undermined his own credibility when he asked Wolverine to murder a teenage mutant who had inadvertently killed an entire town and whose powers, if revealed, seemed certain to stoke uncontrollable anti-mutant hysteria. His trust in Fury and the X-Men eroded by this operation, the President agreed to form public ties with Emma Frost's mutant student body. However, this move finally drove the anti-mutant rebel faction into open treason, and they attacked the President's press conference with Sentinel robots. The X-Men destroyed the Sentinels, and Fury's agent Karma exposed the conspirators, restoring the administration's faith in Fury and the X-Men.

When Earth was plagued by a powerful psionic distress call which sparked mass suicides, Fury and a select team of Ultimates traced the call to an abandoned Russian base in Tunguska. The team discovered an alien android called Vision, sent to Earth nearly a century before to warn humanity of a looming destructive force called Gah Lak Tus. Fury entrusted Vision to one of his contracted specialists, Sam Wilson. The fact that Vision's distress warning had been pre-empted by Russian attempts to cannibalize him for parts in their own super-soldier project was not lost on Fury, who began to feel overwhelmed by the events he had helped set into motion.

Fury has since suffered one setback after another, as his ties with the X-Men grew more tenuous and his friend Spider-Man began to seem more of a potential threat than an ally. His job was further complicated by the alien Kree, who stationed observers (including the defector Captain Marvel) to record Earth's death throes at the mercy of "Gah Lak Tus." With the exposure of the Hulk's connection to the Ultimates and Thor's apparent breakdown, the Ultimates have suffered additional scandal. Their growing international activity has led some to regard Fury as a loose cannon ready to ignite a superhuman world war. To remove a potential wild card, Fury arranged for his own assassination by Mister Nix, perhaps the deadliest political assassin on Earth. Fury killed Nix during the attempt. With the ranks of superhuman criminals growing and threats from outer space rising, Fury's responsibilities to the U.S. and the world seem to get heavier every day, and it remains to be seen how far he will go in fulfilling them.

conflicts and controversies, notably project deputy Bruce Banner's transformation into the monstrous Hulk. Hulk's destructive rampage was halted by the Ultimates, though S.H.I.E.L.D. concealed the Hulk's true identity from the public. Despite this, Fury forged the Ultimates into a unique fighting team just in time to save the world from extraterrestrial Chitauri invaders (thanks in part to last-minute manipulation of the Hulk), guaranteeing the team a place in the world's heart.

An insane Norman Osborn planned to extort young Peter Parker (alias Spider-Man) in to helping him assassinate Fury. Anticipating this move, Fury introduced himself to Parker, taking him into his confidence and promising whatever assistance S.H.I.E.L.D. could legally provide against Osborn. After Spider-Man defeated the Goblin, Fury took Osborn into custody, where he was soon joined by more of Spider-Man's superhuman adversaries. Recognizing his own role in the experiments that mutated these men, Fury planned to give them his personal attention, but was distracted by the return of Magneto, believed dead after a fight with the X-Men months before. When Magneto and his Brotherhood attacked the Brooklyn Bridge, killing hundreds, the X-Men were implicated and Fury directed the Ultimates against both groups while overseeing presidential safety and developing new defenses. The X-Men ultimately defeated Magneto, and Fury, remembering the debt he owed them, arranged for them to come under federal jurisdiction as a specialized peacekeeping unit. However, Fury soon learned that the X-Men would hardly be his most cooperative charges; when decommissioned Weapon X operatives, recruited by an anti-mutant government faction intent on overthrowing the President, targeted Wolverine, the X-Men personally pursued them, unwittingly interfering with S.H.I.E.L.D.'s investigation of the rogue agents.

Meanwhile, Osborn languished in the Triskelion's detention block alongside fellow super-criminals Doctor Octopus, Sandman, Electro, and Kraven the Hunter. Fury intended to hold the five indefinitely, discarding their right to trial, in order to learn their secrets and keep them from harming the public. Under Osborn's leadership, the prisoners escaped and attempted to extort money from the President lest they implicate him in Fury's activities, of which the President had been unaware. Fury rallied the Ultimates and Spider-Man to defeat Osborn's forces, but victory did not blind a shaken Fury to his own role in the fiasco.

HEIGHT: 6'2"
WEIGHT: 231 lbs.
EYES: Brown
HAIR: Black (facial)

ABILITIES AND ACCESSORIES: Fury is an excellent tactician, hand-to-hand combatant, marksman, and athlete. All his clothing is laced with cameras and surveillance devices, guaranteeing that his whereabouts can be tracked at all times. He has access to a wide variety of S.H.I.E.L.D. technology, including stealth gear, which renders him invisible, and protective armor, which enables him to fly.

POWER GRID	1	2	3	4	5	6	7
INTELLIGENCE							
STRENGTH							
SPEED							
DURABILITY							
ENERGY PROJECTION							
FIGHTING SKILLS							

GAH LAK TUS

REAL NAME: Unknown, possibly inapplicable
KNOWN ALIASES: Gah Lak Tus, Reverse of God, Uncreator, Antimessiah, Poison Wave, Universal Endbringer
IDENTITY: Publicly known (various intergalactic civilizations); known to authorities (Earth)
OCCUPATION: Destroyer of life
CITIZENSHIP: Inapplicable
PLACE OF BIRTH: Unrevealed
KNOWN RELATIVES: Unknown, possibly inapplicable
GROUP AFFILIATION: None
EDUCATION: Unknown, possibly inapplicable
FIRST APPEARANCE: Ultimate Extinction #1 (2006)

HEIGHT: (Gah Lak Tus) Approximately 100,000 miles long; (Vision) variable
WEIGHT: (both) Unrevealed
EYES: (Gah Lak Tus) Unrevealed; (Vision) yellow-orange with a red glow
HAIR: (both) None

HISTORY: For millennia, the immense, robotic entity called Gah Lak Tus has traveled the galaxies, destroying all life-bearing planets in its path. It bombards targeted worlds with psychic "fear" broadcasts and a flesh-eating virus, eradicating all life. It then breaks open the dying world to its core and sucks dry all its energy, leaving a permanently lifeless husk. While the extraterrestrial Kree race learned the true nature of Gah Lak Tus, the Eidolon Apparition Vision android contacted worlds in Gah Lak Tus's path, warning them to evacuate or face extinction, while simultaneously recording all information about that culture.

A century ago, Vision tried to warn Earth of Gah Lak Tus, but crash-landed in the sub-arctic Tunguska region of Siberia. Twenty-three years later, Soviet explorers found the Vision in a self-repair coma. The Soviet authorities began a decades-long dissection of Vision, using his technology to supply their Super-Soldier program. Components removed from Vision were grafted onto human subjects, turning many of them into crazed monsters. When their funding collapsed after the fall of the Soviet Union, the project's staff locked away the Vision and their experimental super-soldiers in a bunker.

One decade later, the Vision repaired himself enough to broadcast a signal reaching all Earth communications networks and even higher telepathic frequencies, trying to warn of the coming doom but instead causing fear and mass suicides. Thinking this was a terrorist attack, General Nick Fury of S.H.I.E.L.D. assembled a black ops team consisting of himself, Captain America, Sam Wilson and Black Widow to shut the signal down. Simultaneously, Professor Charles Xavier sent the X-Men Colossus, Marvel Girl, and Wolverine to the same area to rescue what he thought was an abused psychic. Both teams fought their way through hordes of crazed superhuman horrors in the bunker to reach the partially disassembled Vision, who finally delivered its warning. Vision was taken into S.H.I.E.L.D. custody, where Wilson has worked with the android, Kree defector Mahr Vehl, and a captured Kree database, trying to determine what Gah Lak Tus is and how to defend Earth from it.

HISTORY: Remy "Gambit" LeBeau had a hard upbringing: his father abused him, and he fell into the clutches of an abusive man who trained him as a pickpocket. As a young adult, he came under the influence of sinister scientist Nathaniel Essex, who controlled him by threatening a woman Remy loved. Remy eventually ended up living in an abandoned subway car beneath New York, performing card tricks for money. One day, he was approached by a young girl who had witnessed a crooked cop named Hammerhead murder her mother; seeing he could perform "magic," she asked Remy to bring her mother back to life. Gambit took her in while he tried to figure out what to do, but Hammerhead snatched her while Gambit slept, sparing LeBeau since his boss Silvermane owed Essex a favor. Gambit tracked Hammerhead down, and, in a savage fight, apparently blew up the top of Hammerhead's metal skull. Gambit rescued the girl and entrusted her to a homeless shelter, feeling she was not safe around him.

Gambit later began losing control of his powers, charging objects unintentionally. The von Struckers, mutant capitalists who owned Fenris International, fixed his powers in return for his services as a corporate spy. Wishing to recruit the X-Man Rogue, they sent Gambit to kidnap her from Coney Island fairground. After battling her fellow X-Men (notably blowing most of Wolverine's face off), Gambit delivered Rogue to the von Struckers' penthouse, where she stole a kiss from him, thus absorbing his powers and witnessing glimpses of his brutal past. The von Struckers gave her a special suit to control her powers, but she still rejected their job offer. When the von Struckers refused to accept this, Gambit angrily backed her up. Working together, Rogue and Gambit overcame the von Struckers and fought their way out through Fenris' Wolfpack guards. They were confronted at the building exit by Wolverine, eager for a rematch, but Rogue stopped the fight before Gambit was killed. The other X-Men had also come to rescue her, but Rogue explained that she had decided to remain with Gambit, and the pair departed.

They worked their way across the States, robbing Fenris holdings along the way, until they ended up in Las Vegas. The super-criminal Juggernaut, looking for Rogue, challenged them outside the Fenris Resort and Casino. Gambit battled him, eventually bringing a construction site down on both their heads. Rogue dug the dying Gambit out, giving him a final kiss as his last request, absorbing his powers and memories; unlike Rogue's normal transfers, this one seems to be permanent. Though Gambit is dead, his spirit evidently lives on inside of Rogue.

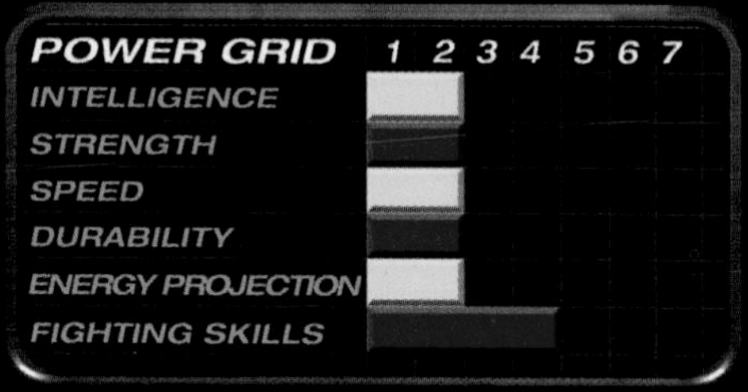

REAL NAME: Remy LeBeau
KNOWN ALIASES: None
IDENTITY: Secret
OCCUPATION: Street performer, thief, corporate spy
CITIZENSHIP: U.S.A.
PLACE OF BIRTH: Louisiana
KNOWN RELATIVES: Unnamed father
GROUP AFFILIATION: Former Fenris International operative
EDUCATION: Little or no formal education
FIRST APPEARANCE: Ultimate X-Men #13 (2002)

HEIGHT: 6'2"
WEIGHT: 165 lbs.
EYES: Red
HAIR: Brown

ABILITIES AND ACCESSORIES: Gambit could charge inanimate objects with energy, causing them to explode or to levitate for brief periods. He was extremely agile, and a skilled marksman with thrown objects.

POWER GRID	1	2	3	4	5	6	7
INTELLIGENCE							
STRENGTH							
SPEED							
DURABILITY							
ENERGY PROJECTION							
FIGHTING SKILLS							

GIANT MAN

REAL NAME: Henry Pym
KNOWN ALIASES: Ant-Man
IDENTITY: Publicly known
OCCUPATION: Research scientist, subversive; formerly superhero, U.S. government super-operative
CITIZENSHIP: U.S.A. with criminal record
PLACE OF BIRTH: Unrevealed
KNOWN RELATIVES: Janet Pym (estranged wife), Grace (aunt)
GROUP AFFILIATION: Formerly Defenders, Ultimates, S.H.I.E.L.D.
EDUCATION: Multiple scientific doctorates, including studies at NYU
FIRST APPEARANCE: Ultimates #2 (2002)

HISTORY: Scientific genius Hank Pym has lived a life of highs and lows, both tied to his wife Janet. College sweethearts, they married despite the insecure and emotionally unstable Hank's occasional physical abuse. The couple worked as scientists at S.H.I.E.L.D.'s Super-Soldier Research Facility under Bruce Banner, in whose scientific shadow Hank lived uneasily. Fearful of anti-mutant prejudice, the self-shrinking, insect-powered Jan concealed her mutant nature, eventually allowing Hank to take credit for creating her powers by scientific means. Pym's genetic studies of Jan helped him make new scientific breakthroughs in the areas of size changing and entomology. The Pyms were later promoted to head the research and development wing of the government's new superhuman strike force, the Ultimates, with Banner as their deputy. The Pyms also became two of the program's founding super-operatives as the Wasp and Giant Man (Hank used his new growth formula). Humiliated and injured in battle by a rampaging Hulk (a transformed Banner), Pym physically recovered, but his shaken confidence sparked a vicious domestic fight with Jan, during which Hank nearly killed her. Pym fled, but he was caught and beaten into traction by Captain America, who soon began dating Jan.

Pym was dismissed from the field team, and his former assistant Eamonn Brankin took over their R&D operations; however, Hank remained on staff, studying captured supercriminals. He formed an unlikely friendship and fertile scientific collaboration with fellow outcast Bruce Banner, while trying unsuccessfully to rejoin the Ultimates field team as the self-shrinking "Ant-Man." When Banner was sentenced to die for the Hulk's crimes, Pym covertly sabotaged the execution, facilitating Banner's secret escape. Finally fired from the Ultimates altogether, a desperate Pym was willing to work for free, even offering them his new Ultron and Vision II robot designs; he was rejected. Pym joined a new amateur super-team, the Defenders, romancing his teammate Valkyrie, but the group's ineptitude soon drove Hank away. Weary of her new boyfriend, Jan secretly renewed contact with Hank. Meanwhile, a desperate Pym has apparently allied himself with a traitor within the Ultimates, eventually using his Ant-Man tech and Ultron robots to help a foreign super-army conquer both the Ultimates and America.

HEIGHT: 6' (variable)
WEIGHT: 185 lbs. (variable)
EYES: Blue
HAIR: Blond (dyed brown)

ABILITIES AND ACCESSORIES: Pym can grow up to sixty feet high and can shrink to the size of an insect. A natural neurological reflex prevents him from growing or shrinking beyond the limits of his body's endurance. Pym is a cybernetics/robotics genius and a genetics expert. His "Giant-Man" costume's shaded goggles protect his enlarged eyes from excess sunlight. His "Ant-Man" helmet communicates with and controls ants via pheromone emissions.

POWER GRID	1	2	3	4	5	6	7
INTELLIGENCE							
STRENGTH							
SPEED							
DURABILITY							
ENERGY PROJECTION							
FIGHTING SKILLS							

HISTORY: A former Olympic archer, Clint Barton became a U.S. intelligence agent over a decade ago. Active around the world, he was present for the liberations of Kosovo and Afghanistan, as well as the fall of the Berlin Wall. He became a close friend and frequent colleague of fellow agent Nick Fury, and the two operatives were key founders of the modern intelligence agency S.H.I.E.L.D. Both rose through the ranks until Fury became the agency's director and Barton (code-named Hawkeye) became an elite agent of S.H.I.E.L.D.'s black ops division, often partnered with ex-KGB espionage legend Natasha Romanov (code-named Black Widow). Despite his dangerous, globe-spanning profession, Barton managed to build a more stable family life than most of his peers, residing for years with his girlfriend Laura (who recently became his wife), with whom he had three children: Callum, Lewis and baby Nicole, named after her godfather, Nick Fury. Hawkeye habitually phoned his family before every mission to say good-bye, just in case he never returned; but he always returned, even after a mission which pitted him, Black Widow, and their support team against two office buildings full of extraterrestrial Chitauri sleeper agents. Most of their team died, but Hawkeye, the Widow and a handful of others survived, wiping out the Chitauri sleepers in the process.

Shortly thereafter, Hawkeye and the Widow were promoted to membership in S.H.I.E.L.D.'s new celebrity superhero team, the Ultimates, complete with newly falsified backgrounds to make them more acceptable public figures. When the Ultimates thwarted a Chitauri plot to destroy Earth, thanks in part to unwitting assistance from the monstrous Hulk, it was a wounded Hawkeye who managed to bring down the rampaging Hulk once the aliens were defeated. Hawkeye participated in many more Ultimates operations before taking part in the team's most controversial mission to date, teaming with the European Super-Soldier Initiative to strip a "rogue" state of its nuclear weapons capability. In response, a traitor within the Ultimates led a black ops team into Hawkeye's home, slaughtering the entire Barton family. Hawkeye himself was taken alive and chemically interrogated, yielding secrets which enabled a foreign super-army to overwhelm the Ultimates.

HEIGHT: 6'3"
WEIGHT: 230 lbs.
EYES: Brown
HAIR: Blond

ABILITIES AND ACCESSORIES: Hawkeye is a master archer with extraordinarily fast reflexes, exceptional dexterity and near-perfect aim. He is also an excellent all-around marksman well versed in conventional firearms, and has an uncanny knack for using miscellaneous hand-held objects as projectile weapons. Hawkeye is a veteran espionage operative, a formidable physical combatant, and an experienced fighter pilot. He typically carries at least one custom bow and a small arsenal of arrows — mostly conventional shafts, but some fitted with specialized tips. He sometimes employs special weapons, such as flamethrowers.

POWER GRID	1	2	3	4	5	6	7
INTELLIGENCE							
STRENGTH							
SPEED							
DURABILITY							
ENERGY PROJECTION							
FIGHTING SKILLS							

REAL NAME: Clint Barton
KNOWN ALIASES: Presumably many espionage aliases
IDENTITY: Publicly known
OCCUPATION: U.S. government super-operative; former conventional intelligence agent, Olympic athlete
CITIZENSHIP: U.S.A.
PLACE OF BIRTH: Unrevealed
KNOWN RELATIVES: Laura (wife), Callum, Lewis (sons) and Nicole (daughter), all deceased
GROUP AFFILIATION: Ultimates, S.H.I.E.L.D.
EDUCATION: Unrevealed
FIRST APPEARANCE: Ultimates #7 (2002)

Art by Bryan Hitch

HELLFIRE CLUB

CURRENT MEMBERS: Arnold, Greenspan, Mr. Marts, Mr. Raicht, Mr. Turner
FORMER MEMBERS: Sebastian Shaw, Seville, several others unidentified
BASE OF OPERATIONS: Manhattan Branch of Hellfire Club
FIRST APPEARANCE: Ultimate X-Men #23 (2002)

HISTORY: Founded by Sir Francis Dashwood in the mid-eighteenth century, the "Order of the Knights of St. Francis of Wycombe," better known as the Hellfire Club, swiftly gained a reputation for upper class debauchery. The club's principles stretched back to ancient Egypt and worship of the Phoenix God. A thousand generations of followers worshipped the ancient force they believed empowered them, and plotted to free it from its many-angled prison. In modern times the Club became a more respectable retreat for the wealthy, where they could conduct business and hold parties. Its members included the most famous names in business, politics, and entertainment. However, a secret conspiracy remained at its heart, ruled by an Inner Circle thirteen strong, and led by their grandmaster Sebastian Shaw. Seeing mutants as a possible way of freeing their lord, they funded Charles Xavier to set up his Xavier Institute and Muir Island hospital, claiming philanthropic motives and hiding their involvement from the public. When one of Charles' students, the telepath Jean Grey, began having terrifying visions and believed she had made contact with an ultra-dimensional entity, the Club understandably took this as a sign that the Phoenix Force had chosen her as a vessel to enter their reality. Informed by their astronomers of an impending alignment, the club invited Xavier and his students to the Manhattan branch for a gala function in their honour, where Shaw claimed they would openly proclaim their support for Xavier to the world press. Xavier, Jean, Storm, and Colossus attended, but the Club's agents ambushed them, overpowering all save Jean, who entered a trance.

The captives were taken to a temple beneath the Club, where Shaw and the Inner Circle conducted a mystic ceremony to free the Phoenix. Though Xavier insisted that Jean's visions were merely a deluded telepath's dreams, the ceremony appeared to work, and Jean, still entranced, was bathed in fire and seemingly possessed. The Phoenix (or perhaps Jean) berated Shaw for daring to command a god; he pleaded that the Hellfire Club had summoned the Phoenix Force in the hopes of serving it, not controlling it. Pointing out that Shaw had given the power to a girl whose friends he had just betrayed, the possessed Jean slew all of the Inner Circle except Shaw. As Shaw begged for mercy, Jean used her new power to transfer all his holdings and wealth to Xavier, and then killed Shaw too. Before she could go too much further, Xavier telepathically restored Jean's personality. Despite the Inner Circle's demise, the Hellfire Club itself remains; it is unclear whether others may replace Shaw and try to pick up where he left off. Recently, Shaw's estate instigated an investigation of Xavier's accounts, attempting to seize back the assets taken from Shaw; this may be a portent of ominous things to come.

Art by Adam Kubert

HULK

HISTORY: Bruce Banner's childhood dream was to be like Captain America: a skinny youth transformed into an athletic hero. Graduating university two years early, he sought to reproduce the lost super-soldier serum, working for the government under S.H.I.E.L.D.'s General Ross. He became head of the Pittsburgh-based Super-Soldier Program, got engaged to Ross' daughter, Betty, and developed a rivalry with fellow scientist Hank Pym. Rumors persisted that he conducted trials on civilians during departmental lean years; he certainly tested formulae on himself more than once. The last test transformed Banner into an intellectually limited, instinct-driven, green-skinned behemoth. Dubbed the Hulk and pursued by Ross' troops, Banner rampaged across the country, briefly reverting to human form during an encounter with Spider-Man.

Eventually restored to human form, and testing negative for Hulk cells, Banner returned to work. When new S.H.I.E.L.D. head Nick Fury expanded the Super-Soldier Program, Banner was demoted to Pym's second-in-command. Dumped and belittled by Betty, and jealous of Pym's successful projects, Banner felt increasingly insecure as he failed to make further progress with his serum. The discovery of the original Captain America, alive and well, provided new data but no breakthrough. Overhearing his colleagues mocking him, Banner cracked; he re-injected himself with his Hulk serum, now laced with Captain America's blood. Becoming a more brutal, gray-skinned Hulk, he slew 852 people on a murderous rampage through Manhattan, trying to reach Betty before the Ultimates finally subdued him.

Banner was sealed away in special high-security prison quarters beneath the Triskelion and kept partially sedated to prevent another transformation. His connection to the Hulk was concealed from the public. The Hulk intrabodies had now bonded with his DNA, leaving an apparently permanent risk of transformation. Betty reconciled with him, seemingly aroused by his darker side; Banner meanwhile worked on curing himself, to no avail. When the extraterrestrial Chitauri threatened Earth, Banner was deliberately provoked into transforming, and battled against the invaders before Hawkeye recaptured him using a tranquillizer arrow.

REAL NAME: Bruce Banner
KNOWN ALIASES: None
IDENTITY: Publicly known
OCCUPATION: Scientist
CITIZENSHIP: U.S.A., with criminal record
PLACE OF BIRTH: Unrevealed
KNOWN RELATIVES: Parents, uncle and cousins (names unrevealed); Jenny (cousin)
GROUP AFFILIATION: None
EDUCATION: PhD
FIRST APPEARANCE: Ultimate Marvel Team-Up #2 (2001)

After Hulk's identity was leaked to the press, a penitent Banner was tried for mass murder and sentenced to death. Banner was sedated and left aboard the decommissioned U.S.S. Constellation to die in a nuclear explosion. A sympathetic Pym reduced Banner's dosage and Bruce awoke, transforming seconds before the explosion. Bruce Banner now wanders a world that thinks him dead, trying to find a way to control the raging monster that dwells within him.

HEIGHT: (as Banner) 5'7"; (as Hulk) 8'1" (variable)
WEIGHT: (as Banner) 120 lbs.; (as Hulk) 1200 lbs. (variable)
EYES: (as Banner) Brown; (as Hulk) Red, with green irises
HAIR: (as Banner) Brown; (as Hulk) Gray

ABILITIES AND ACCESSORIES: Stress or adrenaline can transform Banner into the Hulk. In this form he is superhumanly strong, heals at an accelerated rate, and is capable of superhuman leaps.

POWER GRID	1	2	3	4	5	6	7
INTELLIGENCE							
STRENGTH							
SPEED							
DURABILITY							
ENERGY PROJECTION							
FIGHTING SKILLS							

Art by Bryan Hitch

ICEMAN

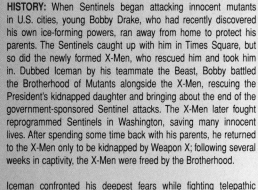

REAL NAME: Robert "Bobby" Drake
KNOWN ALIASES: X6
IDENTITY: Publicly known
OCCUPATION: Student; adventurer
CITIZENSHIP: U.S.A.
PLACE OF BIRTH: Unrevealed
KNOWN RELATIVES: Parents (names unrevealed)
GROUP AFFILIATION: X-Men; formerly Weapon X
EDUCATION: High School (unfinished)
FIRST APPEARANCE: Ultimate X-Men #1 (2001)

HISTORY: When Sentinels began attacking innocent mutants in U.S. cities, young Bobby Drake, who had recently discovered his own ice-forming powers, ran away from home to protect his parents. The Sentinels caught up with him in Times Square, but so did the newly formed X-Men, who rescued him and took him in. Dubbed Iceman by his teammate the Beast, Bobby battled the Brotherhood of Mutants alongside the X-Men, rescuing the President's kidnapped daughter and bringing about the end of the government-sponsored Sentinel attacks. The X-Men later fought reprogrammed Sentinels in Washington, saving many innocent lives. After spending some time back with his parents, he returned to the X-Men only to be kidnapped by Weapon X; following several weeks in captivity, the X-Men were freed by the Brotherhood.

Iceman confronted his deepest fears while fighting telepathic mutant David Xavier (son of X-Men founder Charles Xavier) in Scotland. During a rematch with David in Berlin, Bobby's terror initially immobilized him. Urged on by Professor X, he overcame his fear when his teammate Storm was threatened, only to be severely injured. Bobby spent weeks in the hospital, and his parents withdrew him from the school. The family's medical bills were paid by anti-mutant Senator Andrew Border Turk, who then pushed the Drake family to sue Xavier for $50 million, hoping to put the school out of business. Since Bobby's father lost his job when people found out he had a mutant child, the Drakes agreed. At a live press conference, Bobby refused to read Turk's prepared statement, instead dropping the action, stating he knew the risks of the mission and had learned integrity from Xavier.

When the X-Men became fugitives after it was revealed Xavier had lied about killing Brotherhood leader Magneto, Iceman defied his parents and helped the X-Men escape the Ultimates. The X-Men subsequently captured Magneto and saved the world, publicly redeeming themselves.

Bobby began dating his teammate Rogue, but foolishly kissed Kitty Pryde at the Coney Island fair, hurting Rogue. She soon left the X-Men in the company of Gambit, much to Bobby's distress. Iceman accompanied Marvel Girl, Cyclops and Kitty to Genosha to investigate whether Longshot was truly a murderer, and during the trip he and Kitty became a couple. However, Kitty dumped him when she learned he was still in touch with Rogue by e-mail, and clearly still in love with her.

HEIGHT: 5'5"
WEIGHT: 140 lbs.
EYES: Blue
HAIR: Brown

ABILITIES AND ACCESSORIES: Iceman can generate snow and ice from the moisture in the air. He can use this to bind opponents, slide along at high speed, or cover himself in a layer of ice armor strong enough to stop bullets.

POWER GRID	1	2	3	4	5	6	7
INTELLIGENCE		■					
STRENGTH	■						
SPEED			■				
DURABILITY			■				
ENERGY PROJECTION				■			
FIGHTING SKILLS		■					

Art by Adam Kubert

HISTORY: Blessed and cursed with extraordinary genius, Tony Stark is the son of inventor and defense contractor Howard Stark, and geneticist Maria Stark. The Starks were developing a biological personal armor coating when a lab accident with a regenerative virus fatally infected Maria. The virus mutated her unborn child, Tony, growing additional neural tissue throughout his body which augmented his intelligence while causing chronic pain. Maria died, but Howard saved Tony by coating him in their bacterial bio-armor, which consumed ordinary skin but not Tony's constantly regenerating neural flesh. Business rival Zebediah Stane married Howard's scheming ex-wife Loni, with whom he stole Stark's company, and spent years trying to seize the bio-armor. As a teenager, Tony befriended fellow prep school student Jim Rhodes and began developing his own "Iron Man" armor technology. Becoming a wealthy celebrity and science prodigy, young Tony founded multi-billion dollar design and manufacturing corporation Stark International. He also became an infamous playboy, alcoholic, and womanizer, suffering from recurring depression and secretly learning he was dying from an inoperable brain tumor.

Later, Stark would claim he developed the armor. When he and his shifty cousin Morgan were taken hostage along with other civilians by Guatemalan guerrilla terrorists, their captors demanded Stark's technology in exchange for the hostages' freedom. They killed Morgan when Tony refused to cooperate. Pretending to acquiesce, Stark built makeshift armor and defeated the terrorists with it. Years later, Stark used new Iron Man armor to save the President from an assassination attempt, becoming a bigger celebrity than ever, but refusing to sell or mass-produce his armor technology. When Latverian ambassador Golog tried to steal Stark's "Irontech" with the covert approval of intelligence agency S.H.I.E.L.D., Stark fought off Golog's Mandroids with the aid of Spider-Man. Spurred by his

REAL NAME: Antonio "Tony" Stark
KNOWN ALIASES: Monopoly Man
IDENTITY: Publicly known
OCCUPATION: Inventor, CEO, U.S. government super-operative
CITIZENSHIP: U.S.A.
PLACE OF BIRTH: Unrevealed
KNOWN RELATIVES: Howard & Maria Cerrera Stark (parents, deceased), Morgan Stark (cousin, deceased), Antonio (uncle, deceased), uncle (name unrevealed, deceased)
GROUP AFFILIATION: Ultimates, Stark Industries
EDUCATION: Multiple scientific doctorates, studied at Harvard and MIT
FIRST APPEARANCE: Ultimate Marvel Team-Up #4 (2001)

tumor to make the most of his remaining days, Stark joined the Ultimates, a S.H.I.E.L.D.-sponsored superhero team. Forming an unlikely friendship with anti-corporate teammate Thor, Stark helped defeat the Hulk, the Chitauri and others. Dating teammate Natasha Romanov (Black Widow), Tony eventually proposed to her, creating new armor for her as an engagement gift; however, when a super-army conquered the team, Natasha suddenly attacked Tony, placing him — and their relationship — in jeopardy.

HEIGHT: (unarmored) 6'1", (armored) 7'
WEIGHT: (unarmored) 225 lbs., (armored) 2000 lbs.
EYES: Blue
HAIR: Black

ABILITIES AND ACCESSORIES: Tony Stark is a phenomenal scientific genius and inventor, thanks largely to his body-wide neural tissue, which enhances his intelligence and gives his body fantastic regenerative capacity. His bacterial bio-armor fits his body like a second skin, enhances his durability, and inhibits his chronic neurological pain. He is multilingual, has nearly total recall, and has a seemingly limitless capacity for multitasking. His Iron Man armor grants him tremendous superhuman strength and durability, enabling both supersonic flight and submersible travel, and houses repulsor rays, a uni-beam, mind-impairing "thought-scramblers," "light-negativity" devices allowing short-term invisibility, force field generators, a tracking system, communications tech and onboard computers. He can manually recharge his armor from outside sources or draw additional power from a network of dedicated satellites.

POWER GRID	1	2	3	4	5	6	7
INTELLIGENCE							
STRENGTH							
SPEED							
DURABILITY							
ENERGY PROJECTION							
FIGHTING SKILLS							

LONGSHOT

REAL NAME: Arthur Centino
KNOWN ALIASES: None
IDENTITY: Publicly known
OCCUPATION: Freedom fighter
CITIZENSHIP: Presumably Genoshan, with criminal record
PLACE OF BIRTH: Presumably Genosha
KNOWN RELATIVES: None
GROUP AFFILIATION: Genoshan Mutant Underground
EDUCATION: Unrevealed
FIRST APPEARANCE: Ultimate X-Men #54 (2005)

HISTORY: When the African nation of Genosha passed a law forcing mutant citizens to leave the country a few years ago, Arthur "Longshot" Centino and his mutant girlfriend Spiral were among the few who remained, going underground to promote mutant rights. Longshot's dedication to mutant freedom and his growing hatred of non-powered humans led him to neglect Spiral, who eventually sought solace with Sir Arthur Scheele, a Genoshan politician sympathetic to the mutant cause. Finding them together Longshot was enraged and killed Scheele in a fury before Spiral knocked him unconscious. Hoping to protect Scheele's family from the scandal of her affair, Spiral took both Longshot and Scheele's body to a

secluded area and left them there. Longshot was soon tried and sentenced to death for Scheele's murder.

Longshot was forced to star in the Genoshan government's "Hunt for Justice" television program, overseen by media mogul Mojo Adams and his aide Major Domo, in which condemned mutants were killed on the neighboring island of Krakoa. Released on Krakoa to be hunted down, Longshot survived far longer than the average contestant, becoming a favorite of the viewing public.

When the X-Men learned of "Hunt for Justice," Professor X sent Cyclops, Marvel Girl, Iceman, and Shadowcat to Genosha to investigate Longshot's case. Spiral attacked them, hoping to conceal her involvement with Scheele. Meanwhile, a second team of X-Men disobeyed Professor X's orders and flew to Genosha themselves to rescue Longshot; Dazzler, Colossus, and Nightcrawler fought Arcade, a notorious gamesman selected to kill Longshot. Longshot helped the X-Men defeat Arcade, and they befriended him. However, they soon discovered that their teammate Angel had been captured and was going to be executed unless Longshot surrendered. When Nightcrawler teleported them all into Adams's studio to rescue Angel, Longshot attacked Adams and Domo in a fit of hatred but was restrained by Dazzler. Shortly afterward, his rescuers helped Longshot escape Genosha in a small boat. By that time, Cyclops's team had learned from Spiral that Longshot had indeed killed Scheele.

The X-Men brought Spiral to America to start a new life. Longshot fled to the Savage Land, where he was captured by the Ultimates' Scarlet Witch, after S.H.I.E.L.D. was anonymously tipped off to his location. Taken to the Triskelion, he escaped his cell during Magneto's jailbreak, saving the life of the X-Man Angel en route by breaking the neck of the psychotic cyborg Deathstrike. He then aided Magneto in evading security, becoming the terrorist's newest follower.

HEIGHT: 5'9"
WEIGHT: 100 lbs.
EYES: Blue
HAIR: Blond

DISTINGUISHING FEATURES: Longshot has three fingers on each hand.

ABILITIES AND ACCESSORIES: Longshot can alter probabilities to affect people, objects, or events around him in ways that benefit his survival and goals; his right eye glows when he exercises this ability. He has hollow bones, making him significantly lighter than he appears and contributing to his extraordinary agility and fighting prowess. He customarily carries a knife or razor blades as weapons.

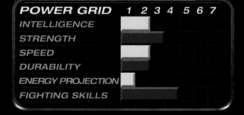

POWER GRID	1	2	3	4	5	6	7
INTELLIGENCE							
STRENGTH							
SPEED							
DURABILITY							
ENERGY PROJECTION							
FIGHTING SKILLS							

Art by David Finch

MOIRA MacTAGGERT

REAL NAME: Moira MacTaggert
KNOWN ALIASES: Moira Xavier
IDENTITY: No dual identity
OCCUPATION: Geneticist
CITIZENSHIP: U.K.
PLACE OF BIRTH: Scotland
KNOWN RELATIVES: David Xavier (son, deceased), Charles Xavier (ex-husband)
GROUP AFFILIATION: None
EDUCATION: PhD
FIRST APPEARANCE: Ultimate X-Men #16 (2002)

HISTORY: Moira MacTaggert met Charles Xavier on a post-graduate genetics course in Glasgow, and, after a three-week whirlwind romance, they married. After four years they were blessed with a son, David. The couple pioneered mutant research, and Moira designed the mutant detection device Cerebro, which they used to track down young mutants who needed medical care. Eventually, their work attracted the attention of adult mutant Erik Lensherr; seduced by their common dream of a new mutant society, Charles abandoned his family to help Erik build that society. The next day David's own mutant powers emerged, and he had to be sedated to prevent those powers from killing him.

A couple of years ago, Charles got back in touch with Moira. He had broken ties with Erik, and was setting up a mutant school in the U.S.A.; he also intended to establish a secret mutant hospital, run by Moira, in part as a way of ensuring David got the best medical attention. Moira accepted, setting up base on Muir Island off the North coast of Scotland.

When David awoke and went on a killing spree, Moira called in Charles and his students, the X-Men. They pursued David to Aberdeen and then Berlin, where he was apparently slain. When the X-Men became fugitives for hiding Magneto's survival from the authorities, Moira went into hiding with her charges. After the X-Men captured Magneto, Moira returned to Muir Island.

HEIGHT: 5'6"
WEIGHT: 124 lbs.
EYES: Blue
HAIR: Light brown

ABILITIES AND ACCESSORIES: Moira is a skilled geneticist and doctor.

POWER GRID	1	2	3	4	5	6	7
INTELLIGENCE							
STRENGTH							
SPEED							
DURABILITY							
ENERGY PROJECTION							
FIGHTING SKILLS							

Art by Bryan Hitch

BETTY ROSS

REAL NAME: Betty Ross
KNOWN ALIASES: None
IDENTITY: No dual identity
OCCUPATION: Director of Communications
CITIZENSHIP: U.S.A.
PLACE OF BIRTH: Unrevealed
KNOWN RELATIVES: General Ross (father)
GROUP AFFILIATION: Ultimates support staff
EDUCATION: Communications degree from Berkeley, studies at NYU
FIRST APPEARANCE: Ultimates #2 (2002)

HISTORY: Daughter of the legendary General Ross, Betty Ross roomed with fellow "army brat" Janet Van Dyne at NYU. Earning a communications degree at Berkeley, Betty dated Bruce Banner, lead scientist in her father's Super-Soldier Research program. His experiments led to his recurring transformations into the monstrous Hulk. Banner managed to suppress his Hulk transformations, but was still demoted when the Super-Soldier program expanded into the Ultimates superhero team. Banner was made deputy to new head scientists Hank and Janet Pym, and Betty was hired as the team's Director of Communications. Betty said nothing about the Pyms' past personal problems at first, but later revealed all after Hank nearly killed Jan during a domestic fight. Meanwhile, Betty routinely belittled Bruce until he finally snapped and went on a destructive rampage as the Hulk, finally halted by the Ultimates. Betty converted this into a public relations triumph by concealing the Hulk's true identity. She also took new romantic interest in Bruce, flattered by his desperate devotion and perversely attracted to his savage Hulk persona. When the Hulk's true identity leaked out, Betty coldly went along with the government's plan to execute Bruce for the Hulk's murders — though she broke down during the trial, declaring her love for Bruce and asking forgiveness. Unaware that Hank Pym secretly helped Banner escape his seeming execution, Betty mourned Bruce's death but continued her work with the Ultimates.

HEIGHT: 5'6"
WEIGHT: 110 lbs.
EYES: Brown
HAIR: Brown

ABILITIES & ACCESSORIES: Betty Ross is a cunning and shameless public relations mastermind with an obsessive work ethic, an almost invariably heartless attitude, and a knack for deceit and manipulation.

POWER GRID	1	2	3	4	5	6	7
INTELLIGENCE							
STRENGTH							
SPEED							
DURABILITY							
ENERGY PROJECTION							
FIGHTING SKILLS							

MAGNETO

REAL NAME: Erik Lensherr
KNOWN ALIASES: None
IDENTITY: Publicly known
OCCUPATION: Terrorist
CITIZENSHIP: Unrevealed
PLACE OF BIRTH: Unrevealed
KNOWN RELATIVES: Father (name unrevealed, deceased), Isabelle (wife), Pietro (son), Wanda (daughter)
GROUP AFFILIATION: Brotherhood of Mutants
EDUCATION: Unknown
FIRST APPEARANCE: Ultimate X-Men #1 (2001)

HISTORY: A magnetic-powered mutant (or "post-human"), Erik Lensherr approached mutant telepath Charles Xavier after hearing of his work saving young mutant patients with uncontrollable powers. Lensherr and Xavier found each other fascinating, neither having met an adult mutant before. They became close friends

and developed an ideology regarding mutants as mankind's replacements. Eventually, both men left their wives to found the Brotherhood of Mutants, a safe haven for persecuted mutants. Erik took his mutant children with him, and would later deny he ever loved his human spouse. A few years later, the Brotherhood moved to a remote Pacific island, the Savage Land, to found a new civilization. Erik even devised a new language for this new world, and through genetic experimentation created dinosaurs to inhabit it. Increasingly convinced humanity would not peacefully relinquish the planet to Homo Superior, Erik became more radical, regarding the Savage Land's citizens as an army. Abandoning his human name, Erik took the title Magneto. Realizing that Xavier didn't agree with his views, a paranoid Magneto took to wearing a helmet to prevent psi intrusion into his mind. Xavier finally fled with a handful of followers, but Magneto decided to teach him a lesson and broke his spine, leaving him crippled. Soon after, Magneto led the Brotherhood in an anti-human campaign of political assassinations and terrorist bombings.

Following an attack on Washington, the U.S. government unleashed robotic Sentinels on the mutant population in retaliation. When Xavier's new students, the X-Men, interfered, Magneto learned Xavier had survived, and sent Wolverine to slay his former friend. He also had the President's daughter kidnapped, which halted the Sentinel campaign; the X-Men soon rescued her. American authorities located the Savage Land and launched a massive Sentinel attack, but Magneto used his powers to reprogram them, leading them back to assault Washington. While the Sentinels decimated the capital, Magneto dragged the President naked onto the Whitehouse lawn. The X-Men intervened, and Magneto was defeated when his son Quicksilver, convinced that genocide was going too far, removed his helmet, leaving him vulnerable to Xavier's powers. Xavier claimed to have killed Magneto, but had instead secretly brainwashed him, hoping to rehabilitate him. For several months the amnesiac Erik lived peacefully as a Manhattan social worker looking after disabled children; however, the Brotherhood eventually learned he was alive, and restored his memories. Magneto resumed the bombing campaign halted by his errant children, simultaneously gathering every mutant he could into a floating Arctic Citadel. His powers enhanced by a machine of Forge's design, Magneto intended to reverse Earth's magnetic field, leaving humanity to perish in the ensuing environmental chaos. The X-Men stopped him, and he was imprisoned in the Triskelion, home of S.H.I.E.L.D. and the Ultimates. He was recently freed by Mystique and Forge.

HEIGHT: 6'2"
WEIGHT: 195 lbs.
EYES: Blue
HAIR: Silver

ABILITIES AND ACCESSORIES: Magneto can manipulate magnetic fields to fly, create force fields, and move metallic objects at will.

POWER GRID	1	2	3	4	5	6	7
INTELLIGENCE							
STRENGTH							
SPEED							
DURABILITY							
ENERGY PROJECTION							
FIGHTING SKILLS							

HISTORY: When Jean Grey's mutant telepathic powers emerged, the voices and visions nearly drove her insane. She had been committed to a psychiatric institution when fellow psi Charles Xavier saved her and taught her to control her powers. Recruited into Xavier's X-Men as Marvel Girl, she in turn enlisted many others. Her teammate Scott Summers (Cyclops) was attracted to her, but too uncertain to act; though Jean knew this, she instead became involved with new recruit Wolverine. When she learned he had originally joined intending to kill Xavier on behalf of the Brotherhood of Mutants, she dumped him. The X-Men were subsequently abducted by Weapon X, Wolverine's former employers. After six weeks in their brutal custody, Jean gained a new perspective on her former lover and forgave him, though they did not get back together. On her first mission with Weapon X, Jean was blackmailed into murdering Indian geneticist Atul Pandya to prevent Weapon X from killing Cyclops; in spite of this, when the X-Men were freed by the Brotherhood, Jean convinced her teammates not to slay their former captors.

Jean finally made the first move on Scott, and they became an item. Around the same time, her seizures returned and she experienced visions of a giant burning Phoenix. She was convinced she had contacted a hostile extra-dimensional entity. This belief was shared by the Hellfire Club, Xavier's mysterious financial backers, who carried out a mystic ceremony to merge Jean with the "Phoenix God," hoping to precipitate the end of the world. The ceremony appeared to work, but instead of granting the Club power, the possessed Jean slew them all. Xavier, insisting she was merely delusional, managed to restore Jean's own personality. No longer overwhelmed by the Phoenix power, Jean continued to access it, once lifting an unstable nuclear reactor in to the atmosphere and atomising it, thus saving the East Coast from devastation. Confident she could control the power, Jean believed the Phoenix had been an illusory manifestation created by her inability to deal with her own immense powers. Thor of the Ultimates advised caution, saying that if he were trying to possess someone, he would try to convince the host he did not exist.

Grey has continued to participate in various X-Men missions: bringing the explosive mutant Geldoff to the Mansion for treatment; trying to track serial killer Sinister by communicating telepathically with surviving victim Jean-Paul Beaubier; locating Rogue when she was kidnapped by Gambit; unintentionally and temporarily

REAL NAME: Jean Grey
KNOWN ALIASES: X12
IDENTITY: Publicly known
OCCUPATION: Adventurer, student
CITIZENSHIP: U.S.A.
PLACE OF BIRTH: Unrevealed
KNOWN RELATIVES: Professor Grey (father)
GROUP AFFILIATION: X-Men; formerly Weapon X
EDUCATION: Taking college level courses
FIRST APPEARANCE: Ultimate X-Men #1 (2001)

swapping Wolverine's mind with Peter Parker's (Spider-Man). Jean recently learned Cyclops lied when he told her that she was his first girlfriend.

HEIGHT: 5'5"
WEIGHT: 135 lbs.
EYES: Green
HAIR: Red

ABILITIES AND ACCESSORIES: Jean can read and transmit thoughts, generate illusions in people's minds, telekinetically move objects, and fly. She can lift thousands of tons in extreme circumstances. She is surrounded by a fiery aura when using telekinesis.

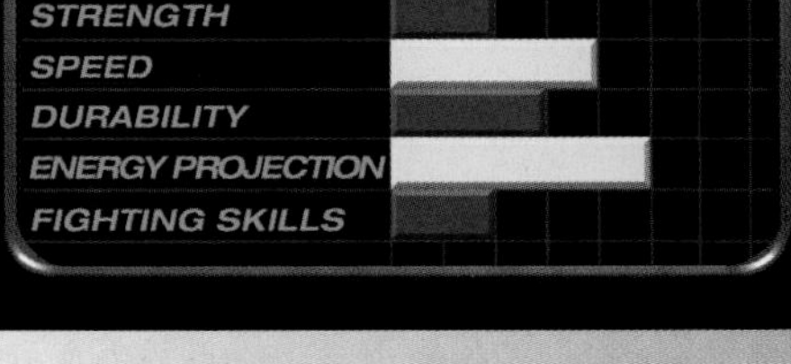

POWER GRID	1	2	3	4	5	6	7
INTELLIGENCE							
STRENGTH							
SPEED							
DURABILITY							
ENERGY PROJECTION							
FIGHTING SKILLS							

Art by Stuart Immonen

NIGHTCRAWLER

REAL NAME: Kurt Wagner
KNOWN ALIASES: Dread Pirate Bluetail, X3
IDENTITY: Known to authorities
OCCUPATION: Adventurer, student; formerly Weapon X agent
CITIZENSHIP: Germany
PLACE OF BIRTH: Germany
KNOWN RELATIVES: None
GROUP AFFILIATION: X-Men; formerly Weapon X
EDUCATION: Taking High school level courses
FIRST APPEARANCE: Ultimate X-Men #7 (2001)

HISTORY: Growing up in the Bavarian Alps, German mutant Kurt Wagner was kidnapped in his early teens by the black ops Weapon X organization. They brutally trained him for months to become their agent. Speaking no English, he was isolated from his fellow captives until the X-Men were likewise kidnapped and the telepathic Marvel Girl communicated with him. When the captives escaped with the assistance of the Brotherhood of Mutants, Weapon X head Colonel Wraith tried to flee in a helicopter. The X-Man Storm blasted it out of the sky in retaliation for his crimes, but Nightcrawler teleported Wraith out, insisting Weapon X had ruined enough lives without turning Storm into killer as well. The ungrateful Wraith was about to shoot Nightcrawler, but the newly arrived Nick Fury killed Wraith first.

Nightcrawler returned to Germany and learned English, ostensibly from watching television. After mutant terrorist Magneto, long believed slain by the X-Men, resurfaced, the X-Men became fugitives. Their enemies sought out their past associates, including Nightcrawler, who found himself pursued by the German authorities. Evading them thanks to his Weapon X training, he headed for Glasgow and Moira MacTaggert, whose contact information had been given to him by X-Men founder Charles Xavier. He nearly made it to her hideout before being captured and taken to Camp X-Factor in Guantanamo Bay. He was freed by a Brotherhood raid. When Magneto overloaded a Miami nuclear reactor, Nightcrawler was one of many mutants who helped evacuate the area. After the crisis was over, he joined the X-Men. During his time with them, he has hunted the serial killer Sinister, attempted to rescue his kidnapped teammate Rogue from Gambit and the von Struckers, bonded with teammate Angel in secret pirate games in the Danger Room as the Dread Pirate Bluetail, and joined an unauthorized expedition to Krakoa to free convicted mutant murderer Longshot.

HEIGHT: 5'8"
WEIGHT: 145 lbs.
EYES: Yellow
HAIR: Blue

DISTINGUISHING FEATURES: Covered in blue fur, Nightcrawler has three fingers and toes on each hand or foot and a prehensile forked tail. His body seems to burn with a golden inner fire which shows through his eyes, nostrils and mouth; his breath is visible as a golden mist.

ABILITIES AND ACCESSORIES: Nightcrawler can teleport up to two miles; he can transport others in this manner, and in extreme circumstances has been seen to move an entire car. He needs to be able to see or clearly visualize his destination point to teleport safely. He can also walk on walls. His toes and tail are prehensile, and he is an accomplished acrobat. He is an experienced fighter, trained with guns and swords.

POWER GRID	1	2	3	4	5	6	7
INTELLIGENCE							
STRENGTH							
SPEED							
DURABILITY							
ENERGY PROJECTION							
FIGHTING SKILLS							

Art by Brandon Peterson

PROFESSOR X

HISTORY: Charles Xavier is one of the world's premiere experts on mutants. A mutant telepath, Charles and his wife Moira wrote the book on post-human medicine, treating young mutants endangered by their own powers. Their mutant son David was born a few years into their marriage, but Charles never felt close to him. He had a strong bond with Erik Lensherr, the first adult mutant he ever met. As Charles and Moira drifted apart, Charles abandoned his family and helped Erik establish the Brotherhood of Mutants. Charles gradually realized Erik, now calling himself Magneto, didn't share his goal of peaceful coexistence with humanity. When Charles and his allies fled the Brotherhood, Magneto impaled Charles with a metal spear, severing his spine.

As the Brotherhood turned to terrorism, Charles worked to oppose them. Offered funding for a mutant school and hospital by the Hellfire Club, Charles asked Moira to take charge of the latter, thus ensuring his now sickly son David had constant treatment. At some point, Charles romanced his adult student Emma Frost, who eventually left him after arguing against what she viewed as plans to turn his students into soldiers. When the government launched the robotic anti-mutant Sentinels in response to the Brotherhood's terrorism, Charles sent his new students, the X-Men, to save mutants from the killer robots. The X-Men rescued the President's kidnapped daughter from the Brotherhood, winning Presidential favor, which was augmented when they saved Washington from destruction and Charles apparently slew Magneto. Charles secretly spared Erik, rendering him an amnesiac in the hope of eventual rehabilitation.

When David went on a murderous rampage, Charles found himself unable to kill his son, so Colossus, one of his X-Men, did it for him. Feeling himself a failure for letting down both David and his student Iceman (whom David hospitalized), Charles nearly disbanded the X-Men. Apparent progress with Magneto's rehabilitation convinced him to persevere. Tragically, Magneto later regained his memories and returned to terrorism. Suspected of collusion because he had lied about Magneto's demise, Xavier was captured by the Ultimates and imprisoned in Camp X-Factor, Guantanamo Bay. Later freed in a Brotherhood raid, he coordinated efforts to contain a nuclear power plant meltdown Magneto instigated, publicly redeeming himself. The X-Men were allowed to continue under S.H.I.E.L.D. jurisdiction.

Xavier is sometimes accused of using his powers to influence people for his own ends; though he denies this, he is not above

REAL NAME: Charles Xavier
KNOWN ALIASES: None
IDENTITY: Publicly known
OCCUPATION: Educator
CITIZENSHIP: U.S.A.
PLACE OF BIRTH: U.S.A.
KNOWN RELATIVES: Moira MacTaggert (wife, divorced), David Xavier (son)
GROUP AFFILIATION: X-Men; formerly Weapon X
EDUCATION: PhD
FIRST APPEARANCE: Ultimate X-Men #1 (2001)

deceit and manipulation. In his own way he is just as fanatical as Magneto. Only his conscience prevents him from being just as ruthless in the pursuit of his goals: protecting his students and achieving mutant-human coexistence.

HEIGHT: 6'
WEIGHT: 165 lbs.
EYES: Blue
HAIR: Bald (brown in childhood)

ABILITIES AND ACCESSORIES: Charles' telepathy allows him to project and read thoughts, locate the position of specific minds, control others' perceptions and, if desired, brainwash them. He is also a low-level telekinetic, able to move objects with his mind.

POWER GRID	1	2	3	4	5	6	7
INTELLIGENCE							
STRENGTH							
SPEED							
DURABILITY							
ENERGY PROJECTION							
FIGHTING SKILLS							

Art by Stuart Immonen

PROTEUS

REAL NAME: David Xavier
KNOWN ALIASES: Betsy Braddock
IDENTITY: Secret
OCCUPATION: Patient
CITIZENSHIP: U.K.
PLACE OF BIRTH: Scotland
KNOWN RELATIVES: Charles Xavier (father), Moira MacTaggert (mother)
GROUP AFFILIATION: None
EDUCATION: High school, unfinished
FIRST APPEARANCE: Ultimate X-Men #16 (May 2002)

HISTORY: The child of mutant telepath Charles Xavier and geneticist Moira MacTaggert, David Xavier grew up believing his father didn't love him. Certainly the intellectual Charles found it difficult to relate to his son, who loved soccer, video games, and wrestling. When Charles left his family to found the Brotherhood of Mutants with Magneto, he firmly believed they wouldn't miss him; yet David did, and the very next day his own mutant powers disastrously emerged. Their slightest use ravaged David's body, so Moira was forced to keep him sedated; he spent several years in his mother's care in the Muir Island hospital. Somehow sensing his father's return to Britain, David suffered a fatal convulsion but survived by transferring his consciousness into nurse Isobel MacLinden. He fled to the mainland, swapping bodies as each host wore out and slaying anyone who got in his way. Confronted by his parents and the X-Men in Aberdeen, he usurped Wolverine's form and fought them with a combination of reality manipulation, telepathic psychological warfare, and his host's natural skills. Since Wolverine's regenerative powers countered the internal damage David's powers caused, David intended to retain his new host permanently; but while attempting to flee, he carelessly leapt in front of an oncoming lorry. David jumped from Wolverine into the driver seconds before his former host was run over. After the vehicle crashed, David secretly possessed telepathic S.T.R.I.K.E. agent Betsy Braddock. Having finally figured out how to slow down his degeneration, he hid within Betsy and lured the X-Men to Berlin, where the Xaviers had held their last family holiday prior to Charles leaving.

As Betsy, he quizzed his father to learn Charles' true feelings for David, unaware that Charles knew his true identity. When Charles revealed this, David abducted him. With his powers growing, David restructured Betsy's body to resemble his original one, overpowered the X-Men and critically injured Iceman, then teleported Charles and himself around the world, blowing up landmarks and murdering innocent people. He taunted his father, claiming Charles didn't care about him, and sarcastically suggesting he might join the X-Men as Proteus. As he prepared to kill Charles, Betsy's mind resurfaced, blocking David's powers. She urged Charles to kill them before David could resume control or escape, but Charles found himself unable to kill his own son. The X-Man Colossus had no such problem, and swiftly crushed Betsy/David beneath a car, apparently killing them both. However, Betsy was reborn in a new body, so David's final fate remains in doubt.

HEIGHT: Variable
WEIGHT: Variable
EYES: Green (glowing)
HAIR: None (originally blond)

ABILITIES AND ACCESSORIES: David could transfer his mind from body to body, overriding the host mind's control; in each form he gained the skills and powers of his host. He was telepathic enough to sense opponents' fears and generate illusions of the same. He could also manipulate reality, allowing him to fly, teleport, and reshape objects around him. Use of his powers slowly burned out his hosts from the inside.

POWER GRID	1	2	3	4	5	6	7
INTELLIGENCE							
STRENGTH							
SPEED							
DURABILITY							
ENERGY PROJECTION							
FIGHTING SKILLS							

HISTORY: Pietro Lensherr, a.k.a. Quicksilver, is the son of mutant supremacist Magneto and twin brother of Wanda. Magneto abandoned their human mother when the twins were children, taking them with him as he founded the Brotherhood of Mutants with Charles Xavier, whom the children regarded as an uncle. Pietro loved his father, but nothing he did was ever good enough for Magneto; perhaps because Pietro was a constant reminder that Magneto had once loved a human. Pietro continued trying to win his father's respect, becoming his lieutenant and participating in the Brotherhood's anti-human terrorism. His father in turn deliberately belittled him. With doubts placed in Quicksilver's mind by the X-Man Cyclops, Quicksilver helped the X-Men defeat his father when Magneto tried to trigger a nuclear holocaust.

With Magneto presumed dead, Quicksilver assumed leadership of the Brotherhood. Feeling guilty about his role in his father's fate, Quicksilver tried to recover Magneto's corpse from the military, but found only his helmet. The X-Men offered the twins membership, but they declined. Still, relations between X-Men and Brotherhood thawed, and when Weapon X captured the X-Men, the Brotherhood rescued them. During this mission, Quicksilver encountered S.H.I.E.L.D. director Nick Fury, whose decision to allow the Brotherhood to leave peacefully may have earned Quicksilver's trust, laying the foundations for their future dealings. Pietro was soon convinced by "Uncle Charles" to shift the Brotherhood's activities from bombings to less violent protests, targeting financial institutions and research facilities experimenting on mutant animals. Many of the Brotherhood quit, feeling his leadership was weak, so Quicksilver led them in stripping Pakistan and India of their nuclear arsenals to prove his strength. He and his sister also brokered a deal with S.H.I.E.L.D. to go on selected black ops missions in return for the release of mutant "political prisoners." In this capacity, they helped repel an invasion by the alien Chitauri.

When Magneto returned, his children feared his wrath and defected to the Ultimates. Magneto breached S.H.I.E.L.D.'s Triskelion base and shot Quicksilver in the kneecaps for his betrayals, though Pietro swiftly healed. Now surrounded by humans, the twins grew closer, affecting an air of detached superiority towards their new teammates. In spite of this attitude, they proved crucial members of the team. Quicksilver played a key role in the capture of rogue teammate Thor, battled fellow speedster Northstar when Emma Frost's mutant students attacked the Triskelion, and even helped the Ultimates disarm a Middle-Eastern nation. Most recently,

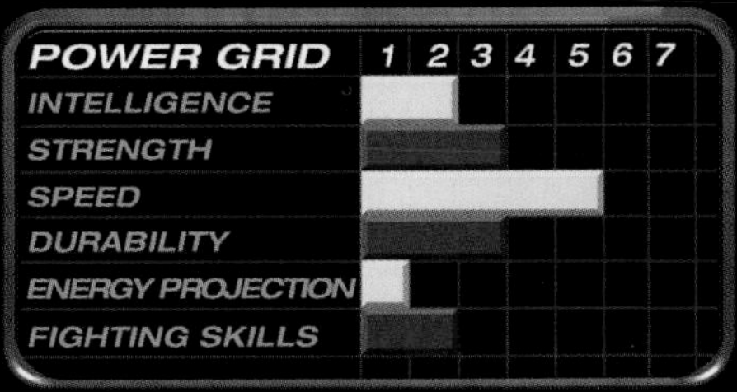

REAL NAME: Pietro Lensherr
KNOWN ALIASES: Pietro Maximoff
IDENTITY: Publicly known
OCCUPATION: Government super-agent; formerly terrorist
CITIZENSHIP: Unknown
PLACE OF BIRTH: Unknown
KNOWN RELATIVES: Isabelle (mother), Erik Lensherr (Magneto, father), Wanda Lensherr (Scarlet Witch, sister), grandfather (name unrevealed, deceased)
GROUP AFFILIATION: Ultimates; formerly Brotherhood of Mutants
EDUCATION: Unknown
FIRST APPEARANCE: Ultimate X-Men #1 (2001)

Wanda and Pietro were among the foremost defenders of both the Triskelion and New York during a foreign super-army's invasion of America.

HEIGHT: 6'
WEIGHT: 150 lbs.
EYES: Blue
HAIR: White

ABILITIES AND ACCESSORIES: Quicksilver is able to move at superhuman speed, fast enough to run across the U.S.A. in a matter of minutes. His perceptions and reflexes are similarly swift.

POWER GRID	1	2	3	4	5	6	7
INTELLIGENCE							
STRENGTH							
SPEED							
DURABILITY							
ENERGY PROJECTION							
FIGHTING SKILLS							

ROGUE

REAL NAME: Marian
KNOWN ALIASES: X7
IDENTITY: Known to authorities
OCCUPATION: Thief; formerly student, agent of Weapon X
CITIZENSHIP: U.S.A.
PLACE OF BIRTH: Unknown
KNOWN RELATIVES: Parents (names unrevealed)
GROUP AFFILIATION: X-Men; formerly Weapon X, Brotherhood of Mutants
EDUCATION: High School (unfinished)
FIRST APPEARANCE: Ultimate X-Men #7 (2001)

HISTORY: Growing up in the South, Marian first ran away after her father's gambling cost them the family home. When her mutant powers emerged, Marian unintentionally rendered a local boy

comatose. She was later captured by Weapon X and inhumanely trained as their agent, codenamed Rogue. In captivity, she bonded with fellow prisoner Cain (Juggernaut). When the Brotherhood of Mutants freed her, she joined them, and as part of a Brotherhood cell, she helped bomb the Brooklyn Bridge. Before they could leave their New Jersey safe house, S.H.I.E.L.D. sent in the Ultimates to arrest them. Rogue was captured by Hawkeye and sent to Camp X-Factor. A Brotherhood raid released her, but when Magneto overloaded a Miami nuclear reactor, Rogue helped X-Men founder Charles Xavier contain the radiation. Because of her heroism, her traumatic past, and her youth, she was reunited with her parents and released into the X-Men's custody rather than face prison.

When the winged Warren Worthington joined the X-Men, Rogue's religious upbringing led her to speculate he was an angel. She became romantically involved with Bobby Drake (Iceman); after the serial killer Sinister broke into the X-Men's home and shot Drake down, Rogue replicated Angel's wings and carried Sinister aloft, threatening to drop him to his death. Fellow X-Man Storm informed her that Bobby was alive, and convinced Rogue not to become a killer.

After catching Bobby kissing Kitty Pryde, Rogue was kidnapped by Gambit on behalf of the von Struckers, who wished to recruit her as corporate spy. Though they offered to help her control her powers, Rogue declined, explaining she believed her lack of control was a punishment for her crimes, and that she was determined to redeem herself. Escaping the von Struckers alongside Gambit, whose memories she had glimpsed, she informed the X-Men she intended to remain with him, much to Iceman's dismay. Rogue and Gambit travelled to Las Vegas, targeting Fenris holdings along the way. Outside the Fenris Resort and Casino, Juggernaut caught up with them, wanting Rogue back. Gambit brought a building down on both himself and Juggernaut; Rogue dug him out of the rubble, but he was fatally injured. At his behest, she kissed him, absorbing his memories and powers. Those powers and memories have not faded with time, and Rogue now has Gambit's mind inside her as a constant companion. Rogue has recently returned to the X-Men.

HT: 5'5"
WEIGHT: 135 lbs.
EYES: Red, formerly blue
HAIR: Brown with white stripes

ABILITIES AND ACCESSORIES: Rogue can duplicate others' memories and powers with a touch; this usually incapacitates her victim. She has no control over this power, which activates automatically with skin-on-skin contact. Since absorbing Gambit, she can charge inorganic matter and make it explode. Trained in hand-to-hand combat, she has absorbed Gambit's acrobatic and throwing skills.

POWER GRID	1	2	3	4	5	6	7
INTELLIGENCE		2					
STRENGTH		2					
SPEED		2					
DURABILITY		2					
ENERGY PROJECTION	1						
FIGHTING SKILLS			3				

HISTORY: Sabretooth was a mutant who believed that as men were crueler than less evolved animals, mutants should naturally be crueler and more monstrous than men. He was recruited into Weapon X, a black ops section of S.H.I.E.L.D. Initially coerced into serving them (he once spent six months as a NASA crash test dummy for disobeying orders), he eventually took a sadistic liking to the work, gaining a degree of authority over his fellow captive mutants. Sabretooth instantly disliked the similarly powered Wolverine, and has made an unverified claim that he slew Wolverine's wife and child. When Wolverine escaped Weapon X, Sabretooth was sent to bring him back; they clashed with one another in the New York subway and in Times Square before Wolverine escaped, thanks to Spider-Man's help.

After Wolverine joined the X-Men, Weapon X located their Mansion base and attacked it, capturing all of them except the absent Wolverine. Weeks later, Wolverine was recaptured in St. Petersburg. Sabretooth, now enhanced with adamantium implants similar to but more extensive than Wolverine's, took Wolverine outside the base to torment him by destroying files detailing the amnesiac Wolverine's past in front of him, unaware his rival had allowed himself to be captured so that Weapon X's location could be uncovered. A tracker implant within Wolverine led the Brotherhood of Mutants to the area to free the X-Men. Wolverine tricked an enraged Sabretooth into cutting his bonds, and the two battled until Wolverine castrated his foe and tackled him off a cliff. Wolverine recovered consciousness first, doing unspecified but non-lethal damage to his downed foe.

After Sabretooth recovered, he joined the terrorist Brotherhood of Mutants. Though he briefly quit in disgust over Quicksilver's weak leadership, he returned when Magneto resumed control, soon becoming his right hand man. He led raids on the Louvre and other museums and galleries, gathering art prior to Magneto's plan to devastate the Earth. He also oversaw missions recruiting oppressed mutants from around the globe. When the X-Men attacked the Brotherhood's Citadel, Sabretooth again clashed with Wolverine, boasting he was bigger, stronger and could heal any wound Wolverine inflicted; in response, Wolverine decapitated him.

REAL NAME: Unrevealed
KNOWN ALIASES: None
IDENTITY: Known to the authorities
OCCUPATION: Terrorist; formerly Weapon X agent
CITIZENSHIP: Unrevealed
PLACE OF BIRTH: Unrevealed
KNOWN RELATIVES: None
GROUP AFFILIATION: Brotherhood; formerly Weapon X
EDUCATION: Unknown
FIRST APPEARANCE: Ultimate Marvel Team-Up #1 (2001)

HEIGHT: 6'5"
WEIGHT: 220 lbs.
EYES: Red
HAIR: Blond

ABILITIES AND ACCESSORIES: Sabretooth had enhanced senses, and could track a target by scent alone. His wounds healed rapidly. His natural claws and fangs were later enhanced with adamantium coating, and four foot-long retractable claws were added to each arm.

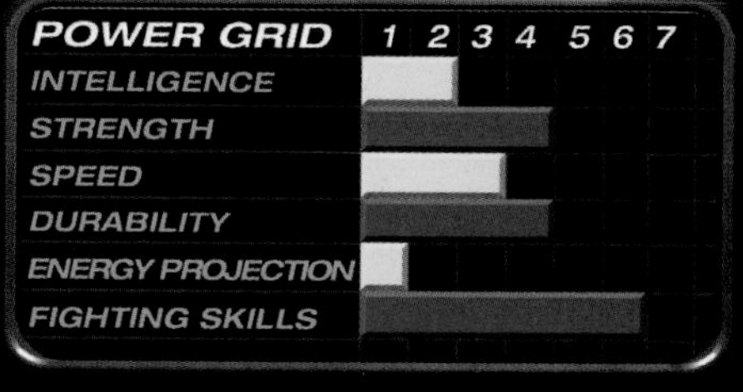

POWER GRID	1	2	3	4	5	6	7
INTELLIGENCE							
STRENGTH							
SPEED							
DURABILITY							
ENERGY PROJECTION							
FIGHTING SKILLS							

Art by Tom Raney

SCARLET WITCH

REAL NAME: Wanda Lensherr
KNOWN ALIASES: Wanda Maximoff
IDENTITY: Publicly known
OCCUPATION: Government super-agent; formerly terrorist
CITIZENSHIP: Unrevealed
PLACE OF BIRTH: Unrevealed
KNOWN RELATIVES: Isabelle (mother), Erik Lensherr (Magneto, father), Pietro Lensherr (Quicksilver, brother), grandfather (name unrevealed, deceased)
GROUP AFFILIATION: Ultimates; formerly Brotherhood of Mutants
EDUCATION: Unknown
FIRST APPEARANCE: Ultimate X-Men #1 (2001)

HISTORY: Wanda is the twin sister of Pietro and daughter of mutant supremacist Magneto, who took the twins away from their human mother and raised them within his Brotherhood of Mutants. The twins were always close, with Wanda generally deferring to Pietro in all things. While her brother bore the brunt of their father's contempt for his children, Wanda was Pietro's confidante, consoling him. After their father was reportedly killed in Washington, Wanda backed Pietro's leadership of the Brotherhood. She helped him try to recover Magneto's corpse from the military, only to discover it was absent. During the course of this mission, Cyclops tried to persuade them to join the X-Men. Wanda nearly convinced Pietro to do so, but the moment was lost when a soldier shot at her. Still, Wanda began to question their militant anti-human campaign. When the X-Men were abducted by Weapon X, the Brotherhood rescued them, and Wanda used her powers to remove the neural implants that controlled the agency's captives.

Under Quicksilver, the Brotherhood became less murderous. The twins also secretly agreed to assist S.H.I.E.L.D. black ops on selected missions in return for the release of mutant "political prisoners," helping to repel a Chitauri invasion of Earth alongside the Ultimates. Magneto subsequently turned back alive, and took back the Brotherhood. Regarded as traitors by their fellow mutants, fearful of Magneto's retribution for Quicksilver's part in his earlier defeat, and branded by working with humans, the twins found sanctuary with S.H.I.E.L.D. Magneto, however, penetrated the agency's Triskelion base and forced Wanda to watch as he shot her brother in the knees. Though Quicksilver recovered, their old ties were irrevocably severed, and they became full time members of the Ultimates.

Wanda is not above exploiting her brother's devotion to her; when the Ultimates fought Thor, she spurred a badly injured Quicksilver back into action by lying, saying that Thor had hurt her, ultimately securing victory for the team. When the murdering mutant Longshot hid out in the Savage Land, where Wanda grew up, she tracked him down and used her own probability manipulation powers to override his. She has since tried to stop Emma Frost's mutant students from breaking into the Triskelion, and helped the Ultimates disarm a Middle-Eastern country. Most recently, Wanda and Pietro were among the foremost defenders of both the Triskelion and New York during a foreign super-army's invasion of America.

HEIGHT: 5'9"
WEIGHT: 145 lbs.
EYES: Brown
HAIR: Brown, formerly dyed black

ABILITIES AND ACCESSORIES: Wanda can manipulate probability to create a wide range of effects. She can fly, teleport targets with surgical exactness, and transform people and objects.

POWER GRID	1	2	3	4	5	6	7
INTELLIGENCE							
STRENGTH							
SPEED							
DURABILITY							
ENERGY PROJECTION							
FIGHTING SKILLS							

Art by Stuart Immonen

SENTINELS

HISTORY: With an increasing number of powerful mutants appearing across the globe, government officials grew concerned. In response, scientist Bolivar Trask devised the Sentinels, a series of gigantic, well-armed robots with mutant detection equipment. After the terrorist Brotherhood of Mutants bombed Capitol Hill and publicly proclaimed their intention to supplant humanity as the dominant species, Senator Andrew Border Turk pushed the President into activating the Sentinels and sending them out to hunt and slay mutants. They struck without warning or mercy, killing anyone they found with a mutant gene, regardless of age, gender, race or creed, innocence or guilt. Beginning in Los Angeles, they swept across the country.

In New York's Times Square they targeted young mutant runaway Robert Drake, who had fled his family, fearful that they might be hurt if the Sentinels tracked him down. Drake was saved by the X-Men, a mutant group gathered by Charles Xavier. They destroyed several Sentinels, and Bobby froze one himself using his ice generating powers. More Sentinels were sent to scour New York, but the X-Men were cloaked from their scans. When the Brotherhood kidnapped the President's daughter and threatened to kill her if the Sentinels killed another mutant, the President temporarily retired the Sentinels. After his daughter was rescued by the X-Men, the President promised to end the indiscriminate Sentinel attacks altogether, but still authorized one last mission to attack the recently discovered Brotherhood stronghold in the Savage Land. A fleet of Sentinels killed many of the Brotherhood until Magneto magnetically reprogrammed the Sentinels to kill normal humans, and then led them against Washington. The X-Men tried to minimize loss of life, gradually whittling down the Sentinels' numbers until Xavier stopped Magneto, ending the attack.

New, human-driven Sentinels were subsequently developed by S.H.I.E.L.D., sixty specially trained agents in high-tech armor made of a non-conductive polymer resistant to Magneto's control, each one powerful enough to destroy a fleet of their predecessors. Used to guard Camp X-Factor, they were apparently killed or disabled when the Brotherhood attacked the base in force to free the captive mutants held within.

FIRST APPEARANCE: Ultimate X-Men #1 (2001)

Anti-mutant factions high up in the government also used Sentinels again, unleashing several at the press launch of Emma Frost's new mutant education campaign. The X-Men made short work of these Sentinels, but not before one slew the Beast. The conspirators behind them were swiftly brought to justice.

HEIGHT: 50'
WEIGHT: 5 tons
EYES: Red
HAIR: None

ABILITIES AND ACCESSORIES: The robot Sentinels could fly at supersonic speeds, were heavily armored against conventional weaponry, possessed immense strength, and were armed with extremely powerful blasters capable of incinerating most targets. The human Sentinels were alleged to have much more powerful weapons, but the only ones apparent were machine guns.

POWER GRID	1	2	3	4	5	6	7
INTELLIGENCE							
STRENGTH							
SPEED							
DURABILITY							
ENERGY PROJECTION							
FIGHTING SKILLS							

SHADOWCAT

REAL NAME: Katherine "Kitty" Pryde
KNOWN ALIASES: None
IDENTITY: Known to the authorities
OCCUPATION: Student, adventurer
CITIZENSHIP: U.S.A.
PLACE OF BIRTH: U.S.A.
KNOWN RELATIVES: Theresa Pryde (mother)
GROUP AFFILIATION: X-Men
EDUCATION: High school student
FIRST APPEARANCE: Ultimate X-Men #21 (2002)

HISTORY: After fourteen-year-old Kitty Pryde's mutant powers emerged, causing terrifying incidents where she uncontrollably phased out of the family apartment in to moving traffic and sewers, her mother Theresa contacted Professor Xavier, who agreed to teach Kitty to control her abilities. Kitty's mother insisted she did not want her going off on dangerous missions like Xavier's other X-Men students, or taking a codename; but Kitty immediately ignored Theresa's wishes, considering calling herself Shadowcat and initially regarding the school as a big heroic adventure. This changed after she stowed away on a mission with Wolverine and Cyclops to the Savage Land. There Kitty unintentionally saved the pair's lives when she phased through a sentient computer controlling zombie cyborg hordes, shorting it out. As they evacuated the area, Cyclops was apparently killed. Kitty and Wolverine returned to the States to find the X-Men wrongly accused of being allied with the terrorist Magneto. The X-Men became fugitives, and Kitty was forced to grow up fast living on the run.

After the X-Men cleared their names, Kitty settled into her new life. Ruled by her hormones, she showed romantic interest in her teammates Colossus and Angel before setting her sights on Iceman (Bobby Drake). She was also a big fan of Spider-Man, and when she met him while in New York tracking down the explosive mutant Geldoff, the star-struck Kitty invited the wall-crawler back to the X-Men Mansion to meet Xavier (much to her teammates' chagrin). En route, Geldoff blew a hole in the jet, and Spider-Man was knocked out. Xavier removed his costume while examining him for injuries, and Kitty was intrigued to discover that he was both cute and near her age.

Kitty subsequently proved herself in combat, downing an attacking Sentinel in Washington and saving teammate Rogue from the serial killer Sinister, even though she was jealous of Iceman's interest in Rogue. Later, while visiting the Coney Island fair, Iceman kissed Kitty. Rogue caught them, knocked Kitty out, and soon left the X-Men to be with Gambit. Kitty and Iceman finally became an item during a later trip to Genosha, but she ended the relationship when she found he was still in e-mail communication and in love with Rogue. Realizing she had been interested in Iceman because he was attracted to her, not because she wanted to be with him, she decided on a whim to call Spider-Man and asked him out on a date. After a pleasant afternoon of conversation and crime fighting, they became a couple.

HEIGHT: 5'4"
WEIGHT: 120 lbs.
EYES: Brown
HAIR: Brown

ABILITIES AND ACCESSORIES: Kitty can turn intangible, allowing her to pass through solid objects and walk on air. When she phases through electronic or mechanical systems, she can cause them to malfunction and break down.

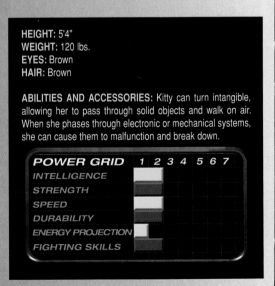

POWER GRID	1	2	3	4	5	6	7
INTELLIGENCE							
STRENGTH							
SPEED							
DURABILITY							
ENERGY PROJECTION							
FIGHTING SKILLS							

Art by Mark Bagley

S.H.I.E.L.D.

HISTORY: It is unclear exactly when the S.H.I.E.L.D. global security agency was founded. Hawkeye once claimed that he and Nick Fury founded S.H.I.E.L.D. late in the Cold War. However, a little over ten years ago, Fury was attached to an army unit (possibly part of S.H.I.E.L.D.) escorting Weapon X, then a single mutant operative. At some point in the last decade, with the global mutant population increasing, S.H.I.E.L.D. expanded into a multi-national organization with thousands of agents worldwide. Within its security remit it policed scientific advances, both technological and genetic; to keep S.H.I.E.L.D. ahead of the opposition, it also ran its own R&D programs. Colonel Wraith headed Weapon X, by then a counter-terrorism unit exploiting captive mutants. Colonel Fury's section handled the Super-Soldier Project (trying to duplicate the process which empowered Captain America) and policed violations of the superhuman test ban treaty. Convinced the next war would be a genetic one, Fury commissioned civilian corporations such as Oscorp to develop a super-soldier serum for S.H.I.E.L.D. Tech and Psi-divisions were established, as well as regional branches, such as Britain's S.T.R.I.K.E. General Ross oversaw all aspects, and also personally monitored the Baxter Building genius hothouse.

After losing S.H.I.E.L.D. funding, Oscorp developed the Oz Compound, which led to several mutations including Norman Osborn and Peter Parker (Spider-Man). Fury took a personal interest in both cases, planting Agent Bradley at Peter's school and covertly monitoring Osborn. Following the mutant terrorist Magneto's attack on Washington, S.H.I.E.L.D.'s budget was expanded; Weapon X was shut down (the current administration did not condone its abduction of innocent mutants), and replaced with a small volunteer superhuman defense unit, the Ultimates. Disapproving of these plans, Wraith attempted to murder Ross. With Ross incapacitated, Fury became the new head of S.H.I.E.L.D., executed Wraith, and closed down Weapon X. Promoted to General, he moved S.H.I.E.L.D.'s main base to the Triskelion in New York harbor.

S.H.I.E.L.D.'s next few months were busy. The Ultimates were publicly launched, while S.H.I.E.L.D. agents arrested Doctor Octopus and the Sandman, closed down Justin Hammer's illegal genetics lab, helped Spider-Man bring down the Green Goblin (a transformed Norman Osborn), and aided the X-Men in hunting down rogue mutant David Xavier. However, S.H.I.E.L.D.'s greatest losses and victories came in repelling the Chitauri, shapeshifting alien infiltrators. A S.H.I.E.L.D. flotilla of helicarriers was destroyed in a nuclear ambush with the loss of 20,000 operatives, but the survivors rallied Earth's forces to destroy the Chitauri armada.

When Magneto threatened global destruction, S.H.I.E.L.D. rounded up mutants connected to the terrorist and imprisoned them in Camp X-Factor, Guantanamo Bay. Following this crisis, the X-Men were brought under Fury's jurisdiction. Meanwhile, S.H.I.E.L.D. illegally housed many genetically modified criminals in a research facility where they could be studied by Hank Pym (Giant Man); eventually, Osborn led a breakout and tried to blackmail the President into firing Fury, but Osborn's "Six" were finally recaptured on the White House lawn. Black ops agent Karma helped uncover a conspiracy within the upper echelons of government, and when Harry Osborn proved to have been mutated like his father, a S.H.I.E.L.D. squad, led by Fury, took him into custody. Most notably, S.H.I.E.L.D. coordinated Earth's defenses against another extra-terrestrial threat, the world destroyer Gah Lak Tus. A foreign super-army recently destroyed the Triskelion, slaughtered countless S.H.I.E.L.D. troops, captured the Ultimates and occupied major American cities; whether S.H.I.E.L.D. can recover from this disaster remains to be seen.

CURRENT MEMBERS: Betsy Braddock, Bradley, Sharon Carter, Crowley, Dugan, Nick Fury, Karma (Xi'an Coy Mahn), McQuillan, Clay Quartermain, Thibodeau, Jimmy Woo
FORMER MEMBERS: Bruce Banner, Black Widow (Natasha Romanov), Eamonn Brankin, Fred, Hawkeye (Clint Barton), Jason, Lange, Liebowitz, Linklater, Hank Pym, Janet Pym, Quicksilver (Pietro Maximoff), Riggs, General Ross, Scarlet Witch (Wanda Maximoff), Tara, Dai Thomas, John Wraith
BASE OF OPERATIONS: Triskelion, New York
FIRST APPEARANCE: Ultimate X-Men #7 (2001)

SINISTER

REAL NAME: Nathaniel Essex
KNOWN ALIASES: Mister Sinister
IDENTITY: Secret
OCCUPATION: Serial killer; former bioengineer
CITIZENSHIP: Unrevealed
PLACE OF BIRTH: Unrevealed
KNOWN RELATIVES: None
GROUP AFFILIATION: None
EDUCATION: Presumed Ph D in bioengineering
FIRST APPEARANCE: Ultimate X-Men #46 (2004)

HISTORY: A bioengineer for Oscorp's New Orleans subsidiary, Nathaniel Essex developed techniques to create a super-soldier who could evade any form of detection and hypnotically persuade others. When his supervisors refused to allow him to test his procedures on human subjects, Essex experimented upon himself. Much like Oscorp's self-mutated president Norman Osborn, Essex developed superhuman abilities accompanied by schizophrenic traits. One of these voices identified itself as Lord Apocalypse, a powerful mutant who intended to usher in "the Final Age" of humanity and, presumably, bring about either mutant rule or the end of the world entirely. It is unclear if Lord Apocalypse was real or hallucinatory, but regardless, Essex was fired from Oscorp for his interaction with his hallucinatory voices.

Calling himself "Sinister" and elaborately tattooed to that effect, Essex relocated to New York, following "Lord Apocalypse's" instructions to slay ten "innocent" mutants, after which Lord Apocalypse would help complete Essex's transformation. Essex murdered four mutant youths but a fifth victim, Jean-Paul Beaubier, survived thanks to his superhuman speed. Under Marvel Girl's telepathic counsel, Beaubier provided the X-Men with information about Sinister. X-Men members Cyclops, Colossus, Storm, Wolverine, Marvel Girl and Nightcrawler dispersed throughout New York in search of Sinister. Having anticipated this response, Sinister snuck into X-Men headquarters, intending to slay the mutants who had remained behind. Sinister threw Professor Xavier down a flight of stairs, then fought Iceman, Angel, Dazzler and Shadowcat to a standstill before Rogue caught him and flew into the air with him. Rogue intended to drop Sinister to his death, but a returning Storm dissuaded her.

Taken into S.H.I.E.L.D. custody, Sinister broke down completely, suffering from sensory disorientation. Lord Apocalypse (or the hallucination thereof) appeared before him in his cell, declaring Sinister unworthy of being his Horseman, and then ordered Sinister to choke himself. Sinister apparently tried, but failed, to kill himself, and is now kept restrained and under suicide watch.

APOCALYPSE

Art by Brandon Peterson

HEIGHT: 6'1"
WEIGHT: 239 lbs.
EYES: Hazel
HAIR: Black

ABILITIES & ACCESSORIES: Sinister can hypnotically immobilize anyone, and compel them to do whatever he says, although this power may be limited to relatively simple commands. He is invisible to any electronic detection, and is incapable of being tracked. Sinister has remarkable strength and endurance, but it is unclear if it reaches superhuman levels. He often carries firearms.

POWER GRID	1	2	3	4	5	6	7
INTELLIGENCE							
STRENGTH							
SPEED							
DURABILITY							
ENERGY PROJECTION							
FIGHTING SKILLS							

HISTORY: Ororo Munroe was raised in Morocco, learning English from American films. Ororo's family was murdered under unknown circumstances, and she fled to America as an illegal immigrant. She stole cars in Harlem before relocating to Texas. Although Storm's mutant powers manifested during her youth, she was too frightened to experiment with them. In Texas, Ororo was mentored and befriended by slightly older car thief Yuriko "Yuri" Oyama. However, Yuri soon saw Ororo as a rival, and their friendship ended in a motorcycle chase which Ororo halted with a sudden rainstorm; Yuri lost control and had a seemingly fatal collision with a truck. Guilt-ridden, Ororo continued thieving in Texas, briefly serving time in juvenile detention. At one point she declined an offer to join Magneto's Brotherhood of Mutants.

Pursued by police after stealing a car, Ororo panicked and lashed out with her powers, almost killing several bystanders before she was caught. Hours later the X-Men arranged her release and recruited her. Still nervous about her abilities, Ororo, now called Storm, learned several new applications of her powers, including the ability to fly, and became attracted to fellow student Hank McCoy, a.k.a. the Beast, whose lifetime of mistreatment made him doubt anyone could love him.

Weapon X imprisoned the X-Men, torturing them and mutating Beast into a furry, animal-like form. When they were eventually freed by the Brotherhood of Mutants, Storm tried to kill Weapon X's Colonel Wraith, but Nightcrawler stopped her. Feeling more unworthy of Storm than ever, the transformed Beast ended their relationship. The rift between them widened when Beast inadvertently helped the Brotherhood free Magneto from Professor X's mental conditioning, but they reconciled during the resulting crisis.

Still feeling inadequate, Beast left the X-Men when new recruit Angel became attracted to Storm. He soon joined Emma Frost's "New Mutants," but their press conference was disrupted by a Sentinel attack, during which Beast perished. Grief-stricken and enraged, Storm lashed out uncontrollably before Professor X calmed her telepathically. In the tragedy's aftermath, Storm drastically altered her hairstyle and clothing to distance herself from her time with Beast. She also became more predisposed to act as the team's conscience, preventing Rogue from killing Sinister just as Nightcrawler prevented Storm from killing Wraith.

REAL NAME: Ororo Munroe
KNOWN ALIASES: None
IDENTITY: Publicly known
OCCUPATION: Student, adventurer; former car thief
CITIZENSHIP: Morocco, criminal record in U.S.A.
PLACE OF BIRTH: Morocco
KNOWN RELATIVES: Unspecified family members (deceased)
GROUP AFFILIATION: X-Men
EDUCATION: Little formal schooling prior to X-Men membership
FIRST APPEARANCE: Ultimate X-Men #1 (2001)

Storm gradually bonded with Wolverine, and they shared a kiss while searching for an abducted Rogue. When Rogue chose to accompany her abductor, rejecting and insulting Wolverine, he left the X-Men. Storm pursued him to Canada, where both were attacked by Yuri, now transformed by Weapon X into Deathstrike. Storm ended their fight with a lightning strike to both women. Storm was resuscitated by Wolverine. They both returned to the X-Men, their feelings still unresolved.

HEIGHT: 5'8"
WEIGHT: 117 lbs.
EYES: Brown
HAIR: White

ABILITIES AND ACCESSORIES: Storm can control weather patterns, creating rain, snow, lightning, and other effects. She is able to fly by manipulating powerful winds; weather conditions in her vicinity are frequently altered in unconscious reflection of her mood. Storm is an exceptional athlete and thief.

POWER GRID	1	2	3	4	5	6	7
INTELLIGENCE							
STRENGTH							
SPEED							
DURABILITY							
ENERGY PROJECTION							
FIGHTING SKILLS							

Art by Andy Kubert

THOR

REAL NAME: Thor or Thorlief Golmen
KNOWN ALIASES: None
IDENTITY: (Thor) Publicly known; (Golmen) known to authorities
OCCUPATION: Guardian deity; formerly psychiatric nurse
CITIZENSHIP: (Thor) Asgard; (Golmen) Norway
PLACE OF BIRTH: (Thor) Asgard; (Golmen) Norway
KNOWN RELATIVES: (Thor) Odin (father), Loki (half-brother); (Golmen) Gunnar Golmen (brother)
GROUP AFFILIATION: Formerly Ultimates
EDUCATION: Unrevealed
FIRST APPEARANCE: The Ultimates #4 (2002)

HISTORY: He claims he is the legendary Norse thunder deity Thor, sent to Earth by his father Odin. Official records say he is Thorlief Golmen, who stole his scientist brother Gunnar Golmen's super-soldier technology. Both accounts agree that he believed he was different from an early age, but only came to believe he was Thor after suffering a nervous breakdown just before turning 30, spending the next 18 months in an asylum. After discovering (or stealing, as the case may be) his powers, Thor began spreading his message of social change through lecture tours and books. He initially refused to join the Ultimates, but did help them subdue the monstrous Hulk after the U.S. President met Thor's demand of doubling the U.S.'s foreign aid budget. Thor began working with the Ultimates thereafter, forming a fast friendship with teammate Tony Stark (Iron Man). He helped the Ultimates in their attempt to recruit Hawk-Owl; though Thor declined fulltime Ultimates duty, he reliably aided the team against serious threats. He helped defeat the extraterrestrial Chitauri invasion force, and neutralized a Chitauri doomsday weapon which would have destroyed the solar system. After failing to prevent Magneto from breaching the S.H.I.E.L.D. Triskelion, Thor battled X-Men members Storm and Colossus, finding the latter's strength matched his own. When Norman Osborn's "Six" attacked the White House, Thor defeated fellow lightning wielder Electro. He also helped the Ultimates and Fantastic Four gather information about the world destroyer Gah Lak Tus.

Thor met (or hallucinated) fellow Asgardian warrior Volstagg the Voluminous, who warned that Thor's evil half-brother Loki had escaped from the "room without doors," and that the Ultimates were pawns of the New World Order. Quitting the Ultimates in protest after they began operating uninvited in foreign countries, Thor was publicly accused by Captain America of leaking team secrets. Thor later intervened to protect protestors from police at an Italian demonstration against the European Defence Initiative's super-soldier program. Persuaded by Gunnar Golmen that Thor was simply a madman using stolen technology, the Ultimates and the E.D.I. hunted down Thor in Norway, attacking him despite his claims that Gunnar was actually Loki in disguise. Thor held his own until Quicksilver removed his belt, depriving him of his powers. Thor currently resides in a high-security cell in the Triskelion, where he is haunted by gloating visions of Gunnar/Loki, warning of a traitor in the Ultimates' ranks.

HEIGHT: 6'5"
WEIGHT: 285 lbs.
EYES: Blue
HAIR: Blond

ABILITIES & ACCESSORIES: Thor possesses immense superhuman strength, endurance, and resistance to injury. Much of his power seems to come from his belt, which is either powered by advanced technology or Norse iconography. His hammer, Mjolnir, enables him to fly, control storms, direct thunder and lightning, and teleport.

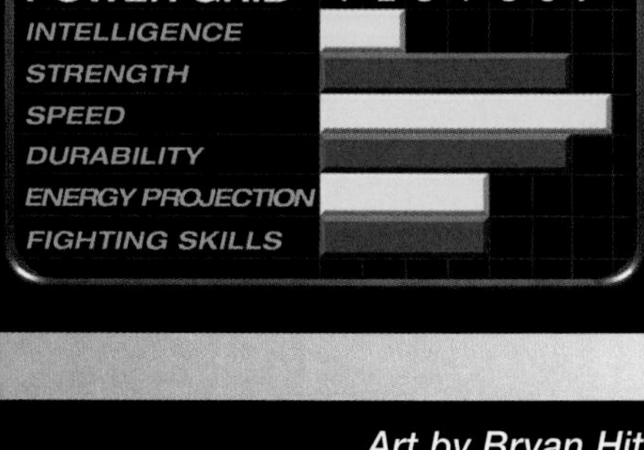

POWER GRID	1	2	3	4	5	6	7
INTELLIGENCE							
STRENGTH							
SPEED							
DURABILITY							
ENERGY PROJECTION							
FIGHTING SKILLS							

Art by Bryan Hitch

HISTORY: The world's foremost superhuman strike force, the Ultimates trace their origins back to World War II super-operative Captain America (Steve Rogers), whom the U.S. government empowered in part to oppose the Nazis' secret extraterrestrial Chitauri allies. Rogers appeared to die while helping destroy the Chitauri/Nazi war effort, and U.S. scientists tried for decades to duplicate his powers. In recent years, the super-soldier program's lead scientist was geneticist Bruce Banner, reporting to General Ross, head of the S.H.I.E.L.D. intelligence agency. Later, new S.H.I.E.L.D. director Nick Fury pushed through a multi-billion expansion of the super-soldier program, though Banner's temporary transformation into the monstrous Hulk resulted in his demotion to deputy under new head scientists Hank and Janet Pym, who did double duty as size-changing super-operatives Giant-Man and Wasp. Altruistic armored billionaire inventor Tony Stark soon joined as Iron Man. Enigmatic left-wing powerhouse Thor refused membership at first, but Captain America himself was found alive and revived from a state of suspended animation to join the team. Together, Rogers, Stark and the Pyms became the Ultimates, headquartered in the high-tech Triskelion complex and backed by a huge support staff, a large conventional military force and black ops agents. Banner's semi-estranged girlfriend Betty Ross (daughter of General Ross) was hired as Director of Communications and helped make the new team into celebrities while making Bruce's life miserable. The depressed Banner finally snapped and transformed into the Hulk again, embarking on a destructive rampage stopped by the Ultimates with the aid of Thor, who began working with the team thereafter.

The Hulk's true identity was concealed from the public, and the Ultimates became beloved national heroes. The group soon expanded: intelligence veterans Hawkeye and Black Widow and mutant ex-terrorists Quicksilver and Scarlet Witch were promoted from the black ops division to the core team. Meanwhile, Hank Pym nearly killed his wife during a violent domestic dispute and was himself beaten into traction by Captain America, who later began dating the Wasp. Pym's former assistant Dr. Eamonn Brankin became the new scientific head of the program. Despite losing Giant-Man, the Ultimates saved the world from a Chitauri plot with the unwitting aid of the Hulk and became bigger icons than ever. They went on to apprehend Kraven, Electro, Luther Manning, the X-Men and Norman Osborn's "Six." Later allied with the European Super-Solider Initiative, the Ultimates became more controversial as they began operating in foreign territory, notably the Middle East. Thor quit, and a traitor within the group outed Banner as the Hulk. Seemingly executed for the Hulk's crimes, Banner secretly survived with the aid of Hank Pym, who was soon fired from the Ultimates altogether. Meanwhile, apparently exposed as a madman, Thor was brutally arrested by the team. The global community grew wary as the Ultimates developed many more superagents as their reserves, and anti-Ultimates sentiment accelerated when the team stripped a small "rogue" Middle Eastern nation of its nuclear capability. The traitor within the

ACTIVE MEMBERS: Black Widow (Natasha Romanov), Captain America (Steve Rogers), Hawkeye (Clint Barton), Iron Man (Tony Stark), Quicksilver (Pietro Maximoff), Scarlet Witch (Wanda Maximoff), Wasp (Janet Pym)
FORMER MEMBERS: Giant-Man (Hank Pym), Hulk (Bruce Banner), Lieberman (deceased reservist), Thor (allegedly Thorlief Golman)
RESERVES: The Four Seasons, the Goliaths, Intangi-Girl, Owen, O'Donohue, Rocketman One (Dexter), Rocketman Two, Rocketman Three, Rusk, Son of Satan (Damien), Thunderbolt, unspecified others
BASE OF OPERATIONS: The Triskelion, Upper Bay, Manhattan
FIRST APPEARANCE: Ultimates #2 (2002)

Ultimates responded by murdering Hawkeye's family, framing Captain America for the crime, and helping a foreign super-army invade America. Assisted by Hank Pym, this foreign force destroyed the Triskelion and occupied major American cities, slaughtering the reserves and capturing the remaining Ultimates in the process.

Art by Bryan Hitch

VON STRUCKERS

REAL NAME: Andreas and Andrea von Strucker
KNOWN ALIASES: None
IDENTITY: Secret
OCCUPATION: CEOs of Fenris International
CITIZENSHIP: Unrevealed (somewhere in Europe, probably Germany or Austria)
PLACE OF BIRTH: Unrevealed
KNOWN RELATIVES: (Andreas) Andrea (sister or wife); (Andrea) Andreas (brother or husband)
GROUP AFFILIATION: Fenris International
EDUCATION: Unknown
FIRST APPEARANCE: Ultimate X-Men #51 (2004)

HISTORY: Andrea and Andreas von Strucker are co-presidents of global investment firm Fenris International, named for the Norse wolf who brought about the twilight of the gods. Nobody is sure whether the pair are siblings or married. Secretly, they are mutants whose powers depend on physical contact with each other. Long believing that economic empowerment was Homo Superior's only chance for true equality with normal humans, they founded their company to end humanity's financial dominance over mutantkind. Feeling they needed "creative measures" to compete in a human-dominated business world, they recruited fellow mutants to use for corporate espionage, sometimes kidnapping them first to ensure that Fenris had not been seen to hire them, allowing deniability if their missions went wrong. One such recruit was the Cajun thief Gambit, whose loyalty they bought by helping him regain control of his powers.

When their scouts determined Rogue of the X-Men would make a useful operative, Gambit abducted her and brought her to their Empire State building penthouse offices. The von Struckers offered to have their bioengineers cure Rogue's inability to control her draining abilities, and train her as a spy, in return for signing an exclusive contract with them. They tried to convince a wary Rogue by having her don a special polymer uniform which dampened her powers, allowing her to touch Gambit without absorbing his powers or memories; if she agreed to work for them, they would graft the material under her skin, allowing her to regulate her powers at will. Rogue still declined, but the von Struckers made it clear that they would not accept her choice. When Gambit backed her up, the Struckers blasted him, then turned on Rogue. Gambit managed to damage her suit, allowing Rogue to drain the von Struckers, stunning them long enough for Rogue and Gambit to flee. Though Andrea was prepared to write them off as bad investments, Andreas took the physical assault more personally, and ordered their Wolfpack operatives to slay the pair before they could leave the building. However, when other X-Men arrived and easily overpowered the von Struckers, the executives decided to back down…at least for now.

HEIGHT: (Andreas) 5'11"; (Andrea) 5'9"
WEIGHT: (Andreas) 160 lbs.; (Andrea) 110 lbs
EYES: (both) Blue
HAIR: (both) Blond

ABILITIES AND ACCESSORIES: By touching hands (or presumably other body parts) Andrea and Andreas can fire twin energy beams of heat and concussive force; they can discharge sufficient energy to knock the Manhattan power-grid offline or atomise a human. They can also generate a protective energy shield.

POWER GRID	1	2	3	4	5	6	7
INTELLIGENCE							
STRENGTH							
SPEED							
DURABILITY							
ENERGY PROJECTION							
FIGHTING SKILLS							

Art by Andy Kubert

HISTORY: Asian-American mutant Janet Van Dyne grew up on a military base near Dusseldorf, Germany, but later went to college in America. Studying science at NYU, she roomed with fellow "army brat" Betty Ross and dated Hank Pym, an unstable scientific genius who sometimes physically abused her. Claiming the good times made the bad times worth it, Jan stuck by Hank despite his abuse, and eventually married him. Her low self-esteem may have stemmed in part from her secret mutant traits (insect-like properties and the power to reduce her own physical size), which she concealed from everyone but Pym. When she and Hank worked at S.H.I.E.L.D.'s Super-Soldier Research Facility under Bruce Banner (later the monstrous Hulk), Jan allowed Hank to take credit for supposedly creating her powers by scientific means, and Pym made various scientific breakthroughs based on his genetic studies of Jan. The Pyms were later promoted to head the research and development wing of the government's new superhuman strike force, the Ultimates, with Banner as their deputy and Betty Ross as the program's Director of Communications. The Pyms also became two of the program's founding super-operatives as the Wasp and Giant-Man (Hank using a new growth formula), and Jan embraced her new status as a celebrity. Humiliated and injured in battle by a rampaging Hulk and jealous of teammate Captain America, Hank nearly killed Jan during a subsequent domestic fight, engulfing the shrunken Wasp in an army of hostile ants.

While Hank fled and Jan recovered, Hank's former assistant Eamonn Brankin took over the Ultimates' R&D operations. Captain America apprehended Hank, beating Pym into traction, but an embarrassed and confused Jan denounced the Captain's meddling and considered quitting the team. After helping the Ultimates save Earth from the extraterrestrial Chitauri, Jan decided to stay on, cutting ties with Hank and dating Captain America. This new relationship was controversial since the Pyms were not yet formally divorced, and Jan gradually wearied of the generation gap between herself and the 1940s-born Captain America. She also began to feel increasingly marginalized and excluded as the Ultimates expanded. Feeling alienated from her team and her lover, Jan

REAL NAME: Janet Pym (née Van Dyne)
KNOWN ALIASES: None
IDENTITY: Publicly known
OCCUPATION: Molecular biologist, U.S. government super-operative
CITIZENSHIP: U.S.A.
PLACE OF BIRTH: Unrevealed
KNOWN RELATIVES: Hank Pym (estranged husband)
GROUP AFFILIATION: Ultimates, S.H.I.E.L.D.
EDUCATION: Two scientific doctorates, including studies at NYU
FIRST APPEARANCE: Ultimates #2 (2002)

began secretly seeing Hank (long since fired from the Ultimates), albeit platonically, and left Captain America after he discovered and denounced this "affair;" however, Pym has since helped a foreign super-army invade America and defeat the Ultimates.

HEIGHT: 5'3" (variable)
WEIGHT: 105 lbs. (variable)
EYES: Purple
HAIR: Black

ABILITIES AND ACCESSORIES: Wasp can shrink to the size of an insect. As she shrinks, she grows insect-like wings that enable her to fly. At miniature sizes, she can discharge "stings" of bioelectric energy. A natural neurological reflex prevents her from shrinking beyond the limits of her body's endurance. She sometimes eats bugs, forms larval nests and produces egg-like constructs, side-effects of her insectoid genetics. Janet is an experienced molecular biologist with training in unarmed combat and marksmanship, and is moderately fluent in German.

POWER GRID	1	2	3	4	5	6	7
INTELLIGENCE							
STRENGTH							
SPEED							
DURABILITY							
ENERGY PROJECTION							
FIGHTING SKILLS							

Art by Chris Bachalo

WEAPON X

FORMER MEMBERS: Beast (Hank McCoy), Colossus (Piotr Rasputin), Dr. Cornelius, Cyclops (Scott Summers), Fred, Iceman (Robert Drake), Juggernaut (Cain), Liebowitz, Linklater, Marvel Girl (Jean Grey), Nightcrawler (Kurt Wagner), Rogue (Marian), Sabretooth, Tara, Wolverine (James Howlett), Colonel John Wraith, Professor Charles Xavier
BASE OF OPERATIONS: Finland; formerly Arizona; Canada
FIRST APPEARANCE: Ultimate X-Men #2 (2001)

HISTORY: Weapon X was founded as S.H.I.E.L.D.'s premier counter-terrorism unit. A little over a decade ago, Weapon X was mutant operative Wolverine's codename; under Colonel John Wraith's control, he was used as a living weapon, kept caged when not in use. The concept of kidnapping and dehumanizing mutants was expanded, and Weapon X became the name of the entire project, 250 men strong.

Wraith, operating largely autonomous of his S.H.I.E.L.D. superior General Ross, took sadistic pleasure in torturing his captives. A few years ago Wolverine escaped, covertly assisted by Nick Fury, whose life he had saved many years earlier. Wolverine repeatedly evaded his pursuers, once escaping Sabretooth and a couple of agents in New York thanks to the intervention of Spider-Man. Wraith later ambushed Wolverine at JFK airport, but Wolverine was rescued by the X-Men. Wolverine left Wraith with facial scars in this last encounter, and would have killed him had the X-Men's Marvel Girl not stopped him.

Weapon X continued to "recruit" new agents, including Nightcrawler, Rogue, and Juggernaut, replacing ones lost on missions in Bosnia and other parts of the world. Despite the X-Men becoming national heroes, Weapon X invaded their home and abducted them all, except the absent Wolverine. Weapon X tortured and trained the X-Men, controlling them with neural implants. After Nick Fury was captured during an Indian mission, General Ross ordered Wraith to send in Weapon X to rescue Fury and end an Indian genome project; the X-Men succeeded in both missions, but Wraith forced Marvel Girl to murder an Indian scientist. Ross was horrified to learn of the X-Men's kidnappings, and decided to phase out Weapon X. Getting wind of this, Wraith attempted to assassinate him, planning to seize control of S.H.I.E.L.D.

Wolverine let himself be recaptured, leading the Brotherhood of Mutants to Weapon X's base. With the X-Men freed, Wraith attempted to flee, but Storm downed his helicopter; not wishing her to become a murderer, Nightcrawler saved Wraith from the explosion. The ungrateful Wraith was about to shoot his savior when he was killed by Nick Fury, who, called in by Wolverine, had just arrived with a contingent of S.H.I.E.L.D. agents to shut Weapon X down.

Though officially decommissioned, elements of Weapon X persisted in targeting Wolverine, backed by senior government officials who feared mutant domination. One squad, led by Tara, a woman who claimed to be Wolverine's wife, hunted him through New York, battling both Spider-Man and Daredevil. Wolverine and the X-Men subsequently tracked them down to their base, but, abandoned by their secret backers, Tara killed her team and committed suicide rather than face capture.

More recently, Dr. Cornelius attempted to kill Wolverine, transforming paralyzed teenager Yuriko Oyama in to the cyborg assassin Deathstrike. She confronted Storm and Wolverine in a remote part of Canada. When they gained the upper hand, Weapon X agents and Cornelius moved in for the kill, but Storm and Wolverine together brought down their attack helicopter. Whether any more remnants of Weapon X will return remains to be seen.

HISTORY: Howlett's past is mostly unknown, but during World War II he participated in military airdrops with Captain America. Decades later, he was abducted and experimented upon by a covert government unit, who bonded unbreakable adamantium to his skeleton and implanted three claws in each arm. Initially designated Weapon X (later the name of the entire unit), Howlett was renamed both "Logan" and "Wolverine." Weapon X held him for at least a decade. Supposedly programmed to kill any human he saw, he proved his humanity was intact by saving Nick Fury's life in the Middle East. He grew to hate his captors and also his fellow prisoner, Sabretooth.

Fury eventually helped him escape, and Wolverine became a mercenary, frequently working for Magneto's Brotherhood of Mutants. He was constantly pursued by Weapon X, on one occasion evading them with the aid of the young adventurer Spider-Man. A year and a half after his escape, Wolverine was assigned by Magneto to assassinate Charles Xavier, leader of the X-Men. Successfully infiltrating the X-Men, Wolverine delayed his mission in order to romance Marvel Girl, but in the succeeding weeks he embraced Xavier's cause and turned on Magneto, fighting the Brotherhood alongside the X-Men.

Soon afterward, Weapon X captured and enslaved most of the X-Men; Wolverine informed Nick Fury of the abductions, and then allowed himself to be captured in order to lead rescuers to Weapon X's secret base. While Wolverine was drawn into a grudge match with Sabretooth, the Brotherhood of Mutants raided the base, and Fury arrived to kill Wraith and guarantee the X-Men's freedom.

Wolverine remained jealous of Marvel Girl's boyfriend Cyclops, and when they investigated Magneto's abandoned Savage Land lair together, Wolverine left Cyclops to die. Wolverine helped the other X-Men battle Magneto and the Ultimates, but as the multi-front conflict reached its conclusion, Cyclops returned, exposing Wolverine's misconduct and kicking him off the team. Retreating into isolation, Wolverine was surprised when Cyclops, feeling Wolverine's rehabilitation outweighed their feud, invited him back and informed him S.H.I.E.L.D. had discovered evidence of his earlier life: a wedding ring.

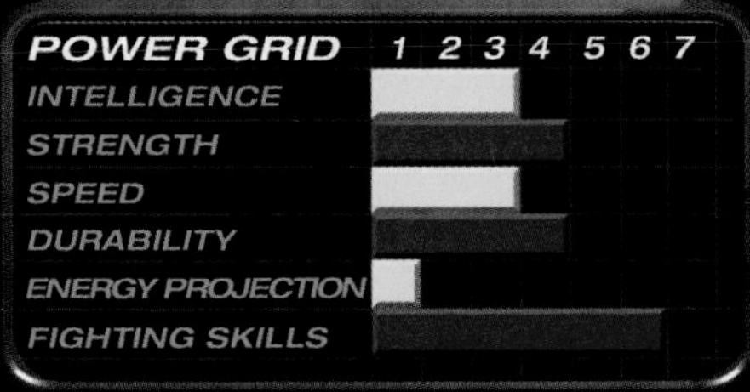

REAL NAME: James Howlett
KNOWN ALIASES: Logan, Weapon X, Lucky Jim
IDENTITY: ("Logan") publicly known; (James Howlett) Known to the authorities
OCCUPATION: Student, adventurer; formerly mercenary, government operative, corporal in Canadian Special Forces, otherwise unrevealed
CITIZENSHIP: Presumably Canada
PLACE OF BIRTH: Unrevealed, probably somewhere in Canada
KNOWN RELATIVES: Wife (name and status unconfirmed); son (allegedly, supposedly deceased)
GROUP AFFILIATION: X-Men; formerly Brotherhood of Mutants, Weapon X, 1st Canadian Parachute Battalion
EDUCATION: Unrevealed
FIRST APPEARANCE: Ultimate X-Men #1 (2001)

Troubled by the revelation, Wolverine departed again, but was targeted by Weapon X renegades whom he defeated alongside Spider-Man and Daredevil. Wolverine has gradually regained the X-Men's trust, and been startled by a growing attraction between him and Storm, battling alongside her against Deathstrike.

More recently, Nick Fury has called upon Wolverine to hunt down and kill the fugitive Dr. Bruce Banner (Hulk), a mission Wolverine accepted because it sounded like a fun challenge.

HEIGHT: 5'9"
WEIGHT: 292 lbs. (including adamantium)
EYES: Blue
HAIR: Black

ABILITIES AND ACCESSORIES: Wolverine's mutant healing factor enables him to recover from virtually any injury in a matter of minutes to hours. His enhanced senses make him an excellent tracker. His bones have been bonded with unbreakable adamantium, and he has six claws made of the same material. Wolverine's physiology has been altered so he is invisible to radar, and most telepaths are unable to read his thoughts.

POWER GRID	1	2	3	4	5	6	7
INTELLIGENCE							
STRENGTH							
SPEED							
DURABILITY							
ENERGY PROJECTION							
FIGHTING SKILLS							

Art by Adam Kubert

X-MEN

CURRENT MEMBERS: Colossus (Piotr Rasputin), Cyclops (Scott Summers), Dazzler (Alison Blaire), Iceman (Bobby Drake), Marvel Girl (Jean Grey), Nightcrawler (Kurt Wagner), Rogue (Marian), Shadowcat (Kitty Pryde), Storm (Ororo Munroe), Wolverine (James Howlett), Professor Charles Xavier
FORMER MEMBERS: Angel (Warren Worthington III), Beast (Hank McCoy)
BASE OF OPERATIONS: Xavier Institute for Gifted Children, Salem Center
FIRST APPEARANCE: Ultimate X-Men #1 (2001)

HISTORY: Leaving the radical Brotherhood of Mutants and obtaining secret financial backing from the Hellfire Club, Charles Xavier established the Xavier Institute for Gifted Children in New York. He gathered Cyclops, Marvel Girl, Colossus, Storm and Beast as his X-Men, defending mutants while promoting peaceful co-existence with humanity. Iceman joined them after being saved from Sentinels, and Wolverine after the X-Men rescued him from Weapon X.

When the Brotherhood kidnapped the U.S. President's daughter, the X-Men freed her, gaining the President's favor and ending Sentinel attacks on innocent mutants. Cyclops briefly defected to the Brotherhood, unhappy Xavier was dealing with "the Evil Empire," but when Magneto attempted to destroy Washington with reprogrammed Sentinels, Cyclops returned to the fold. Weapon X soon abducted all the X-Men except Wolverine, coercing them to become operatives until the Brotherhood freed them.

When the X-Men were called in to hunt down Xavier's murderous mutant son David, Iceman was badly injured and Colossus was forced to kill David. Iceman's parents removed him from the school and tried to sue Xavier, pressured by an anti-mutant senator; however, Iceman refused to co-operate, and dropped the suit. Shortly after Kitty Pryde joined the X-Men, Xavier sent Wolverine and Cyclops on a mission to the Savage Land; while there, Wolverine deliberately left Cyclops to die, jealous of his relationship with Marvel Girl. Meanwhile, the Hellfire Club revealed their true motivations when they tried to merge Marvel Girl with a hostile extra-dimensional entity, the Phoenix Force.

Magneto returned and the Brotherhood resumed its anti-human terrorism. Implicated as Magneto's allies since they had falsified reports of his death, the X-Men became fugitives, battling the Ultimates and escaping only due to the surprise return of Iceman. The X-Men located Magneto thanks to Cyclops, who had been found and healed by the Brotherhood. Defeating Magneto and saving Florida from nuclear destruction, the X-Men became national heroes; the White House pardoned them but placed them under the supervision of S.H.I.E.L.D. In the wake of this adventure, Nightcrawler and Rogue were recruited into the X-Men, and Cyclops fired Wolverine. Cyclops later relented, feeling Wolverine's best chance of redemption was with the X-Men.

The next few months saw a visit to the mansion from Spider-Man, an incursion by remnants of Weapon X, and the addition of Angel to the group. Beast left to join Emma Frost's rival mutant educational program, but was killed in a Sentinel attack; Dazzler, one of Frost's other recruits, joined the X-Men, though her rock chick ways irritated Xavier. The serial killer Sinister nearly slew Xavier and Iceman before Rogue defeated him. Believing a worldwide spate of horrendous nightmares might be a telepathic mutant's distress call, Xavier sent several X-Men to Siberia, where they encountered the Ultimates and learned of the coming of Gah Lak Tus; Xavier subsequently helped oppose the world destroyer.

After Rogue left the team to be with mutant thief Gambit, Xavier sent several X-Men to Genosha to find out if convicted murderer Longshot had been framed by the anti-mutant regime. They learned he was guilty, but not before an unauthorized mission led by Dazzler freed him. The X-Men recently tried to prevent some of Emma Frost's new students from breaking into S.H.I.E.L.D.'s Triskelion, bringing them into conflict with the Ultimates and Magneto once more.

U - Ultimates	USec - Ultimate Secret
UI - Ultimate Iron Man	USix - Ultimate Six
UMT - Ultimate Marvel Team-Up	USM - Ultimate Spider-Man
	UW - Ultimate War
UN - Ultimate Nightmare	UX - Ultimate X-Men

ACADEMY OF TOMORROW
First Appearance: UX #44 (2004)
Significant Issues: First class assembled (UX #43-45, 2004); used to free Magneto (UX #61-65, 2005)

ANGEL
First Appearance: UX #40 (2004)
Significant Issues: Joined X-Men (UXM #40, 2004); injured during Krakoa mission, started dating Dazzler (UXM #54-57, 2005)

BEAST
First Appearance: UX #1 (2001)
Significant Issues: Joined X-Men, battled Magneto (UX #1-6, 2001); mutated by Weapon X (UXM #8-12, 2001-2202); unwittingly informed Brotherhood of Magneto's survival (UXM #23, 2002); left X-Men, killed (UXM #42-45, 2004)

BLACK WIDOW
First Appearance: UMT #14 (2002)
Significant Issues: Manipulated Spider-Man and joined SHIELD (UMT #14, 2002); joined Ultimates, fought Chitauri (U #7-13, 2002-2004); got engaged, obtained armor (U 2 #3, 2005)

BETSY BRADDOCK
First Appearance: UX #16 (2002)
Significant Issues: Hunted David Xavier, possessed, body killed (UX #16-19, 2002); returned in Kwannon's body (UX #33, 2003)

BROTHERHOOD
First Appearance: UX #1 (2001)
Origin: UX #26 (2003)
Significant Issues: First fought X-Men (UX #3, 2001); rescued X-Men from Weapon X (UX #11-12, 2001-2002); Magneto resumed leadership, defeated (UX #25-33/UW #1, 2003)

CAPTAIN AMERICA
First Appearance: U #1 (2002)
Significant Issues: Led attack on Nazi base, frozen, revived in modern day (U #1-3, 2002); fought Chitauri (U #10-13, 2003-2004)

CAPTAIN BRITAIN
First Appearance: (as Braddock) UX #19 (2002); (as Captain Britain) U 2 #2 (2005)
Origin: U 2 #4 (2005)
Significant Issues: Helped raise submarine (U 2 #2, 2005); helped capture Thor (U 2 #4-5, 2005)

CAPTAIN MAHR VEHL
First Appearance: USec #1 (2005)
Origin: USec #2-4 (2005)
Significant Issues: Sent to spy on humanity, defected instead (USec #1-4, 2005)

CHITAURI
First Appearance: U #8 (2002)
Significant Issues: Conflict with Ultimates, flashbacks to World War II (U #8-13, 2002-2004)

COLOSSUS
First Appearance: UX #1 (2001)
Significant Issues: Briefly resigned from X-Men, returned (UX #16-18, 2002); fought Ultimates (UN #1-5, 2004-2005)

CYCLOPS
First Appearance: UX #1 (2001)
Significant Issues: Defected to Brotherhood, convinced Quicksilver to betray Magneto (UX #5-6, 2001); left for dead by Wolverine (UX #29, 2002)

DAZZLER
First Appearance: UX #42 (2004)
Significant Issues: Chosen for Frost's mutant PR group (UX #42-45, 2004); fought Sinister (UX #49, 2004); led Longshot rescue (UX #54, 2005); became involved with Angel (UX #57, 2005)

DEFENDERS
First Appearance: U 2 #6 (2005)
Significant Issues: Recruited Giant-Man, humiliated by cigarette thieves, Nighthawk injured (U 2 #6, 2005); recruited Whiz-Kid, spied upon by Son of Satan (U Annual #1, 2005)

FALCON
First Appearance: UN #1 (2004)
Significant Issues: Accompanied Ultimates to Russia, fought Colossus, established contact with Vision (UN #1-5, 2004-2005)

NICK FURY
First Appearance: UMT #5 (2001)
Significant Issues: Delhi mission, rescued by X-Men, shot Wraith (UX #9-12, 2001-2002); organized Ultimates against Chitauri (U #2-13, 2002-2003); warned Spider-Man about Osborn (USM #24, 2002); led Ultimates mission to Tunguska (UN #1-5, 2004-2005); learned of Kree presence on Earth (USec #2, 2005)

GAH LAK TUS
First Appearance: UEx #1 (2006)
Significant Issues: Vision arrived on Earth to warn of coming doom (UN #1-5, 2005); Gah Lak Tus database stolen from Kree starship (USec #1-4, 2005)

GAMBIT
First Appearance: UX #13 (2002)
Significant Issues: Faced Hammerhead (UX #13-14, 2002); kidnapped Rogue for Fenris (UX #50-53, 2005); died (UX Annual #1, 2005)

GIANT MAN
First Appearance: U #2 (2002)
Significant Issues: Became Giant-Man (U #2, 2002); injured by Hulk, abused Wasp (U #5-6, 2002); beaten by Cap (U #9, 2002); Ant-Man guise, fired from Ultimates (U 2 #1-3, 2005); joined Defenders, allied with traitor (U 2 #6, 2005)

HAWKEYE
First Appearance: (mentioned) U #4 (2002), (cameo) U #7 (2002), (full) U #8 (2002)
Significant Issues: Wiped out Chitauri nest alongside Black Widow, joined Ultimates, fought Chitauri (U #7-13, 2002-2004); Barton family slaughtered by Ultimates traitor (U 2 #7, 2005)

HELLFIRE CLUB
First Appearance: UX #24 (2003)
Significant Issues: Merged Jean Grey with Phoenix, then destroyed (UX #24-25, 2003)

HULK
First Appearance: UMT #2 (2001)
Significant Issues: Encountered Spider-Man (UMT #2-3, 2001); caused New York massacre (U #5-6, 2002); fought Chitauri (U #12-13, 2003-2004); trial and "execution" (U 2 #2-3, 2005)

ICEMAN
First Appearance: UX #1 (2001)
Significant Issues: Injured by Proteus (UX #19, 2002); dropped lawsuit against Xavier (UX #24, 2003); rescued X-Men from Ultimates (UW #4, 2003)

IRON MAN
First Appearance: UMT #4 (2001)
Origin: UI limited series (still in progress)
Significant Issues: Met Spider-Man (UMT #4-5, 2001); joined Ultimates, fought Hulk & Chitauri, met Black Widow (U #2-13, 2002-2004); engaged to Black Widow (U 2 #3, 2005)

LONGSHOT
First Appearance: UX #54 (2005)
Origin: UX #57 (2005)
Significant Issues: "Hunt for Justice" participant, freed by X-Men (UX #54-57, 2005); captured by Scarlet Witch (UX #62, 2005)

MOIRA MACTAGGERT
First Appearance: UX #16 (2002)
Origin: UX #18 (2002)
Significant Issues: Called in X-Men to pursue David (UX #16-19, 2002); went into hiding (UX #27-32, 2003)

MAGNETO
First Appearance: UX #1 (2001)
Significant Issues: First confronted X-Men (UX #1-6, 2001); memories restored, plotted to reverse Earth's magnetic field (UX #25-33, 2003)

MARVEL GIRL
First Appearance: UX #1 (2001)
Significant Issues: Killed Atul Pandya (UX #10, 2001); gained Phoenix power (UX #25, 2003); saved Florida (UX #32-33, 2003)

NIGHTCRAWLER
First Appearance: UX #7 (2001)
Significant Issues: Tried to escape Weapon X (UX #7, 2001); joined X-Men (UX #32, 2003)

PROFESSOR X
First Appearance: UX #1 (2001)
Origin: UX #18, 26 (2002, 2003)
Significant Issues: Co-founded Brotherhood (UX #26, 2003); stopped Magneto's attack on Washington (UX #6, 2001)

PROTEUS
First Appearance: UX #16 (2002)
Origin: UX #17 (2002)
Significant Issues: Went on killing spree, slain by Colossus (UX #16-19, 2002)

QUICKSILVER
First Appearance: UX #1 (2001)
Significant Issues: Betrayed his father (UX #6, 2001); rescued X-Men (UX #11-12, 2001-2002); joined Ultimates (U #8, 2002/UW #1-2, 2003)

ROGUE
First Appearance: UX #7 (2001)
Significant Issues: Weapon X agent (UX #7-12, 2001-2002); captured by Hawkeye (UW #1, 2003); helped save Florida, pardoned, joined X-Men (UX #30-31, 2003); departed with Gambit (UX #53, 2005); absorbed dying Gambit's memories (UX Annual #1, 2005)

BETTY ROSS
First Appearance: (mentioned) U #2 (2002); (pictured) U #3 (2002)
Significant Issues: Publicized Ultimates, spun Hulk disaster into good PR (U #3-6, 2002); interest in Banner rekindled (U #13, 2004); broke down during Banner's trial (U 2 #2-3, 2005)

SABRETOOTH
First Appearance: UMT #1 (2001)
Significant Issues: Fought Wolverine in Times Square (UMT #1, 2001); helped Weapon X capture and train X-Men (UX #8-12, 2001-2002), with Brotherhood (UX #26-30, 2003)

SCARLET WITCH
First Appearance: UX #1 (2001)
Significant Issues: Considered joining X-Men (UX #1/2, 2002); joined Ultimates (U #8, 2002/UW #1-2, 2003); captured Longshot (UX #62, 2005)

SENTINELS
First Appearance: UX #1 (2001)
Significant Issues: Sentinels initiative launched, halted following Washington debacle (UX #1-6, 2001); Attacked press launch (UX #44-45, 2004)

SHADOWCAT
First Appearance & Origin: UX #21 (2002)
Significant Issues: Destroyed evolved computer (UX #24, 2003); first met Spider-Man (USM #42-44, 2003); began dating Peter Parker (USM Annual #1, 2005)

S.H.I.E.L.D.
First Appearance: UX #2 (2001)
Significant Issues: Closure of Weapon X, Fury replaces Ross as head of agency (UX #9-12, 2001-2002); formation of Ultimates (U #1-6, 2002); vs. Chitauri (U #7-13, 2002-2004); escape and recapture of Osborn's "Six" (USix #1-7, 2003-2004)

SINISTER
First Appearance: UX #46 (2004)
Origin: UX #49 (2004)
Significant Issues: Shot Jean-Paul Beaubier (UX #46, 2004); fought X-Men (UX #49, 2004)

STORM
First Appearance: UX #1 (2001)
Origin: UX #59 (2005)
Significant Issues: Almost killed Wraith (UX #12, 2002); reacted to Beast's death (UX #44-45, 2004); expressed feelings for Wolverine (UX #51-52, 2004); fought Deathstrike (UX #59-60, 2005)

THOR
First Appearance: U #4 (2002)
Significant Issues: Fought Hulk in New York (U #5-6, 2002); fought Chitauri (U #7-13, 2002-2004); captured by Ultimates (U 2 #4-5, 2005)

ULTIMATES
First Appearance: U #1 (2002)
Significant Issues: Fought Hulk in New York (U #5-6, 2002); fought Chitauri (U #7-13, 2002-2004); took down Thor (U 2 #4-5, 2005)

ANDREA AND ANDREAS VON STRUCKER
First Appearance: UX #51 (2004)
Significant Issues: Tried to recruit Rogue (UX #50-53, 2004-2005)

WEAPON X
First Appearance: UX #2 (2001)
Significant Issues: Abducted X-Men, closed down (UX #8-12, 2001-2002); survivors targeted Wolverine (UX #34-39, 2003-2004); unleashed Deathstrike (UX #59-60, 2005)

WASP
First Appearance: U #2 (2002)
Significant Issues: Joined Ultimates (U #2, 2002); brutalized by Hank (U #6, 2002); fought Chitauri, spurned Hank, romanced Cap (U #10-13, 2003-2004); wearied of Cap (U 2 #1-7, 2005)

WOLVERINE
First Appearance: UX #1 (2001)
Significant Issues: Joined X-Men (UX #2-6, 2001); freed X-Men from Weapon X (UX #8-12, 2001-2002); battled Weapon X renegades (UX #33-39, 2003-2004)

X-MEN
First Appearance: UX #1 (2001)
Significant Issues: Brought down Magneto (UX #1-6, 2001); abducted by Weapon X (UX #8-12, 2001-2002); fought Ultimates & Magneto (UW #1-4/UX 27-33, 2003)

POWER RATINGS

INTELLIGENCE
Ability to think and process information
1 Slow/Impaired
2 Normal
3 Learned
4 Gifted
5 Genius
6 Super-Genius
7 Omniscient

STRENGTH
Ability to lift weight
1 Weak: cannot lift own body weight
2 Normal: able to lift own body weight
3 Peak human: able to lift twice own body weight
4 Superhuman: 800 lbs-25 ton range
5 Superhuman: 25-75 ton range
6 Superhuman: 75-100 ton range
7 Incalculable: In excess of 100 tons

SPEED
Ability to move over land by running or flight
1 Below normal
2 Normal
3 Superhuman: peak range: 700 MPH
4 Speed of sound: Mach-1
5 Supersonic: Mach-2 through Orbital Velocity
6 Speed of light: 186,000 miles per second
7 Warp speed: transcending light speed

DURABILITY
Ability to resist or recover from bodily injury
1 Weak
2 Normal
3 Enhanced
4 Regenerative
5 Bulletproof
6 Superhuman
7 Virtually indestructible

ENERGY PROJECTION
Ability to discharge energy
1 None
2 Ability to discharge energy on contact
3 Short range, short duration, single energy type
4 Medium range, duration, single energy type
5 Long range, long duration, single energy type
6 Able to discharge multiple forms of energy
7 Virtually unlimited command of all forms of energy

FIGHTING ABILITY
Proficiency in hand-to-hand combat
1 Poor
2 Normal
3 Some training
4 Experienced fighter
5 Master of a single form of combat
6 Master of several forms of combat
7 Master of all forms of combat-

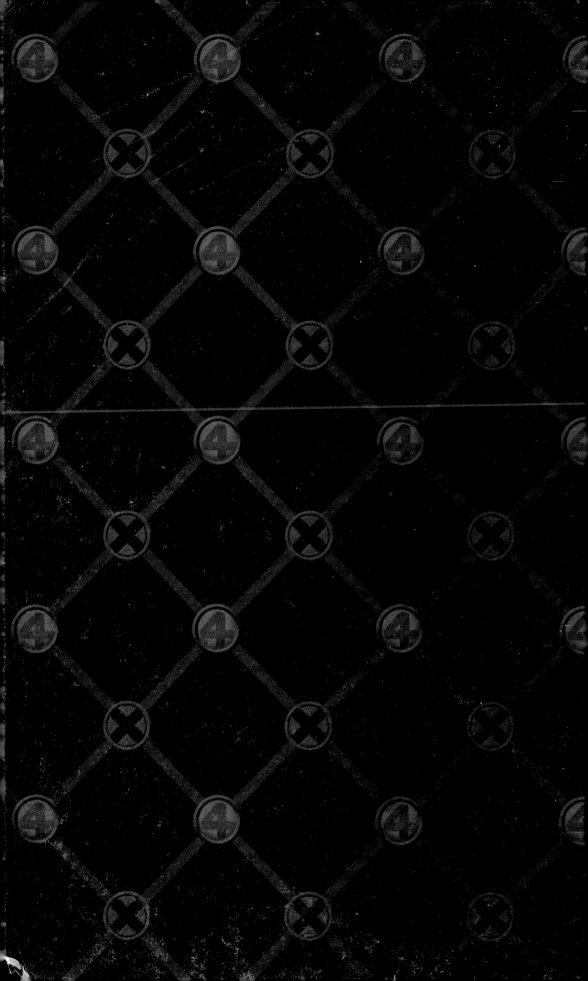